Advances in Experimental Philosophy of Causation

Advances in Experimental Philosophy

Series Editor
James Beebe, Professor of Philosophy, University at Buffalo, USA

Editorial Board
Joshua Knobe, Yale University, USA
Edouard Machery, University of Pittsburgh, USA
Thomas Nadelhoffer, College of Charleston, UK
Eddy Nahmias, Neuroscience Institute at Georgia State University, USA
Jennifer Nagel, University of Toronto, Canada
Joshua Alexander, Siena College, USA

Empirical and experimental philosophy is generating tremendous excitement, producing unexpected results that are challenging traditional philosophical methods. *Advances in Experimental Philosophy* responds to this trend, bringing together some of the most exciting voices in the field to understand the approach and measure its impact in contemporary philosophy. The result is a series that captures past and present developments and anticipates future research directions.

To provide in-depth examinations, each volume links experimental philosophy to a key philosophical area. They provide historical overviews alongside case studies, reviews of current problems and discussions of new directions. For upper-level undergraduates, postgraduates and professionals actively pursuing research in experimental philosophy these are essential resources.

Titles in the series include
Advances in Experimental Epistemology, edited by James R. Beebe
Advances in Experimental Moral Psychology, edited by Hagop Sarkissian and Jennifer Cole Wright
Advances in Experimental Philosophy and Philosophical Methodology, edited by Jennifer Nado
Advances in Experimental Philosophy of Aesthetics, edited by Florian Cova and Sébastien Réhault
Advances in Experimental Philosophy of Language, edited by Jussi Haukioja
Advances in Experimental Philosophy of Logic and Mathematics, edited by Andrew Aberdein and Matthew Inglis
Advances in Experimental Philosophy of Mind, edited by Justin Sytsma
Advances in Religion, Cognitive Science, and Experimental Philosophy, edited by Helen De Cruz and Ryan Nichols
Experimental Metaphysics, edited by David Rose
Methodological Advances in Experimental Philosophy, edited by Eugen Fischer and Mark Curtis
Advances in Experimental Philosophy of Free Will and Responsibility, edited by Thomas Nadelhoffer and Andrew Monroe
Advances in Experimental Philosophy of Causation, edited by Alex Wiegmann and Pascale Willemsen

Advances in Experimental Philosophy of Causation

Edited by
Pascale Willemsen and Alex Wiegmann

BLOOMSBURY ACADEMIC
LONDON • NEW YORK • OXFORD • NEW DELHI • SYDNEY

BLOOMSBURY ACADEMIC
Bloomsbury Publishing Plc
50 Bedford Square, London, WC1B 3DP, UK
1385 Broadway, New York, NY 10018, USA
29 Earlsfort Terrace, Dublin 2, Ireland

BLOOMSBURY, BLOOMSBURY ACADEMIC and the Diana logo are trademarks
of Bloomsbury Publishing Plc

First published in Great Britain 2022
This paperback edition published 2024

Copyright © Pascale Willemsen, Alex Wiegmann and Contributors, 2022

Pascale Willemsen and Alex Wiegmann have asserted their right under the Copyright, Designs and Patents Act, 1988, to be identified as Editors of this work.

For legal purposes the Acknowledgments on p. xii constitute an
extension of this copyright page.

Cover design by Catherine Wood
Cover photograph © Dieter Leistner / Gallerystock

All rights reserved. No part of this publication may be reproduced or transmitted in any form or by any means, electronic or mechanical, including photocopying, recording, or any information storage or retrieval system, without prior permission in writing from the publishers.

Bloomsbury Publishing Plc does not have any control over, or responsibility for, any third-party websites referred to or in this book. All internet addresses given in this book were correct at the time of going to press. The author and publisher regret any inconvenience caused if addresses have changed or sites have ceased to exist, but can accept no responsibility for any such changes.

A catalogue record for this book is available from the British Library.

A catalog record for this book is available from the Library of Congress.

ISBN: HB: 978-1-3502-3580-9
PB: 978-1-3502-3584-7
ePDF: 978-1-3502-3581-6
eBook: 978-1-3502-3582-3

Series: Advances in Experimental Philosophy

Typeset by RefineCatch Limited, Bungay, Suffolk

To find out more about our authors and books visit www.bloomsbury.com
and sign up for our newsletters.

Contents

List of Illustrations	vi
List of Tables	viii
List of Contributors	ix
Acknowledgments	xii
Introduction *Pascale Willemsen and Alex Wiegmann*	1
1 Revisiting Hume in the Twenty-first Century: The Possibility of Generalizable Causal Beliefs Given Inherently Unobservable Causal Relations *Nicholas Ichien and Patricia W. Cheng*	7
2 Mysteries of Actual Causation: It's Complicated *James Woodward*	35
3 Juggling Intuitions about Causation and Omissions *Carolina Sartorio*	63
4 Causal Perception and Causal Inference: An Integrated Account *David Danks and Phuong (Phoebe) Ngoc Dinh*	81
5 The Interplay between Covariation, Temporal, and Mechanism Information in Singular Causation Judgments *Simon Stephan and Michael R. Waldmann*	101
6 Cause, "Cause," and Norm *John Schwenkler and Eric Sievers*	123
7 The Responsibility Account *Justin Sytsma*	145
8 Causation in the Law and Experimental Philosophy *Karolina Prochownik*	165
9 Children and Adults Don't Think They Are Free: A Skeptical Look at Agent Causationism *Lukas S. Huber, Kevin Reuter, and Trix Cacchione*	189
Index	211

Illustrations

1.1 Illustration of Michotte's (1946/1963) Experiments 1 (top sequence) and 21 (bottom sequence).   11

1.2 Three views of the same collision event from three different inertial reference frames   12

1.3 Distributions of the relative sensitivity of S, M, and L cones to electromagnetic waves with wavelengths in the range that give rise to human color vision. Peak sensitivities are normalized to 1.0.   14

1.4 The color sensations reported by subjects when viewing a small spot of 550-nm light.   15

1.5 Occurrences of headaches in patients who did not receive the medication (top) and in patients who did receive the medication (bottom) in Context 1.   21

1.6 Occurrence of headaches in patients who did not receive the medication in Context 2 (top) and occurrence of headaches in patients receiving the medication in this context as predicted, respectively, by the causal power estimated in Context 1.   25

1.7 Occurrence of headaches in patients who did not receive the medication in Context 1 (top left) and occurrence of headaches in patients receiving the medication in this context as predicted, respectively, by the causal power estimated using the causal-invariance decomposition function (middle left) and by the causal strength estimated using the additive decomposition function (bottom left) based on the event frequencies in Context 2 shown in Figure 6 and duplicated here for easier visual comparison (top right).   26

1.8 Occurrences of headaches in patients who did not receive the medication in Context 1 (top left) and Context 3. Occurrences of headaches in patients receiving the medication in Context 1 (bottom left) and in Context 3 (bottom right).   29

1.9 w_M according to the logistic decomposition function in various causal contexts. Each pair of cause-present and control events (light grey and dark grey points) represents a different causal context.   30

1.10 Causal estimates (y-axes) as a function of outcome probability in control events (x-axes), holding constant $\Delta P = .2$.   31

Illustrations

2.1	Simple Pre-emption: (Ex5.1).	48
2.2	Over determination: (EX5.2).	48
4.1	Graphical model for monist inference.	89
4.2	Screenshots of successful Launch (top row) and successful Blink (bottom row) events. In unsuccessful events, the recipient remained stationary.	93
5.1	Different causal models in which C and A represent root causes of a common target effect E.	103
5.2	Predictions of the standard power PC model of causal attribution for different levels of w_c and w_a.	104
5.3	Model predictions and results of Experiment 1a from Stephan and Waldmann (2018).	106
5.4	Illustration of how the causes' strengths and their causal latencies determine the predictions of the generalized power PC model of singular causation judgments.	109
5.5	Illustration of the scenario used in Experiment 1 in Stephan and Waldmann (2022).	113
5.6	Model predictions and results (means and 95% CIs) of a subset of test cases used in Experiment 1 in Stephan and Waldmann (2022).	114
6.1	Results of Experiment 1.	130
6.2	Results of Experiment 2.	131
6.3	Results of Experiment 3.	134
6.4	Illustration of the animation used in Experiment 4.	136
6.5	Results of Experiment 4.	138
7.1	Histograms for each rank ordering for the questions in Studies 1a (top) and 1b (bottom).	157
9.1	Means of agreement ratings across conditions.	202
9.2	Distribution of agreement ratings across conditions (a–c).	202
9.3	The results of Study 2 threaten a successful inference from the experience to the belief in causal agency.	207

Tables

6.1 The 100 most commonly used English verbs according to the Corpus of Contemporary American English.   123

6.2 Results of Experiment 4.   137

7.1 Summary of the scope of the norm effect for each view along the dimensions of context, judgments, and norms.   154

9.1 Examples of two cases.   195

9.2 Features of different cases.   195

9.3 Number and percentages (in brackets) of "choose to" responses, separated by age groups.   196

9.4 Pairwise comparisons between age groups using Fisher's exact test.   197

List of Contributors

Trix Cacchione is a professor at the University of Applied Sciences and Arts Northwestern Switzerland. She is specialized in developmental psychology, with a focus on conceptual development. Her research interests span from psycholinguistics to comparative psychology, and include cross-specific work aiming to trace back the evolutionary origins of human cognition.

Patricia W. Cheng is a professor of psychology at the University of California, Los Angeles. She is interested in how an intelligent system can come to represent and understand the world as we humans do.

David Danks is L.L. Thurstone Professor of Philosophy and Psychology at Carnegie Mellon University. In July 2021 he was appointed Professor of Data Science and Philosophy at the University of California, San Diego. His research interests are at the intersection of philosophy, cognitive science, and machine learning, using ideas, methods, and frameworks from each to advance our understanding of complex, interdisciplinary problems.

Phuong (Phoebe) Ngoc Dinh is a Ph.D. student in the Department of Psychology at Carnegie Mellon University. Phuong's research program draws on cognitive, developmental, and philosophical work in causal cognition to characterize the cognitive processes and representations that underlie human causal learning across tasks and over development, with a special interest in building bridges between disparate islands of research traditions and paradigms (causal perception and causal inference being one example). Currently, Phuong is fascinated by the prominent but ill-defined role of domain knowledge in causal cognition and how to delineate domain knowledge in the first place.

Lukas S. Huber is a master's student in cognitive and developmental psychology at the University of Bern. He aims to combine different perspectives to gain a multidisciplinary understanding of topics relating to cognitive development and philosophy of mind. Currently, he is studying the differences and similarities in data processing between children and artificial neural networks at the University of Tübingen.

Nicholas Ichien is a graduate student in cognitive psychology at the University of California, Los Angeles. He is interested in the flexibility of human thought and researches human processing of similarity, analogy, metaphor, and causality.

Karolina Prochownik is a senior researcher at the Center for Law, Behavior, and Cognition at the Faculty of Law, Ruhr-University Bochum. She holds a Ph.D. in law and a Ph.D. in philosophy. Her research focuses on experimental legal philosophy and the cognitive science of religion.

Kevin Reuter is an SNSF Eccellenza Professor at the Institute of Philosophy, University of Zurich. His research interests are in the philosophy of mind, language, cognitive and social sciences, and experimental philosophy. Currently, he studies evaluative concepts, the nature and concepts of pains and emotions, as well as (ir)rational decision-making processes.

Carolina Sartorio (Ph.D. MIT, 2003) is Professor of Philosophy at the University of Arizona. She works at the intersection of metaphysics, the philosophy of action, and moral theory. She is the author of *Causation and Free Will* (Oxford University Press, 2016), and of articles on causation, agency, free will, and moral responsibility, among other topics.

John Schwenkler is Professor of Philosophy at Florida State University. He is the author of *Anscombe's 'Intention': A Guide* (Oxford University Press, 2019) and co-editor, with Enoch Lambert, of *Becoming Someone New: Essays on Transformative Experience, Choice, and Change* (Oxford University Press, 2020). His research is in the philosophy of mind, action, and language.

Eric Sievers earned a J.D. from Elon University in 2015 and began graduate study in the philosophy department at Florida State University in 2018. He received his M.A. in 2020 and is currently in enrolled in the doctoral program. His interests primarily lie in the nexus of the philosophy of law and the philosophy of causation.

Simon Stephan is a postdoctoral researcher in the field of cognitive science at the University of Göttingen, Germany, where he currently works in Michael R. Waldmann's lab of Cognitive and Decision Sciences. The focus of his research is on higher-level cognition, including causal learning and reasoning, categorization, and explanation.

Justin Sytsma is an associate professor in the philosophy programme at Victoria University of Wellington. Justin's research focuses on issues in philosophy of psychology and philosophy of mind. As a practitioner of experimental philosophy, Justin's research into these areas often involves the use of empirical methods.

Michael R. Waldmann is Professor of Psychology at the University of Göttingen, Germany. He is a Fellow of the Association for Psychological Science and the Cognitive Science Society. The focus of his research is on higher-level cognitive processes, including causal and moral reasoning, categorization, judgment and decision-making, and learning.

Alex Wiegmann is a postdoctoral researcher in the Emmy Noether Research Group Experimental Philosophy and the Method of Cases (EXTRA) at the Institute for Philosophy II at Ruhr-University Bochum. Before that, he was a postdoctoral researcher at the Department of Cognitive Science at University of Göttingen. His works focuses on moral judgments and the concept of lying.

Pascale Willemsen is a postdoctoral researcher at the University of Zurich and Principle Investigator of the SNSF-funded research group, Investigating Think Ethical Concepts. Her research interests are in causal cognition, philosophical moral psychology, metaethics, philosophy action, normativity in language, as well as experimental philosophy. She is further involved in projects concerning the relationship between agency, moral responsibility and free will; the folk concept of lying; the ethics of omissions; and the relationship between moral responsibility and causal responsibility.

James Woodward is Distinguished Professor in the Department of History and Philosophy of Science at the University of Pittsburgh. He works mainly in general philosophy of science, with a particular interest in causation, among other topics. He is a Fellow of the American Academy of Arts and Sciences.

Acknowledgments

We would like to express our gratitude to all those people involved in making this volume possible. First and foremost, we thank James Beebe as the series editor for excellent advice and guidance. We are also grateful to the editorial board of the *Advances in Experimental Philosophy* series who generously provided feedback on the outline of this volume. We would like to thank the anonymous reviewers of this volume who contributed their expertise and skillfulness, and who offered invaluable suggestions for improvements.

Our greatest thanks and appreciation is due to the authors of this volume who provided excellent chapters that stand out in terms of their accessibility, originality, and both philosophical and scientific curiosity. We would like to acknowledge that all these invaluable pieces of work have been produced during the Covid-19 pandemic, which put a heavy burden on all of us, and especially on those committed to taking care of friends and family.

Finally, we would like to thank the German National Foundation for financially supporting the work of Alex Wiegmann (Grant Number: 391304769), and the Swiss National Science Foundation for funding Pascale Willemsen's research (Grant Numbers: PCEFP1_181082 and PZ00P1_201737).

Introduction

Pascale Willemsen and Alex Wiegmann

Causation is a classical topic in metaphysics, with an extensive literature on the nature of causal relata and the causal relation itself. Experimental philosophers have contributed to these debates by offering new perspectives and applying new tools to old problems. In September 2021, forty-three papers on PhilPapers.org were categorized as Experimental Philosophy: Metaphysics, subsection "Causation." This number might seem surprisingly low, given that much experimental-philosophical work has been done on causation.

On second thought, this number might not be surprising at all, given how diverse the experimental literature on causation actually is. Thinking of causation as merely a matter of metaphysics would be underestimating the omnipresence of causal considerations and the pervasive impact they have on various topics in philosophy, psychology, the natural sciences, and our ordinary life. For instance, questions about causal relationships are central to ethical considerations. Many moral and legal philosophers believe that to be morally or legally responsible for an event, a person needs to have caused this event. In reaction to these debates, experimental philosophers have examined the role of causation for moral and legal judgments. In addition, questions about free will often revolve around questions of whether or not the agent had sufficient control over bringing about the outcome or preventing it from occurring. Taking this idea to the experimental level, experimental philosophers investigate the relevance of various causal chains for the attribution of free will. The highly interdisciplinarity and broad nature of research on causality is reflected in this volume. It presents cutting-edge research from (experimental) philosophers, psychologists, and cognitive scientists on a wide range of topics.

Chapter outlines

The volume begins with three chapters that discuss the relationship between traditional, philosophical questions about causation, intuitions, and empirical work.

In Chapter 1, Nicholas Ichien and Patricia Cheng address a question that is motivated by two key issues raised by David Hume. First, our beliefs about causal relations are formed based on non-causal data—what we can observe are events in the world following one another, but we don't observe their causal relationship. Second, experience with causal relationships of the past is only useful if the future resembles the past. Based on these two issues, Ichien and Cheng ask: How is it possible to tease apart a target candidate cause's influence from that due to background causes, in a way that yields causal knowledge that generalizes across the learning and application contexts? In answering this question, Ichien and Cheng first review Hume's first issue from a modern scientific perspective, including cognitive psychology, cognitive neuroscience, and also discussing perceived causality in different contexts and inertial reference frames, and cognitive causal "illusions." In a second step, the authors argue for a causal-invariance constraint. Without such a constraint, intuitive causal induction and normative statistical inference both fail to aim at generalizable causal beliefs. In this innovative and interdisciplinary chapter, Ichien and Cheng provide new, empirically-informed access to a classical, philosophical text on causation.

In Chapter 2, James Woodward provides an overview of issues that arise in the context of formal and empirical work on actual causation. It is argued that claims about actual causation have various features that distinguish them from claims about type-level causation. As a consequence, claims about actual causation should not be regarded as grounds or foundations for type-level causal claims. Instead, actual causal claims should be thought of as answers to distinctive questions about causal structure but not as providing answers to the sorts of causal questions that are instead associated with other sorts of causal claims. Furthermore, it is not clear that there is a single unitary notion of actual causation. In his chapter, Woodward suggests that some actual causal claims have to do with *causal selection,* that is picking out certain causes from a larger set of causally relevant factors. Such selection-based judgments are influenced by normality considerations. By contrast, in other cases, actual cause judgments seem less influenced by considerations related to normality and instead seem to track a distinct notion that Woodward calls actual causal contribution. Furthermore, he briefly considers the consequences of this for modelling actual cause judgments and for their empirical investigation.

In Chapter 3, Carolina Sartorio discusses the relevance of intuitions for philosophical theorizing about causation and distinguishes four different roles that these intuitions play: (1) There are causal intuitions: intuitions to the effect that something is or is not a cause of a given outcome. (2) Explanatory intuitions concern the question of whether something is part of the explanation of something else (where this tracks something potentially broader than causation). (3) Responsibility intuitions are those intuitions that agents are or are not morally responsible for a given outcome. Finally, (4) grounding intuitions speak to whether or not agents are morally responsible for a given outcome because of their causal or explanatory connection to the outcome. Sartorio discusses how these different intuitions interact with one another and how and whether these interactions inform our theorizing about causation. She argues that causation theorists mostly focus on causal intuitions. However, intuitions of the other kinds are also relevant to philosophical theorizing about causation. According to Sartorio, causation is not an isolated concept but one that is connected with other theoretically useful concepts, such as explanation and moral responsibility. Cases of omission (failures to act) and overdetermination are used as interesting case studies to support this conclusion.

Chapters 4 and 5 share a strong cognitive focus and examine the cognitive processes underlying causal cognition.

Chapter 4 adds to the discussion about causal learning. David Danks and Phuong (Phoebe) Ngoc Dinh critically examine the empirical evidence for a widely-shared assumption about causal learning, namely the idea that causal learning can be divided into two distinct types of cognitive processes and representations: causal perception versus causal inference. However, Danks and Dinh argue there is not much empirical evidence in support of this assumption. For one thing, research on causal learning has largely proceeded in two different paradigms, and so there are systematic methodological confounds that can explain the appearance of distinct processes. Moreover, the few experiments to investigate the relationship between causal perception and causal inference rather suggest that causal perception and causal inference are not distinct after all. Danks and Dinh suggest that there are natural theoretical options that have not yet been systematically explored, and they focus on one unexplored possibility in more detail: an integrated account based on inference to shared representations. In particular, this proposal holds that causal learners opportunistically use a wide range of features to infer the existence and strength of unobserved causal connections, and then explain, predict, and reason about the world around them on the basis of those inferred connections.

In Chapter 5, Simon Stephan and Michael Waldmann focus on singular causation relations between cause-and-effect events that occurred at a particular spatiotemporal location (e.g., "Mary's having taken this pill caused her sickness"). They argue that while the analysis of singular causation has received much attention in philosophy, relatively few psychological studies have investigated how laypeople assess these relations. Initially inspired by the power PC (probabilistic contrast) model of causal attribution proposed by Cheng and Novick, Stephan and Waldmann developed and tested a new computational model of singular causation judgments which integrates covariation, temporal, and mechanism information.

Chapters 6, 7, and 8 discuss findings strongly suggesting that normative considerations influence people's causal judgments. While Chapters 5 and 6 offer explanations for this phenomenon, Chapter 7 discusses it in the context of law.

In Chapter 6, John Schwenkler and Eric Sievers argue that much empirical evidence on how laypeople make causal judgments is based on agreement ratings with so-called "cause" statements of the form "X caused …." These studies often report effects of normative considerations on causal judgments. Schwenkler and Sievers explore the extent to which previously observed effects of normative considerations extend as well to other forms of causal queries of the form "X V-ed Y," where V is a lexical causative. The principal findings are that in many cases the effects do not extend in this way. Moreover, in those cases where the same patterns are found, the causal verb has a negative valence of its own. Schwenkler and Sievers draw two main conclusions from this finding. First, it reveals how the almost exclusive focus on "cause"-statements in the experimental study of causal judgment has led to findings that are unrepresentative of the full range of ordinary causal thinking and provides a proof of concept as to how this thinking can be studied in its full variety. Second, the results of these experiments provide significant indirect support for the contention that the effect of moral considerations on agreement with "cause"-statements reflect the fact that these statements are most often used to assign responsibility for an event, and not just to describe the causal structure of what happened. It is not *causal judgments in general* that result from a process in which normative considerations play a role, but perhaps only those judgments that express a determination of moral responsibility.

In Chapter 7, Justin Sytsma spells out a way in which causal statements of the form "X caused Y" might in fact be strongly related to considerations about moral responsibility. Sytsma argues that is now a great deal of evidence that norm violations impact people's causal judgments, but it remains contentious how best to explain these findings. This includes that the primary explanations on offer differ with regard to how broad they take the phenomenon to be. Sytsma details how the explanations diverge with respect to the expected scope of the contexts in which the effect arises, the types of judgments at issue, and the range of norms involved. One account, so Sytsma argues, turns out to be especially compatible with the existent data, namely the responsibility account. Two studies add to the evidence in favor of the responsibility account by employing a novel method: participants were asked to rank order compound statements combining a causal attribution and a normative attribution.

In Chapter 8, Karolina Prochownik examines the basic components of normative theories of causation in legal philosophy and criminal law. Those theories assume that assessment of the causal link between the agent's action (or omission) and a harmful outcome somewhat depends on the evaluations of norm violations. Prochownik discusses to what extent these theories are compatible with folk causal intuitions. In particular, this analysis aims to shed new "empirical" light on frequent statements in legal philosophy and doctrine that legal criteria for assessing the causal link are modeled on the lay notion of causation. Prochownik argues that recent empirical research on the folk concept of causation supports general congruence between the normative theories of causation and the folk causal intuitions. She examines the explanatory potential of different psychological models of the link between causation and norms ("competence," "bias," "pragmatics," and "responsibility" accounts) for the normative theories of causation. In conclusion, so Prochownik argues, the competence account can explain the basic components of these theories to the greatest extent.

Finally, in Chapter 9, Lukas Huber, Kevin Reuter, and Trix Cacchione direct the focus to the role of causation in debates about free will. They identify two strands of evidence that supposedly exist in support of the claim that people think of themselves as agent causationists, that is, as agents who can start and prevent causal chains. First, results from developmental studies suggest that children between the ages of four and six undergo a transition towards thinking of themselves as unconditional free agents. Second, experimental studies indicate that adults think of themselves as agents who, having made some choice, could have done otherwise under exactly the same circumstances. Huber, Reuter, and Cacchione present new evidence that tells against both strands of evidence. They collected new empirical data with children aged four to six (Study 1) and argue that six-year-old children only endorse freedom of choice if they are presented with at least two conflicting desires which are compatible with their own desires. This undermines any strong conclusion to the claim that children think of themselves as agent causationists. Study 2 reveals that adults indeed agree that they "could have done otherwise" given the same circumstances, but only when this phrase is interpreted as a matter of ability. When people are asked whether it is possible that an agent does otherwise, holding the circumstances exactly the same, a majority of people think not. Given that belief in agent causationism is one of the main motivations for the metaphysical account of agent causation, Huber, Reuter, and Cacchione's results also can be seen as evidence against agent causation.

1

Revisiting Hume in the Twenty-first Century: The Possibility of Generalizable Causal Beliefs Given Inherently Unobservable Causal Relations

Nicholas Ichien and Patricia W. Cheng

The present chapter is an introduction to a basic problem in causal induction: how is generalizable causal knowledge possible? We first present the problem of causal induction as posed by David Hume (1739/1987, 1748/1975) and clarify three confusions surrounding this problem. We go on to review empirical evidence from four perspectives that all provide support for Hume's view: Causal relations are not in the input to the reasoner/cognitive system. What is in the input are merely the states of the candidate causes and the state of the outcome-in-question due to all its causes present in the context. Making a causal inference about a target candidate cause therefore requires decomposing the observed outcome into contributions from the target cause and from other causes of the outcome in the context. Nature does not tell the reasoner how to decompose the observed outcome—the task is up to the reasoner. After establishing the problem of causal induction from the perspective of cognitive science, we explain what the assumption of causal invariance is and why it is a necessary constraint for rational causal induction. We end the chapter by relating our analysis of causal invariance to normative causal inference in statistics. This chapter does not assume any background knowledge of work on causal induction in philosophy or psychology. Our intention is for it to be of interest to upper-level undergraduate students, graduate students, and anyone else who enjoys thinking through the problem our mind solves when it aims to infer a generalizable causal relation.

People often have the compelling intuition that they directly "see" causation, and thus have no need to *infer* causation. If they see an unfortunate person killed by a volcanic eruption, overtaken by a pyroclastic flow, it may seem hard to deny that they perceived the reality of the volcanic eruption killing the person.[1] If they see a moving ball hit a stationary ball, and the stationary ball starts to move away, they "see" the true "launching" into motion of one ball by motion in the other. If their right-hand fingers scratch a mosquito bite on their left arm, and their left arm feels relief from the itch, they directly perceive the relieving of the itch by their scratching.

Hume (1739/1987) argues that counter to our compelling intuition that a moving ball launches a stationary ball when we observe the former hitting the latter, the causal aspect of that intuition is an inference in our mind and is absent in the observation itself. Hume (1748/1975, p. 37) also brings attention to an assumption so intuitive that we may be unaware of making it: Whenever we generalize from a learning context to an application context, we assume, "the future will resemble the past." He goes on to state its implication, "If there is any suspicion that the course of nature may change, ... all experience becomes useless ..." Together, Hume's two points raise the question: If causal perceptions and beliefs are mental constructs absent in the observations in our experience, on what basis would one expect these mental constructs to capture the unchanging course of nature, such that experience is not useless?

Three confusions clouding the nature of the problem of causal induction

It is tempting to conclude that the compelling perception of causal relations renders inference unnecessary, at least in cases in which causation appears "observable." However, the conclusion that causation is observable involves three sources of confusion.

The first is a confusion between the input of the causal induction process and its output. The conclusion mistakes the compelling perception of causation, as illustrated in our examples, to be the *input* to the causal induction process, when it is in fact the *output to be explained* (see Henle, 1962, for an example in which confusion about the input to a cognitive process, deductive inference in her case, creates confusion about the process itself). This confusion may be due to the vagueness of Hume's criterion for what he does or does not find "evident" in the observations (1739/1987, pp. 649–50). In contemporary information-processing language, a paraphrase of Hume's thesis that causal relations are not evident in the observations would be: Causal relations are not in the input available to a process that infers cause and effect—the construct we label the causal-induction process. Given that our sensory input does not contain causal relations, but we "know" causal relations, there must be a downstream process that does the work of arriving at the causal output from its noncausal input.

The unobservability of causation is a specific form of the general challenge of formulating adaptive knowledge: reality in the world does not come represented (Goodman, 1955; Hawking and Mlodinow, 2010; Kant, 1781/1965). All our perceptions and conceptions of reality are our representations of it, formulated within an infinite search space. Consider our perception of a cube. The 2-dimensional image cast by a cube on our retina is ambiguous in that it can map onto an infinite number of differently shaped 3-dimensional objects (e.g., see Pizlo, 2001). Yet, despite the inherent underdetermination of the distal object, we perceive a cube. Narrowing down to this adaptive percept in the infinite space of possible distal objects illustrates the application of potent constraints in the form of *a priori* assumptions, in this case the default assumption that the distal object has the simplest form that is consistent with the image (i.e., the object is a "parsimonious explanation" of the image).

Thus, with respect to the stereoscopic vision process, 3-dimensionality is "unobservable"—a shorthand for "being absent in the input to a process"—and is the to-be-explained output of the process. Likewise, causation is "unobservable" with respect to the causal induction process, and the perceived "necessary connection" between a cause and an effect is the to-be-explained output (Hume, 1739/1987).

A second source of confusion is that the apparent examples of observable causation often involve prior causal knowledge at a more abstract level than the particular causal relation in question. Although a reasoner may be witnessing a pyroclastic flow hitting someone for the first time, they almost certainly know, at a more general level, from knowledge of landslides and fires, that being struck by massive flows of hot or heavy matter can be fatal. Lien and Cheng's (2000) hierarchical consistency hypothesis explains how consistency and inconsistency of covariations between potential cause and effect variables across representations at different levels of abstraction can explain conclusions of causality or noncausality ostensibly based on a single instance. Their paper presents evidence showing that information beyond what is in the single instance gets recruited, more specifically, that judgments involving a single instance can be explained by retrieval from causal schemas in long-term memory formed by past causal inferences, rather than by "observable" causality. (See Rips (2011) for a review of evidence and arguments against perception of causality as the source of the causal knowledge.)

A third source of confusion is that examples of observable causation concern situations in which only one cause is perceived to be present (i.e., the reasoner assumes no background causes). In such cases, an inferential process, either inductive (Cheng, 1997) or deductive, can account for the causal percept. Deduction such as the following would reach our intuitive causal conclusions:

Premises:
1. effect e occurred in situation x
2. effects do not occur without a cause
3. c is the only candidate cause in situation x

Conclusion: c caused e. In other words, the fact that we humans are able to judge causation in situations involving one single plausible cause does not imply that we do not have a general causal-induction process capable of inferring new causal knowledge in situations involving more than one plausible cause. The single-cause situation may be regarded as a trivial case of the application of that inference process.

To illustrate that causation in situations with a single plausible cause is not observed but inferred, we review the striking "phantom hand" phenomenon (Armel and Ramachandran, 2003; Botvinick and Cohen, 1998; Ramachandran and Hirstein, 1998). More generally, the phenomenon is a good reminder of the inferential nature of our conception of reality. Armel and Ramachandran report that participants with normal sensation and perception perceived touch sensations as arising from a rubber hand. This occurred when both the rubber hand in view and participants' own out-of-view real hand were repeatedly tapped and stroked in a random sequence in synchrony. In other words, participants perceived the tapping and stroking of the rubber hand as causes of their perceived touch sensations, as if the rubber hand is part of their body. An analogous illusion was obtained even when a table top was similarly tapped. The perceived causal relation could not have been an "observation" of causation, because no such actual causation existed in the experimental setup. The perception was so internalized that when the rubber hand or table was then "threatened" with potential injury, participants winced and sweated. It was as if the participant perceived a threat to the table as a threat to their hand. Consistent with their behavioral response, participants displayed a strong skin conductance response (SCR)[2] in the real hand, even though no threat was issued to it. Notably, when there is only one plausible cause of our sensations, even something so fundamental as the perceived boundary of our body is mutable to allow attribution of the sensations to that single cause. Armel and Ramachandran write (p. 1499), "one's body image is itself a 'phantom': one that the brain constructs for utility and convenience."

Thus, for the hypothesis of "observable causation" to be tenable, processes such as deduction and the recruitment of prior causal knowledge must be ruled out as explanations of the causal conclusion. We propose that, to provide clear evidence for observable causation, the critical discriminating test is to compare causal judgment between two situations: (A) a single-cause situation and (B) a situation in which a second cause is introduced without disturbing the causal sequence in situation A. When multiple plausible causes are present, from either current information or prior knowledge, it would no longer be possible for deduction to narrow down to one cause as the compelling conclusion, but if a causal relation is "observable," the relation should be just as discernable, whether there is one cause or two causes present. If we can see an apple in a bowl, we should still be able to see it when another apple is placed in the bowl. We presently review some empirical evidence comparing the two types of situations.

Four perspectives in support of the unobservability of causal relations (Hume, 1739/1987)

Now that we have clarified the three common sources of confusion, let us turn to empirical evidence in favor of causal relations being unobservable rather than observable. We examine this issue from four perspectives: (1) psychological evidence on the perception of causality when there is more than one cause, (2) the relativity principle with respect to the invariance of laws of motion across inertial reference frames (Newton, 1687/1713/1726/1999), (3) the visual input to our cognitive system and its relation to the cognitive neuroscience of color perception and, by extension, causal perception, and (4) causal inference about internal psychological outcomes.

Perspective 1: When a second cause is introduced, the compelling perception of causation disappears

We compare two situations below, a single-cause and a two-cause situation, summarizing the discussion of them in Cheng (1993).

Michotte's (1946/1963) Experiment 21 provides a clear demonstration that perceived launching is not the result of a direct perception of causation. Because Experiment 21 differs from the basic version of Michotte's often-cited launching experiments in only

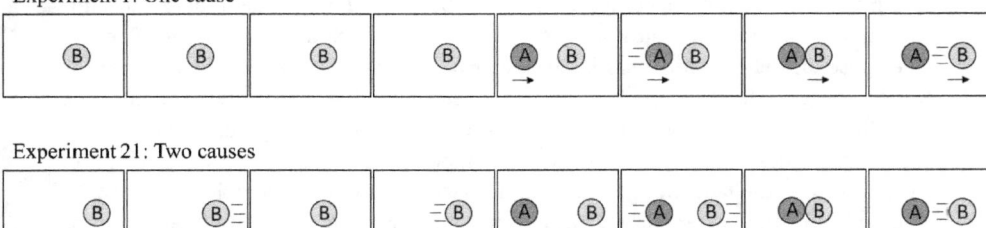

Figure 1.1 Illustration of Michotte's (1946/1963) Experiments 1 (top sequence) and 21 (bottom sequence). The visual stimuli are identical in the two experiments from the moment of impact on (represented in the two rightmost frames in the top and bottom panels). Arrows under Objects A and B indicate motion in the direction of the arrow (see a video of the two demonstrations at https://youtu.be/ZVZpggGXl08).

one respect, we first describe the basic version in Experiment 1. In Experiment 1 (see top sequence in Figure 1.1), an Object B is in the middle of the screen, and the subject fixates on it. At a given moment, Object A enters the screen from the left and moves toward B at a constant speed. Object A stops at the moment it comes into contact with B, while B then starts and moves to the right. The blow by A is often perceived to "send B off," "transfer its momentum to B," "cause B to move," or "launch B."

Describing his results when the collision satisfies some fairly strict spatio-temporal constraints (e.g., B has to start moving within a few tenths of a second of the collision, A cannot stop before touching B), Michotte (1946/1963) writes, "The impression is clear: it is the blow given by A which makes B go, which produces B's movement" (p. 20). He regards his findings as refuting Hume's (1748/1975, Section VII, part ii, p. 74) claim that "we never can observe any tye between 'a cause and an effect.'" Instead, the cause that produces motion can be "directly experienced" (Michotte, p. 21).

In the launching phenomenon, the effect may be characterized as "Object B moving away starting at the moment of collision," and the cause may be characterized as "Moving Object A hitting Object B." Note that the input to the perceptual process consists of the activities of a mosaic of photoreceptors that change over time, nothing more. "Launching" is not in the activity of any of the photoreceptors, and there is no homunculus. Experiment 21 shows results consistent with this information-processing perspective.

Experiment 21 illustrates the two-cause situation (see bottom sequence in Figure 1.1). One often overlooked finding is that the perception of launching is critically dependent on the state of B *before* A collides with it. The stimuli in Experiment 21 (Michotte, 1946/1963) is identical to those in Experiment 1, except that B moves to and fro before A enters. B's oscillation is timed so that A collides with B just as B comes to a rest and is about to move to the right. The sequence at impact and thereafter is identical to that in Experiment 1. Because the effect of impact by A on B cannot precede the impact itself, B's to-and-fro motion before the impact cannot be part of the "effect" in question. Instead, it indicates a cause other than the blow by A.

Michotte (1946/1963) reports that there is no perceived launching with the set-up in Experiment 21: B's movements "seemed entirely independent of the movement performed by A" (p. 74). In comparison with Experiment 1, it is evident that B's to-and-fro motion before the collision eliminates the impression of launching. Because the cause-and-effect sequences in the two experiments are identical, if causation is indeed observable, launching should be perceived equally in both experiments. The fact that it is not indicates that, even in the case of compelling causal perception, causality cannot be present in the sensory input. To conclude from the perception of causality in the launching phenomenon that causality is "observable" is to mistake the output of the perceptual system for its input. Crucially, that causal perception is truly a perceptual phenomenon is entirely consistent with our claim that causation is not observable, and we fully acknowledge that researchers of causal perception do not take the phenomenon as evidence for the observability of causation (e.g., Scholl and Tremoulet, 2000). Our present point is that this phenomenon necessitates explanation. Specifically, how is it that, in the case of causal perception, our perceptual system takes non-causal sensory input and reliably generates the compelling visual representation of "launching" in cases like Experiment 1 but not in cases like Experiment 21?

Perspective 2: If causation is not a mental construct, perceived causality should not change across inertial reference frames (Cheng and Lu, 2017)

We next consider the compelling perception of causality in ball collision episodes (Michotte, 1946/1963) from the perspective of the postulate of relativity in Newtonian physics. Consider the perception of causality in each of three horizontal motion episodes involving the collision of two balls. Assume an idealized world in which there is no friction and no background scene to convey the position of the balls relative to the background. The issue concerns which ball is perceived as the cause of what happens in each of the episodes in Figure 1.2:

Figure 1.2 Three views of the same collision event from three different inertial reference frames (see a video of the episodes at https://www.youtube.com/watch?v=H7ukG3OAT7I).

Episode 1: Ball B is stationary at the center of the screen. Ball A appears from the left, moves toward Ball B with constant velocity v and collides with it. Ball A stops and B moves to the right with velocity v.

Episode 2: Now, Ball A instead is stationary at the center. Ball B appears from the right, moves toward A with velocity v and collides with it. (The negative sign indicates movement from right to left.) B stops as A moves to the left with velocity v.

Episode 3: Balls A and B simultaneously enter from the left and from the right, respectively, *at half the speed* ($v/2$) as in the other two episodes. They collide and move away in opposite directions at the same speed after their collision as before.

In accordance with Michotte's (1946/1963) findings, virtually everyone perceives that in Episode 1 Ball A "causes" Ball B to move. The reverse holds in Episode 2: here Ball B "causes" Ball A to move. In Episode 3, the perception is that each ball causes the other to rebound after their collision. If the balls were real objects rather than cartoons, the preceding perceptions of causality would hold just the same.

Although we perceive the three collision episodes as involving different configurations of causal roles, these episodes can depict the same event viewed from different inertial reference frames. An inertial reference frame is a system of coordinates that moves at a constant velocity. A postulate in Newtonian physics is that laws of motion are invariant across inertial reference frames (Newton, 1687/1713/1726/1999).

To see the three episodes as views of an identical physical event from three inertial reference frames, imagine watching the top episode from clouds moving respectively with constant velocity v and $v/2$, one cloud at a time. The two clouds represent different inertial reference frames. Watching the top episode from each of these two "clouds" transforms that episode respectively into the middle and bottom episode. The exact same event necessarily involves the same causation. Shifting the viewpoint across three inertial frames does not change the event, because the laws of motion are invariant across such frames, but the two balls' causal roles are perceived to differ across episodes. If causation is observable, why would an identical event, involving identical causation, give rise to three compellingly different causal perceptions?

Our three episodes illustrate that, counterintuitively, even in this compelling case of colliding balls, our perception of causation is not a direct reflection of nature. Nature does not come defined by variables or concepts. The concept of an inertial reference frame, for example, is a human construct. Perceived or conceived causation is a matter of how our cognitive processes "choose" to represent reality, in everyday thinking and in science. Whereas intuitive constructs describe these episodes as different events involving different causal roles, Newtonian constructs treat the three episodes as equivalent. Newton's choice yields greater causal invariance, covering a broader explanatory scope (Woodward, 2000). Our example illustrates that the reasoner's goal cannot be to "accurately" represent reality. It is instead to construct more useful, more predictive representations of reality, so that experience is not useless.

Perspective 3: If an activated cone does not know which combination of photons activated it, can "launching" be present in the sensory input to our visual system? (e.g., Hofer, Singer, and Williams, 2005; Mitchell and Rushton, 1971)

From a cognitive neuroscience perspective, causal relations cannot possibly be in the input to our cognitive system. Consider the nature of the input to our receptors, the ultimate and sole source of information about the material world (ourselves included in the material world). Here we review findings on human vision, because sensory input to the visual system is precisely specifiable. The perception of color is perhaps even more compelling than that of causal relations, but the confusion between the input and the output of a system may be more tempting for causal induction, as it may be easier to see that color is in our head, not in the electromagnetic waves.

It is common knowledge that daytime vision in normal human vision is based on the activation of three types of cones, photoreceptors sensitive to electromagnetic waves in the light spectrum. We denote them S, M, and L cones to indicate their respective maximum sensitivity to short, medium, and long wavelengths of light.

Each cone type is sensitive to a range of wavelengths, with overlap between their distributions of relative sensitivities (see Figure 1.3). The overlap in relative sensitivity between the M and L cones is especially large. For example, for rays of 550-nm light, M and L cones are both likely to be activated. Thus, although the cone types are activated with different probabilities by light of different wavelengths, the overlaps imply that when a cone is activated, it would not "know" which wavelength of light activated it.

As vision researchers Mitchell and Rushton (1971, p. 1041) note in their "Principle of Univariance," an activated cone *does not know* which combinations of photons activated it—*it only "knows" that it is activated and the intensity of its activation.* The

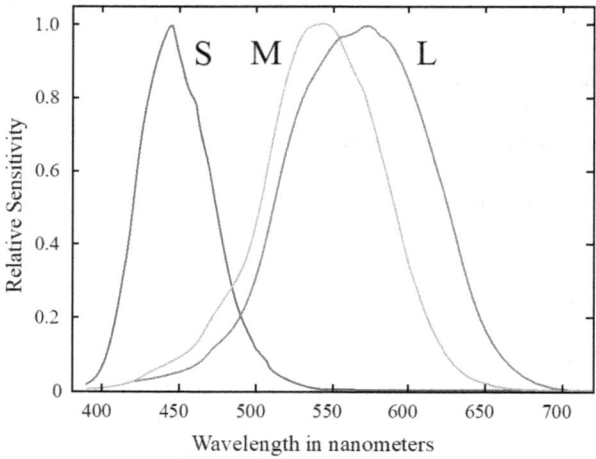

Figure 1.3. Distributions of the relative sensitivity of S, M, and L cones to electromagnetic waves with wavelengths in the range that give rise to human color vision. Peak sensitivities are normalized to 1.0.

distal stimulus is under-determined by the proximal stimulus: An infinite set of wavelength-intensity combinations of electromagnetic waves can elicit an identical response from a cone or a single type of cone. Stepping back from color perception to causal perception, in view of what an activated cone can only know, and thus what it *cannot* know, it should be clear that none of the activated cones can know that some object is "launching" another object.

Findings reported by Hofer, Singer, and Williams (2005) illustrate the remarkable vagueness of the color information encoded in each cone. When human subjects viewed a minuscule spot of 550-nm light that activates a single cone, so that S cones are unlikely to be involved, each subject gave a wide range of verbal responses across trials indicating their perception of color for the same 550-nm light (see Figure 1.4 from Hofer, Singer, and Williams, below). The most common overall response is "white," in addition to at least five other color categories for each subject. Even though S cones are very unlikely to be involved in the detection, "blue" was a quite frequent response for three of the five subjects. If color is not represented in any cone, even less so are other features of our conception of the world; features such as causation, object-hood, and 3-dimensionality are not represented in any of the photoreceptors that inform our daytime vision. There is no homunculus downstream, only more neurons communicating with each other via synapses. Thus, from what is known about the nature of the sensory input, causality is not in the input to our cognitive system from the external world.

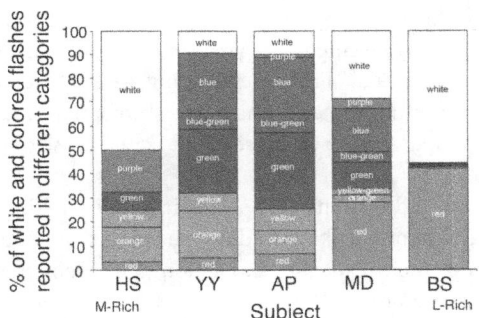

Figure 1.4 A grayscale rendition of Figure 4 in Hofer et al. 2005. The color sensations reported by subjects when viewing a small spot of 550-nm light. At this wavelength only L and M cones participate in detection, with individual subjects varying in how richly populated their retinae are with L cones (i.e., L-Rich) or M cones (i.e., M-Rich). Shown are the percentages of white and colored responses that were placed in each response category, interpolated at 50% frequency of seeing. Percentages for the thin, unlabeled bands for BS are: yellow-green, 0.7%; green, 0.7%; blue-green, 0.3%; and blue, 0.8%. In addition to white, each subject used at least five different hue categories.

Perspective 4: People are unaware of the causes of internal psychological or physical outcomes when multiple plausible causes were present (e.g., Brasil-Neto et al., 1992; Nisbett and Wilson, 1977)

Inducing the causes of internal events is not different from inducing those of external events. Just as causation in external events is inherently not in the input to the processes that give rise to the causal understandings of those events, neither is causation in internal events in the input to the analogous processes. Recall that scratching a mosquito-bite involves proprioceptive input from the fingers, hand, and arm, together with visual input on the cones, enabling the integration across the inputs. No sensory receptor involved in the judgment "knows" the causal perception that the scratching relieved the itch.

If causation in internal events *were* present in the input, one would expect people to be aware of the causes that bring about their voluntary actions, not only in situations when there is one single plausible cause of an action present, but also when multiple plausible causes are present. To provide experimental evidence that causation in internal events is not in the input, we review some findings concerning multiple-cause type situations. In this critical test case, people are remarkably clueless about the causes of their voluntary actions.

In an experiment on the effect of transcranial magnetic stimulation on motor response, normal adult participants were asked to extend the index finger on either their left or right hand at will (Brasil-Neto et al., 1992). They were asked to choose which hand to move upon hearing a go-signal. When magnetic stimulation was delivered to the motor area, participants more often moved the hand contralateral to the site stimulated. This response bias was independent of handedness and of the cerebral hemisphere stimulated. The researchers note that although the influence of magnetic stimulation on hand choice was clear and predictable, no participant was aware of the influence. They conclude (p. 964), "It is possible to influence endogenous processes of movement preparation externally without disrupting the conscious perception of volition." From their finding, we see that when there were two plausible causes of finger movement—magnetic stimulation and participants' own choice of hand—participants were unaware of the actual cause of their "willed" finger movement.

Similarly, in Nisbett and Wilson's (1977) classic article, "Telling more than we can know," they review numerous striking findings showing that people not only cannot articulate the causes of their behaviors and actions, but even when the true cause is revealed, people refuse to believe that such can be the case. For example, in a study conducted in a commercial establishment under the guise of a consumer survey, passersby were invited to appraise articles of clothing and choose one. In one condition, subjects saw four identical pairs of nylon stockings in an array and were asked to evaluate their quality. Once they announced a choice, they were asked to explain why they had chosen what they chose. There was a pronounced position effect, such that the rightmost item in the array was heavily over chosen. The right-most stockings were chosen almost four times as often as the left-most. When asked about the reasons for their choice, no subject ever mentioned the position of the stocking in the array. Even when asked directly whether they chose the article because of its right-most position in the array, "virtually all subjects denied it, usually with a worried glance at the interviewer suggesting that they felt either that they had misunderstood the question or were dealing with a madman" (p. 244).

These examples illustrate that people can be unaware of the causes of their decisions, in simple choices in everyday life or in the laboratory. To our knowledge, there has not been evidence showing that when multiple plausible causes were present, the internal causal relation was "observable."

The four diverse perspectives just reviewed converge in showing that causal understandings are our representations of reality, rather than "direct reflections" of reality. If causal understandings are not directly given by reality, then how and why do we humans develop the causal representations that we do? We do so because we need generalizable/useable causal knowledge, and our causal-induction process aims at formulating such knowledge. The representational nature of causal knowledge implies that the search for such knowledge occurs in an infinite space of possible causal representations (recall the analogous issue in the perception of a cube). In the following, we address two questions arising from that challenge: (1) how is it possible to reduce the search space to avoid paralysis, and (2) how is it possible to tease apart a target candidate cause's influence from that due to potentially unobserved background causes? The rest of our chapter examines an answer to these questions in terms of a constraint on causal induction, which we term causal invariance (Cheng and Lu, 2017; Woodward, 2000).

Causal invariance as a rational constraint on causal induction

In the following, we explain how analytic knowledge of causal invariance plays an essential role in inducing *useable* causal representations, "analytic" in the sense that the knowledge logically follows from the meaning of the concept, namely, the *sameness* of causal influence across contexts, and "useable" in the sense that the acquired knowledge holds when it is applied. We do so by comparing causal induction that is constrained by causal invariance with an associative foil of causal induction that is not so constrained. In an extended example, we show that the former yields useable causal representations and that the latter does not. Because this difference occurs for causal representations involving discrete outcomes and is simple to show for binary outcomes (e.g., a light is either on or off), for which "additivity" is distinct from "invariance" as we explain later, the rest of our chapter concerns binary outcomes.

Terminology and background information

We first clarify some terminology and present some background information. In the previous section, we argued that causal relations are not present in the input to the cognitive system. Given that people do "know" causal relations, such knowledge of causality must therefore emerge somewhere along the pathway from the sensory input to its ultimate output. Under the modularity assumption in cognitive science (Marr, 1982), we designate the causal induction module, the focus of this chapter, to be the segment deep in the computational pathway that begins with an input layer, the layer closest to the causal output that is not yet causal. This module takes as input heterogenous noncausal information encompassing event frequencies and variable intensities and generates as its output *causal representations* and judgments about them. The goal of the module is to induce useable causal representations.

We assume that, for the module, a *causal representation* consists of a cause with one or more component factors, an outcome, and the causal relation between the cause and the outcome. A cause (e.g., stormy weather) influences an outcome occurring in an entity (e.g., an airplane's safe landing). Causal influence can be generative (e.g., increasing the probability of a safe landing) or preventive (reducing that probability). Causal relations are asymmetric in that a cause brings about its outcomes, but an outcome does not bring about its causes. The temporal order of causal relata is asymmetric in that causes precede, or, in some cases, occur simultaneously with the outcomes they bring about (e.g., a wall's blocking of the sun causing the occurrence of a shadow on the ground), but outcomes never precede their causes.

The process of causal induction does its work in situations where available domain-specific causal knowledge does not favor whether or not the candidate is indeed a cause of the outcome (i.e., the input is noncausal in that sense), so that the resulting causal judgment regarding that relation is new knowledge. To be sure, causal knowledge can be transmitted from one reasoner to another (e.g., via verbal communication) after that knowledge has already been induced. However, causal knowledge is ultimately induced based on some individual's experience, through observations of particular events involving the states of candidate causes and of an outcome. (For counterexamples, see Garcia and Koelling, 1966, for evidence of causal knowledge that is not acquired due to individuals' experience, but via the process of evolution based on species' experience.)

We take the view that causation is represented as taking place in individual entities (token causation), but, because causation is "unobservable," no judgment can be made regarding what caused an outcome based on the state of the candidate cause and of the outcome in an individual entity. Causal induction therefore concerns causes and outcomes that are categories (type causation). They are categories in the sense that each is characterized by one or more properties that are common across multiple particular cause and outcome events. These categories are diverse, reflecting reasoners' concerns: They might represent some external event (e.g., rainy weather), some overt action (e.g., a person taking ibuprofen), some enduring state of an entity (e.g., oxygen being present on the surface of the Earth), or an entity's having or not having some property (e.g., a person having or not having a headache), or some other kind of event. In other words, type causal judgments are inferences about relations between cause- and effect-categories based on observations of sets of events across time in which instances (tokens) of cause-categories variously present or absent in sets of entities are, with various probabilities, associated with instances (tokens) of an outcome category occurring in those entities (see Woodward, 2003, for a discussion of the relation between type and token causation; see Stephan and Waldman, 2018, this volume; and Stephan, Mayrhofer, and Waldman, 2020, for discussion of how reasoners can apply their generic, type-level, causal knowledge about causal strength to assess token or singular causation).

Prerequisites for evaluating the influence of a candidate cause on an outcome

No judgment about the influence of a candidate cause on a target outcome can be made based solely on what we term *cause-present* information—that is, information on the relative frequency with which the outcome occurs in multiple entities in which the candidate cause is present. This is so because causation is unobservable. The outcome could have occurred due to *background causes*, various other (known and unknown) causes of the outcome present in the context. The influence of the candidate cause therefore needs to be teased apart from that due to the background causes. Doing so requires an estimate of the probability of the outcome due to background causes.

The influence due to background causes in the cause-present events can be estimated, counterfactually, by the relative frequency of the outcome in *control events*, those in the same causal context—that is, with the same background causes present—but lacking the candidate cause (i.e., *cause-absent* events). In other words, to infer the relation between a candidate cause and an outcome, a reasoner relies on the observation of two relative frequencies: the relative frequency with which an outcome occurs in cause-present events *and* that in control events. Situations in which background causes are held constant—where there is "no confounding"—are the only ones that license causal induction based on contrasting the probabilities of the outcome in the cause-present and cause-absent events (Cheng, 1997). The probability of the outcome in control events, due to satisfaction of the "no confounding" prerequisite, provides an estimate of the probability of the outcome in cause-present events (assuming that sample sizes are sufficiently large). With that estimate, it becomes possible for a reasoner to *decompose* the occurrence of the outcome in the cause-present events into an estimate of the proportion brought about by the candidate cause and the proportion brought about by the background causes, with a potential overlap between the two subsets of events. Given that causation is never observable, decomposition is essential to causal induction.

In the following, we will go through an example where a medication taken by human patients constitutes the candidate cause of headache, the target binary outcome. We partition all causes of headache into the candidate cause and a *composite* of all other (known and unknown) causes in the context (i.e., the background causes), which may affect the occurrence of headache independently of the medication or interacting with the medication. To use the headache example, the composite of background causes might include stress, dehydration, or sleep deprivation.

Because causes and effects are categories, causal induction involves hypothesizing and evaluating representations of a candidate cause, a process that may be parallel to the process involving judgments about causal structure and causal strength (Kemp, Goodman, and Tenenbaum, 2010; Lien and Cheng, 2000; Marsh and Ahn, 2009; Waldmann and Hagmayer, 2006; Waldmann, et al., 2010). This is an important aspect of causal induction which we do not address in the present chapter.

Estimates of causal strength depend on the assumed decomposition function

This process of decomposing the probability of a binary outcome into contributions by its various causes to estimate the causal strength of the candidate can be formally specified using a *decomposition function*. Importantly, given observations of the same event frequencies, different decomposition functions yield different estimates of a candidate's causal strength. This divergence between commonly considered decomposition functions in the psychological literature does not pertain to continuous outcomes (e.g., a light can have varying degrees of brightness), because the dominant decomposition function, additivity, is the causal-invariance function for continuous outcomes.[3] In the following, we focus on causal events featuring a binary outcome in order to contrast two decomposition functions: (1) the *causal invariance* decomposition function, and (2) an associative foil that we label the *additive* decomposition function. Empirical evidence comparing the two decomposition functions shows that the former but not the latter function is descriptive of human causal induction (e.g., Buehner, Cheng, and Clifford, 2003; Cheng, 1997; Liljeholm and Cheng, 2007; Lu, Yuille, Liljeholm, Cheng, and Holyoak, 2008).

Our goal in contrasting these two decomposition functions is to demonstrate that analytic knowledge of causal invariance, in the form of the causal-invariance decomposition function applied to a candidate cause and the composite of other causes in the context, is a rational constraint on causal induction. We show that use of only the causal-invariance decomposition function during learning will result in a logically consistent indication of whether the target causal relation indeed generalizes to other contexts, judging by the criterion of *symmetry*: a causal relation that generalizes from a learning context to an application context should also generalize in the reverse direction, from the application context back to the original learning context.

Please note that the extended example to follow makes use of headache as a *binary outcome*. We acknowledge that headaches do, indeed, vary in their intensity and are more realistically understood as a continuous outcome. Our reason for using headache in our example is simply that their presence and absence is easy to represent in visual diagrams. For more realistic examples of a binary outcome, consider outcomes such as a woman being pregnant or not, a reader subscribing to a magazine or not, a car's motor being on or off, an organism being alive or dead, or a protestor being infected with COVID-19 or not.

Let us consider the following situation, which we will call Context 1: The candidate cause is the medication M taken by human patients and the outcome is these patients having a headache. Patients are randomly assigned to two groups: one that received medication M, another that does not. No relevant causal knowledge about individual patients is available. Here, it is important to note that *individual patients* are the meaningful units within which the medication exerts its causal influence.

Figure 1.5 depicts the occurrence of headaches in patients who did not (top panel) and who did receive the medication (bottom panel) in Context 1. As the figure shows, when patients each take the medication (i.e., in cause-present events), 30/36 of them develop a headache, and when patients do not take the medication (i.e., in control

Revisiting Hume in the Twenty-first Century

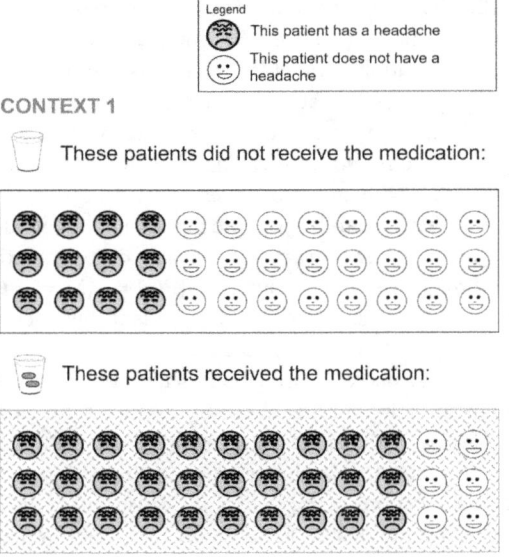

CONTEXT 1

Figure 1.5 Occurrences of headaches in patients who did not receive the medication (top) and in patients who did receive the medication (bottom) in Context 1.

events), 12/36 of them develop a headache. (We leave the fractions unreduced so that they readily correspond to the relative frequencies in the figures.) These relative frequencies of headache are best understood on a ratio scale—each expresses the proportion of individual patients who has a headache relative to the entire group of patients in each kind of event. Assume that there are no preventive causes. When considered in an experimental setting, each of these cause-present and control events might be considered an experimental trial.

Let us consider the causal strengths inferred by the two decomposition functions. An *additive* decomposition function represents the probability of patients having a headache (H) after having taken the medication M in the cause-present events ($P(H = 1|M = 1, B = 1) = 30/36$) as the sum of (1) an estimate of the probability across patients that headache occurs attributable to[4] the composite of background causes B ($p_B = 12/36$) and (2) an estimate of the probability that taking the medication brings about a headache across patients ($p_{M_{Additive}} = 18/36$):

$$P(H = 1 | M = 1, B = 1) = p_B + p_{M_{Additive}} \tag{1}$$

$$\frac{30}{36} = \frac{12}{36} + \frac{18}{36}$$

The additive decomposition function instantiates an exertion of causal strength where each patient is only susceptible to developing a headache from *either* background causes *or* the medication, but not both. To put the point differently, the additive decomposition function implies that in events where the background causes exert their causal strength, the medication *withholds* exerting its causal strength, and in events where the medication exerts its causal strength, the background causes *withhold* exerting their casual strength. Such an absurd state of affairs would involve the medication and the background causes *knowing* in which patients each causes headaches and having the ability to *control* when they themselves do so. In other words, the medication and the background causes are not acting independently.

On the other hand, a *causal invariance* decomposition function represents the probability of this same cause-present outcome (P(H = 1|M = 1, C = 1) = 30/36) as specified in Eq. 2: as a superposition of the independent influences of the medication and the background. $p_{M_{Invariance}}$ in Eq. 2 is the causal power of the medication. *Causal power* is a theoretical, unobservable probability which represents the capacity for an instance of a cause in an entity to bring about an instance of an outcome in that entity (Cartwright, 1989; Cheng, 1997). In the absence of relevant causal knowledge about the individual entities exposed to the candidate cause, the induction of causal power of the candidate based on observations of the state of the cause and of the outcome in a set of entities is constrained by the default assumption that the power of the candidate is *independently and identically distributed* (*iid*) across those entities (e.g., Casella and Berger, 2002). Each particular instantiation of a given cause in an entity is assumed to independently exert the *same* causal power to bring about an instantiation of its outcome across all entities in the set exposed to the same candidate cause. There is no reason to assume otherwise in the absence of relevant causal knowledge. The independent exertion of causal power across individual patients is captured in the intuition that the medication in one patient does not know what the medication in another patient does.

The terms on the right-hand side of Eq. 2 are respectively: (1) an estimate of the probability that headache occurs across patients attributable to background causes (p_B = 12/36), (2) an estimate of the probability that taking the medication brings about a headache across patients ($p_{M_{Invariance}}$ = 27/36), and (3) the counterfactual probability that headache would be produced by taking the medication if it had not already occurred due to the background causes ($p_{M_{Invariance}\cdot B}$ = 9/36), estimated by the product of the preceding two terms:

$$P(H=1\,|M=1, B=1) = p_B + p_{M_{Invariance}} - p_{M_{Invariance},B} \qquad (2)$$

$$\frac{30}{36} = \frac{12}{36} + \frac{27}{36} - \frac{9}{36}$$

The causal invariance decomposition function arrives at $p_{M_{Invariance}}$ = 27/36 as the causal power of taking medication. Under this interpretation, every patient taking the medication in this context is just as susceptible as any other patient to develop headache from background causes, and likewise, independently from taking the medication. This means that there are 9/36 cases in this context where patients' experiencing relief from headache is *causally overdetermined*. Those are the cases in which the background causes and taking medication are *independently* sufficient to cause headache such that, counterfactually, the absence of either one would still have resulted in headache. Those cases are represented by the $p_{M_{Invariance} \cdot B}$ term (which is subtracted in accordance with probability theory to avoid counting those cases twice).

It should be clear that the additive decomposition's estimates of causal strength (i.e., of background causes and of taking medication on developing headaches) *violate* the iid condition across patients. Whereas we refer to the estimate that instantiates the iid assumption as causal power, we use *causal strength* as the theoretically neutral term when an estimate does not necessarily instantiate the iid assumption. We therefore refer to $p_{M_{Additive}}$ as a *causal strength* estimate.

Our present aim is to explain why the iid assumption is a rational constraint on inducing useable causal representation. To gain an intuitive sense of the superposition, consider: What causal strength of medicine M would most likely result in the outcome depicted in the experimental group in Figure 1.5 (the bottom panel)—assuming that M and the background do not interact—if patients in the control group in that figure (the top panel) had received medicine M? We hope it is intuitive that the answer is 3/4, the maximum-likelihood estimate of medicine M producing headache (Griffiths and Tenenbaum, 2005) under the assumptions of the causal power theory (Cheng, 1997).

Are causal strengths inferred without the iid assumption generalizable?

Thus, we see how different decomposition functions arrive at different estimates of causal strengths. To illustrate that causal strengths that violate the iid assumption would not be usable causal knowledge, we explore generalization to a different causal context, which we will call Context 2. Context 2 is the *application context* to which we apply the causal strengths inferred in Context 1, the *learning context*. We continue with the same candidate cause (i.e., taking medication) and the same target outcome (i.e., experiencing headache) as Context 1. We show that, unlike $p_{M_{Invariance}}$, $p_{M_{Additive}}$ does not satisfy even the minimal generalization requirement: specifically, after $p_{M_{Additive}}$ successfully generalizes to Context 2, it fails to generalize from Context 2 back to Context 1, the original context in which it was inferred. To illustrate that $p_{M_{Additive}}$ fails to satisfy this minimal requirement, we chose Context 2 to be a situation in which all associative and causal models agree on the predicted outcome from introducing a cause with any given strength. In Context 2, 0/36 patients have a headache without any medication (see Figure 1.6), indicating that there are no background causes, so that any candidate cause introduced is the only cause present. As before, assume that there are no preventive causes.

An *integration* function uses estimates of causal influence induced from prior experience (e.g., from observing event frequencies in Context 1) to predict frequencies of some outcome in a new context (e.g., the occurrence of headache in patients having taken the medication in Context 2). Importantly, an integration function *generalizes* an estimate of causal strength to a novel context, in which we have no information yet on whether and how the background causes in that context interact with the target cause.

Without any such information, the only reasonable default assumption is that the target cause brings about the outcome of interest with the *same* capacity on each event, and this assumption is captured by the iid nature of causal power. In other words, an integration function that instantiates this iid nature of causal power is the only justifiable integration function to apply as a default. An integration function assuming iid specifies the inverse operation as the causal-invariance decomposition function. We use this function below to generate predictions of headache occurrence in Context 2, for both $p_{M_{Invariance}}$ and $p_{M_{Additive}}$. Because medication M is the only cause in Context 2, no superposition is involved. The applications of this integration function we illustrate below are therefore trivial, and the resulting predictions do not differ from those resulting from applying an additive integration function.

Recall that the causal strength estimate from the additive decomposition function in Context 1 was 18/36 and that the causal power estimate from the causal invariance decomposition function was 27/36. Also recall that 0/36 patients develop a headache without the medication in Context 2. Incorporating this outcome frequency with the causal strength estimated by the additive decomposition function in Context 1 yields the prediction that 18/36 patients will develop a headache after taking the medication:

$$p_B + p_{M_{Additive}} - p_{M_{Additive},B} = P(H=1 \mid M=1, B=1)_{Additive} \tag{3}$$

$$\frac{0}{36} + \frac{18}{36} - \frac{0}{36} = \frac{18}{36}$$

And doing the same but instead using the causal power estimated by the causal-invariance decomposition function in Context 2 yields the prediction that 27/36 patients will develop a headache after taking the medication:

$$p_B + p_{M_{Invariance}} - p_{M_{Invariance},B} = P(H=1 \mid M=1, B=1)_{Invariance} \tag{4}$$

$$\frac{0}{36} + \frac{27}{36} - \frac{0}{36} = \frac{27}{36}$$

We now compare how the predictions generated using the two causal strength estimates generalize the respective strengths back to Context 1, the learning context.

Across the causal events to which the same causal representation applies, an agent may use their observations of some causal events to *induce* that causal representation, or they may *apply* their causal representation to either explain or predict outcome occurrences in other causal events. We refer to the cognitive processes underlying the former phenomenon as *causal induction* and those underlying the latter phenomenon as *causal reasoning*. While both processes may operate in a given event, for the purpose of exposition it is worthwhile to distinguish between *learning contexts* where an agent engages in causal induction and *application contexts* where an agent engages in causal reasoning.

Even though the distinction between the learning and application contexts is natural with respect to a reasoner's cognitive history, this same distinction is completely incidental with respect to *rationally generated* causal representations. Specifically, if the same causal representation holds across two causal contexts, which of those contexts

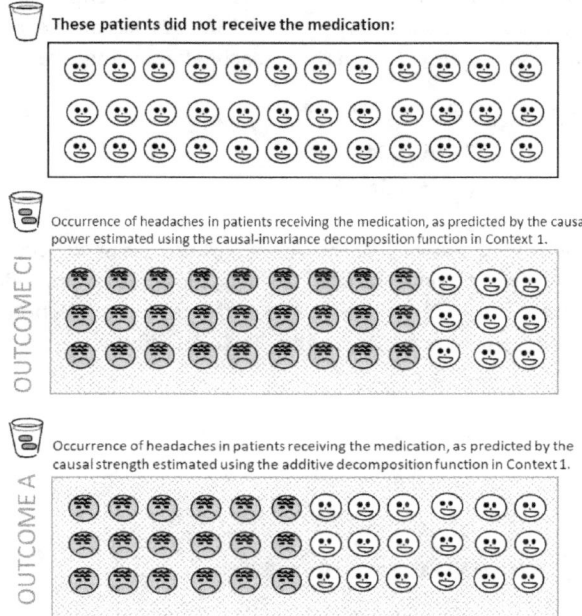

Figure 1.6 Occurrence of headaches in patients who did not receive the medication in Context 2 (top) and occurrence of headaches in patients receiving the medication in this context as predicted, respectively, by the causal power estimated in Context 1 using the causal-invariance decomposition function (middle) and by the causal strength estimated in Context 1 using the additive decomposition function (bottom).

was a learning context and which was an application context for a particular reasoner should make no difference. Returning to our example above, while Context 1 served as a learning context and Context 2 served as an application for a hypothetical reasoner, reversing their roles (i.e., so that Context 2 serves as a learning context and Context 1 serves as an application context) should yield consistent inferences. In other words, causal induction should accommodate symmetry between learning and application contexts. It is logically inconsistent for a causal strength to be *both* "the same" and "not the same" across two contexts: if a cause operates the same way in an application context as in its learning context, its causal strength should remain the same across the two contexts, regardless of that context's epistemic relation to the reasoner. In the following, we show that causal induction assuming causal invariance as the decomposition function does accommodate this symmetry, but that assuming the additivity decomposition function or any other non-causal invariance decomposition function fails to accommodate this symmetry. Let us now flip the learning and application contexts of our previous example, treating Context 2 as a learning context and Context 1 as an application context.

Figure 1.7 depicts the results of flipping the learning and application contexts for the additive and causal invariance functions. The causal strength estimated by the additive decomposition in Context 2, $p_{M_{Additive}}$ = 18/36, makes an incorrect prediction that 24/36 of patients in Context 1 will have headache after having taken the medication:

$$p_B + p_{M_{Additive}} - p_{M_{Additive},B} = P(H=1 \mid M=1, B=1)_{Additive} \tag{5}$$

$$\frac{12}{36} + \frac{18}{36} - \frac{6}{36} = \frac{24}{36}$$

And as should be obvious, because of the inverse relation between decomposition and integration, the causal power estimated by the causal invariance decomposition function in Context 2, $p_{M_{Invariance}}$ = 27/36, makes the correct prediction that 30/36 of patients in Context 1 will have headache after having taken the medication:

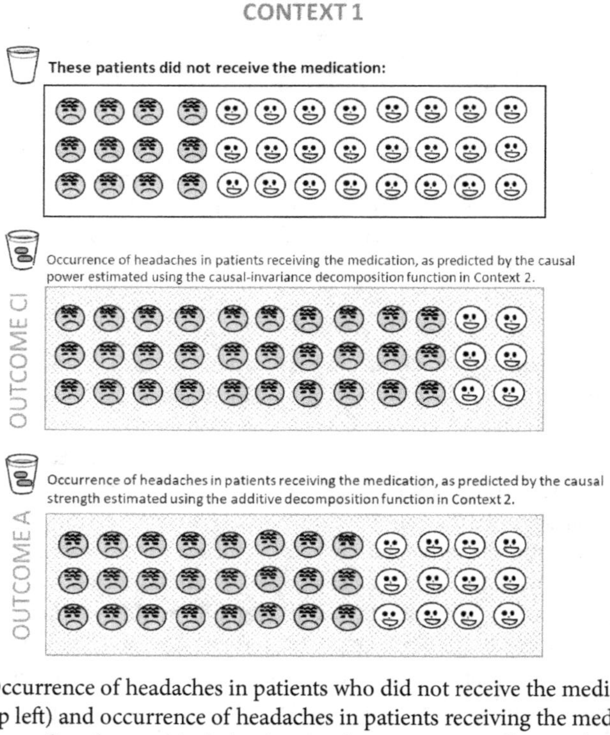

Figure 1.7 Occurrence of headaches in patients who did not receive the medication in Context 1 (top left) and occurrence of headaches in patients receiving the medication in this context as predicted, respectively, by the causal power estimated using the causal-invariance decomposition function (middle left) and by the causal strength estimated using the additive decomposition function (bottom left) based on the event frequencies in Context 2 shown in Figure 1.6 and duplicated here for easier visual comparison (top right).

$$p_B + p_{M_{Invariance}} - p_{M_{Invariance},B} = P(H=1 \mid M=1, B=1)_{Invariance} \tag{6}$$

$$\frac{12}{36} + \frac{27}{36} - \frac{9}{36} = \frac{30}{36}$$

Here, we see that generalizing from Context 2 to Context 1 using the causal invariance decomposition function, but not the additive decomposition function, accommodates the symmetry between learning and application contexts. Specifically, the predicted occurrence of headaches in patients taking the medication in Context 1 using the causal power estimated by the causal-invariance decomposition function in Context 2, but not that estimated by the additive decomposition function, yields the actual observed frequency in Context 1 (Figure 1.5). This difference in the satisfaction of the symmetry requirement follows from (1) the inverse relation between a decomposition function and an integration function, and (2) the inherent assumption when a reasoner applies causal knowledge to a new context where potentially different unobserved or unknown causes occur: the causal relations being generalized operate the same way across the learning and application contexts. That inherent assumption renders the causal-invariance function the only rational integration function to apply in causal reasoning. As an example, we have shown that the additive decomposition function fails to be logically consistent across transpositions of the arbitrary "learning" and "application" context labels for inducing causal relations involving a binary outcome, illustrating that the causal-invariance function is the only rational decomposition function to apply in causal induction.

A careful reader may notice that the additive decomposition function that we have discussed thus far is the one that underlies a linear regression model. Considering that our example features a binary outcome, such a reader might protest that it is inappropriate to use linear regression to estimate binary outcomes (but see Gomilla, 2020 for advocation for this very practice) and question the relevance of problematizing the additive function for such situations. In the following, we show that the inconsistency described above is also characteristic of the logistic model, whose use in predicting binary outcomes is much more conventional. By extending our analysis to the logistic model, we argue that this logical inconsistency is inherent to any decomposition function that violates the iid assumption (i.e., any non-causal-invariance function).

Is logical inconsistency a problem for generalized linear models?

The logical inconsistency across contexts is true not only of the additive decomposition function, for which this problem may be obvious. Here we illustrate the general problem with a concrete example where it is easy to see the problem for the logistic function, a generalized linear function:

$$f(z) = \frac{e^z}{1+e^z}, \tag{7}$$

where z may be interpreted as the weighted sum of the predictor variables (in this interpretation the causal variables), and $f(z)$ is the probability of the binary outcome in question. The logistic function (Eq. 7) is assumed by "normative" associative models such as logistic regression, a widely used statistical method in medical and business research, where binary outcomes (e.g., a tumor is either malignant or benign, a bone is either fractured or intact) are common.

One interpretation of the logistic model is that: (1) the predictor variables exert their independent influences, not directly on the binary outcome, but on a latent mediating variable s—a continuous variable with values on an interval or ratio scale—so that s is a weighted sum of the predictor variables, (2) the probability $f(z)$ in Eq. 7 can be conceptualized as being due to noise n being added to the latent variable s to produce a decision y representing the binary outcome; n has a logistic distribution (i.e., density function) with a mean of 0 and a scale parameter equal to 1, and (3) when $s + n$ is greater than a threshold—0 in this case, the binary outcome occurs, otherwise the outcome does not occur; that is:

$$y = \begin{cases} 1 & s+n > 0 \\ 0 & \text{else.} \end{cases}$$

We do not dispute that hypotheses with a mediating variable should be considered. However, the principle of parsimony would be violated if the continuous mediating variable is postulated as a default, bypassing consideration of a simpler hypothesis. In cases in which the simpler independent-influence hypothesis is in fact the better explanation, it would never be found. For this reason, the common usage of logistic regression as the standard statistical method for analyzing data with a binary outcome is likely to have contributed to the replicability crisis (Ioannidis, 2005; Open Science Collaboration, 2015).

A shared mediating variable can strain credulity in some cases. Consider one of the binary outcomes introduced briefly earlier: Pregnancy. Pregnancy is likely to have dissociable, independent causes. Two such causes might include, (1) whether or not someone has received a medical procedure to improve their fertility and (2) whether or not someone lives in a country with a policy that limits child-rearing (e.g., China and its one-child policy). The mechanism by which someone having received a medical procedure to improve their fertility influences their chances of getting pregnant is biological and internal to their bodily function. On the other hand, the mechanism by which someone's living in a country with a policy that limits child-rearing is social and external to their bodily function. A latent variable that elides the clear distinction between these two causal mechanisms seems implausible. To what would this latent variable refer?

It is our understanding that the simpler hypothesis, the independent *direct* causal-influences hypothesis without the continuous mediating variable, is typically not in the repertoire of potential models to evaluate in popular statistical-analysis software (e.g., SPSS, R). The software user has no choice but to posit the more complex hypothesis, which implies foregoing deviation from independent direct causal influences as a criterion for hypothesis revision, instead treating independent influences on the continuous intervening variable as the aspiration. Beyond the logistic model's relative lack of parsimony, it fails to estimate causal strengths that generalize across distinct contexts when the simpler hypothesis holds, as we now move on to show.

To see the problem with the logistic function as a decomposition function for sets of events with a binary outcome, let us consider yet another context, which we will call Context 3, alongside the previously discussed Context 1 (see Figure 1.8). In Context 3, 6/36 patients develop a headache without receiving the medication, and 24/36 patients develop a headache after having taken the medication.

We constructed the outcome frequency for control events in Context 1 to be the complement of the outcome frequency for cause-present events in Context 3, and the outcome frequency for control events in Context 3 to be the complement of the outcome frequency for control events in Context 1. We use this complementary pattern as an obvious example to illustrate the general violation of the iid assumption by this model. In this model, the probability of a binary outcome is a logistic function of z, the weighted sum of the predictor variables, the causal variables in the case of our example:

$$z = B_1 * w_{B_1} + M * w_M \tag{8}$$
$$B_1 \in \{0, 1\}$$
$$M \in \{0, 1\}$$

B_1 refers to *Context 1*, and M refers to the medication. Each are binary variables where a value of 1 represents the presence of their referent, and a value of 0 represents its absence.

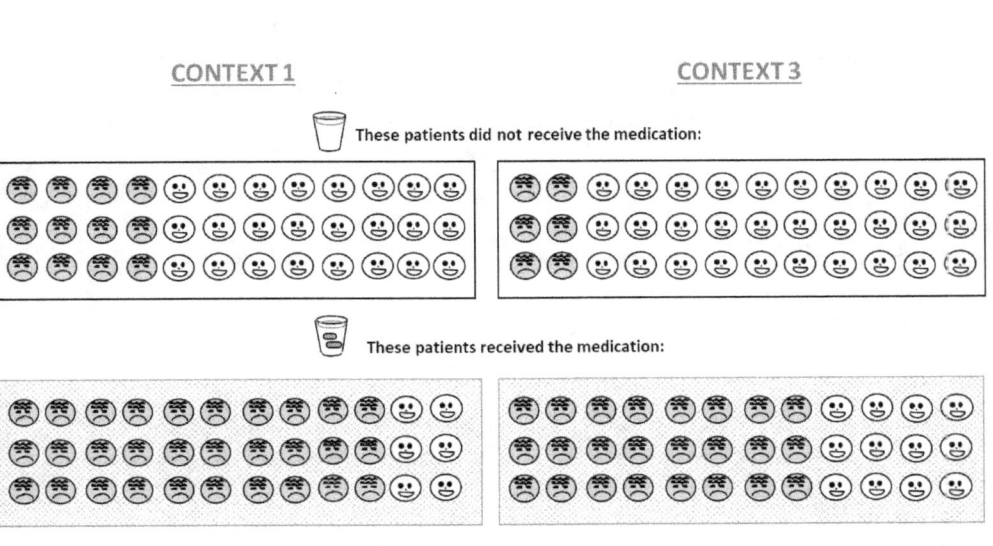

Figure 1.8 Occurrences of headaches in patients who did not receive the medication in Context 1 (top left) and Context 3. Occurrences of headaches in patients receiving the medication in Context 1 (bottom left) and in Context 3 (bottom right).

w_{B_1} and w_M represent the causal weights associated with the *Context 1* background causes and the medication, respectively. w_{B_1} is the same as p_B from the additive decomposition function applied to the respective causal context. Decomposing using Eqs. 7 and 8, the logistic function, like the additive decomposition function, characterizes the medication as an invariant cause across Context 1 and 3, in that w_M is constant across these contexts. It should be clear that this characterization is mistaken. For each of these contexts, consider: What causal strength of medicine M would most likely result in the outcome depicted in the experimental group in Figure 1.8 (the bottom panel)—assuming that M does not interact with the background in either context—if patients in the control group in that figure (the top panel) had received medicine M? The answers are not the same for the two contexts. They instead correspond to $p_{M_{Invariance}}$ in Context 1 and in Context 3.

We will now explain the general divergence between the logistic decomposition function and the causal invariance decomposition function by examining the logistic function graphically, as shown in Figure 1.9. Each of the four pairs of light grey and dark grey points represents a different causal context. Here, we see that the four depicted causal contexts that are symmetric about $z = 0$ or $f(z) = .5$ (e.g., the two contexts represented by the two inner pairs of points or the two contexts represented by the two outer pairs of points in the figure), w_M will be identical across contexts, and the medication will be represented as an invariant cause. This explains the point made earlier: *Context 1* and *Context 3* in Figure 1.8 were constructed to be symmetric about $z = 0$ or $f(z) = .5$. (But note that Figure 1.9 does not illustrate Contexts 1 and 3, but instead illustrates points on the left panel of Figure 1.10.)

Let us now shift attention to the whole logistic curve. Notice that each causal context in Figure 1.9 has the same ΔP (vertical dashed lines), that is, the *difference* in headache probability between cause-present events and the control events is held constant across contexts. Let us now focus on w_M (horizontal dashed lines) across contexts. Notice that, for causal events with the same ΔP, as the observed headache probability for control events (light grey points) approaches .5, w_M decreases, and that as the observed

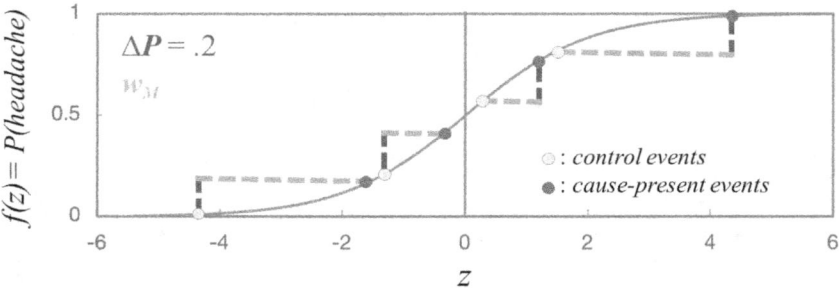

Figure 1.9 w_M according to the logistic decomposition function in various causal contexts. Each pair of cause-present and control events (light grey and dark grey points) represents a different causal context.

headache probability for control events increases beyond .5, w_M increases. This trend is shown in the left panel of Figure 1.10, which depicts causal strength estimate from the logistic decomposition function, w_M (horizontal dashed lines in Figure 1.9), as a function of headache probability in control events (y-values of the grey dots in Figure 1.9), holding ΔP constant. For comparison, the right panel of Figure 1.10 depicts the causal power estimate from the causal invariance decomposition function, $p_{M_{Invariance}}$, as a function of headache probability in control events, holding ΔP constant. In sharp contrast to w_M, $p_{M_{Invariance}}$ monotonically increases as the outcome probability in control events increases. Intuitively, this is because increases in the outcome probability in control events, by counterfactual reasoning, imply a larger *proportion* of patients who would have been *without* headaches in the cause-present events who are caused to have headache, as expressed by $p_{M_{Invariance}}$.

In showing this divergence between the logistic decomposition function and the causal invariance decomposition function across Contexts 1 and 3, we have demonstrated that generalized linear models such as logistic regression are logically inconsistent with causal generalization, and do not yield usable causal knowledge. Further, in showing their incompatibility with causal invariance, we have shown that estimates of causal strength that are consistent with generalized linear models diverge from human causal induction (Buehner, Cheng, and Clifford, 2003; Cheng, 1997; Liljeholm and Cheng, 2007; Lu et al., 2008).

Through discussing event frequencies across Context 1, 2, and 3, we have argued for causal invariance as a rational constraint on the formulation of useable causal knowledge. Causal invariance assumes the identical and independent exertion of causal power within and across causal contexts. Specifically, we have shown (1) how different quantitative estimates of causal strengths assuming non-causal-invariance and causal-invariance decomposition functions respectively violate and accommodate this constraint, and (2) violation of the constraint leads to logical inconsistency, resulting in false alarms and misses in the hypothesis testing and hypothesis revision process. The violation is not specific to the cases we illustrated, but inherent to non-causal-invariance functions.

In conclusion, revisiting Hume's (1739/1987) radical insight that causation is "unobservable," we see that it is strongly supported by findings and theoretical

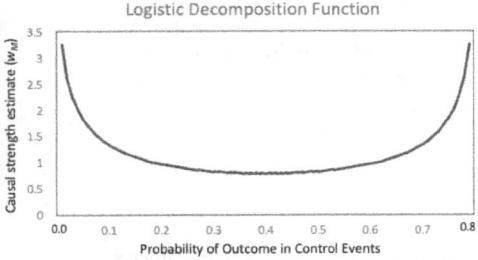
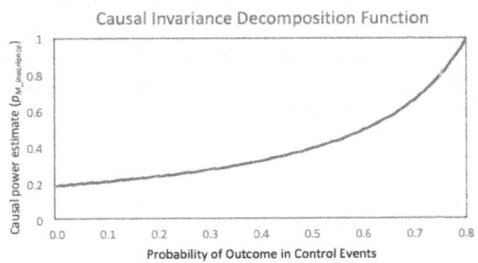

Figure 1.10 Causal estimates (y-axes) as a function of outcome probability in control events (x-axes), holding constant $\Delta P = .2$.

developments from diverse perspectives. These perspectives—psychological science, physics, vision science, and neuroscience—converge in clarifying that causation is a representation of the empirical world by and in our mind. Grounded in a representation-dependent conception of reality, we see that the unobservability of causal relations demands an explanation of how useable causal knowledge is attainable in a search for such knowledge within an infinite space of possible representations. Our analysis shows that it is attainable only if a cognitive process adopts causal invariance as the default decomposition function, in other words, implements the assumption that there exist invariant causal relations in the world, and (implicitly) aims to construct such knowledge. This assumption narrows the search space to representations that are (1) candidates for serving our species' subjective goal of possessing useable causal knowledge and (2) logically consistent with that goal. Omitting the constraint results in logical inconsistency during the search in that vast space. It follows that "normative" statistical inference, whether frequentist or Bayesian, will not yield useable causal knowledge if it violates the causal invariance constraint.

Acknowledgments

We thank Hongjing Lu and Simon Stephan for very helpful comments on a draft of this chapter. We thank George Sperling for a very helpful discussion.

Notes

1. Our thanks to an anonymous reviewer for the example.
2. SCR is a physiological measure of psychological and autonomic arousal that is not under voluntary control.
3. Different outcome-variable types (e.g., binary, continuous, vectors, waves) have different causal-invariance functions, depending on how superposition of causal influences (i.e., independent influences) is normatively expressed in mathematical form. Vector addition, for example, is the causal-invariance function for vectors.
4. We distinguish the interpretation of p_B mentioned in the text from an alternative interpretation in which it is the probability with which background causes bring about headache. The latter is not estimable because of the inherent lack of information about the probability of the occurrence of unobserved and unknown background causes in the context.

References

Armel, K.C., and V.S. Ramachandran (2003). "Projecting sensations to external objects: Evidence from skin conductance response." *Proceedings of the Royal Society of London B, 270*: 1499–506.

Botvinick, M. and J. Cohen (1998). "Rubber hands 'feel' touch that eyes see." *Nature, 391*: 756–756.

Brasil-Neto, J.P., A. Pascual-Leone, J. Valls-Sole, L.G. Cohen, and M. Hallett (1992). "Focal transcranial magnetic stimulation and response bias in a forced-choice task." *Journal of Neurology, Neurosurgery, and Psychiatry, 55*: 964–6.

Buehner, M., P.W. Cheng, and D. Clifford (2003). "From covariation to causation: A test of the assumption of causal power." *Journal of Experimental Psychology: Learning, Memory, and Cognition, 29*: 1119–40.

Cartwright, N. (1989). *Nature's Capacities and their Measurement*. Oxford: Clarendon Press.

Casella, G., and R.L. Berger (2002). *Statistical Inference*. Duxbury Press.

Cheng, P.W. (1993). "Separating causal laws from causal facts: Pressing the limits of statistical relevance." In D.L. Medin (ed.), *The Psychology of Learning and Motivation*, Vol. 30 (215–64). New York: Academic Press.

Cheng, P.W. (1997). "From covariation to causation: A causal power theory." *Psychological Review, 104*: 367–405.

Cheng, P.W. and H. Lu (2017). "Causal invariance as an essential constraint for creating a causal representation of the world: Generalizing the invariance of causal power." In M.R. Waldmann (ed.), *The Oxford Handbook of Causal Reasoning*. New York: Oxford University Press.

Garcia, J., and R.A. Koelling (1966). "Relation of cue to consequence in avoidance learning." *Psychonomic Science, 4*(3): 123–4. https://doi.org/10.3758/BF03342209

Gomilla, R. (2020). "Logistic or linear? Estimating causal effects of treatments on binary outcomes using regression analysis." *Journal of Experimental Psychology: General*.

Goodman, N. (1955). *Fact, Fiction, and Forecast*. Cambridge, MA: Harvard University Press.

Griffiths, T.L., and J.B. Tenenbaum (2005). "Structure and strength in causal induction." *Cognitive Psychology, 51*: 354–84.

Hawking, S., and L. Mlodinow (2010). *The Grand Design*. New York: Bantam Books.

Henle, M. (1962). "On the relation between logic and thinking." *Psychological Review, 69*(4): 366–78.

Hofer, H., B. Singer, and D.R. Williams (2005). "Different sensations from cones with the same photopigment." *Journal of Vision, 5*: 444–54.

Hume, D. (1739/1987). *A Treatise of Human Nature*. 2nd ed. Oxford: Clarendon Press.

Hume, D. (1748/1975). *An Enquiry Concerning Human Understanding*. (L.A. Shelby-Bigge and P.H. Nidditch, eds.) 3rd ed. Oxford: Clarendon Press.

Ioannidis, J.P.A. (2005). "Why most published scientific findings are false." *PLoS Medicine, 2*(8): e124.

Kant, I. (1781/1965). *Critique of Pure Reason*. London: Macmillian.

Kemp, C., N.D. Goodman, and J.B. Tenenbaum (2010). "Learning to learn causal models." *Cognitive Science, 34*(7): 1185–243.

Lien, Y. and P.W. Cheng (2000). "Distinguishing genuine from spurious causes: a coherence hypothesis." *Cognitive Psychology: 40*: 87–137.

Liljeholm, M. and P.W. Cheng (2007). "When is a cause the 'same'?: Coherent generalization across contexts." *Psychological Science, 115*(4): 955–84.

Lu, H., A. Yuille, M. Liljeholm, P.W. Cheng, and K.J. Holyoak (2008). "Bayesian generic priors for causal learning." *Psychological Review, 18*(11): 1014–21.

Marr, D. (1982). *Vision*. New York: Freeman.

Marsh, J.K. and W. Ahn (2009). "Spontaneous assimilation of continuous values and temporal information in causal induction." *Journal of Experimental Psychology: Learning, Memory, and Cognition, 35*: 334–52.

Michotte, A. (1946/1963). *The Perception of Causality*. New York: Basic Books.

Mitchell, D.E. and W.A.H. Rushton (1971). "Visual pigment in dichromats." *Vision Research*, 11: 1033–43.

Newton, I. (1687/1713/1726/1999). *The Principia: Mathematical Principles of Natural Philosophy.* (I.B. Cohen and A. Whitman, eds.). Berkeley and Los Angeles: University of California Press.

Nisbett, R.E., and T.D. Wilson (1977). "Telling more than we can know: Verbal reports on mental processes." *Psychological Review*, 84(3): 231–59.

Open Science Collaboration (2015). "Estimating the reproducibility of psychological science." *Science, 349*: 943. DOI: 10.1126/science.aac4716

Pizlo, Z. (2001). "Perception viewed as an inverse problem." *Vision Research*, 41: 3145–61.

Ramachandran, V.S. and W. Hirstein (1998). "The perception of phantom limbs: The D.O. Hebb lecture." *Brain 121*: 1603–30.

Rips, L.J. (2011). "Causation from perception." *Perspectives on Psychological Science*, 6: 77–97.

Scholl, B.J. and P.D. Tremoulet (2000). "Perceptual causality and animacy." *Trends in Cognitive Sciences*, 4(8): 299–309.

Stephan, S. and M.R. Waldmann (2018). "Preemption in singular causation judgments: A computational model." *Topics in Cognitive Science*, 10(1): 242–57.

Stephan, S., R. Mayrhofer, and M.R. Waldmann (2020). "Time and singular causation—a computational model." *Cognitive Science*, 44(7): e12871.

Waldmann, M.R. and Y. Hagmayer (2006). "Categories and causality: The neglected direction." *Cognitive Psychology*, 53: 27–58.

Waldmann, M.R., B. Meder, M. von Sydow, and Y. Hagmeyer (2010). "The tight coupling between category and causal learning." *Cognitive Processing*, 11: 143–58.

Woodward, J. (2000). "Explanation and invariance in the special sciences." *British Journal of the Philosophy of Science*, 51: 197–254.

Woodward, J. (2003). *Making Things Happen: A Theory of Causal Explanation (Oxford Studies in the Philosophy of Science)*. Oxford: Oxford University Press.

2

Mysteries of Actual Causation: It's Complicated

James Woodward

1 Introduction

This chapter explores some issues concerning actual cause judgments—judgments that some particular event caused another, as in "the impact of the rock caused the shattering of the bottle" or "Smith's smoking caused his lung cancer." This topic has received a great deal of attention recently in a number of different disciplines. In philosophy, computer science, and psychology there are a number of more or less formal models of such judgments, often (but by no means always) making use of directed graphs and structural equations (e.g., Hitchcock, 2001; Woodward, 2003; Halpern and Hitchcock, 2015; Halpern, 2016; Icard, Kominsky, and Knobe; 2017). These models can be understood either as *descriptive* (as attempting to represent and in some cases to explain the judgments people make) or, in some cases, as *normative* (as characterizing the actual cause judgments people *ought* to make). In a number of cases they have *both* descriptive and normative aspirations—for entirely defensible reasons, as I explain below. At the same time there is an ever-expanding body of empirical work, from psychology and experimental philosophy on the people's actual cause judgments.

Actual cause judgments (although not always under that name[1]) have also been a topic of ongoing interest in more traditional philosophical discussion. Here there tends to be less use of formal models but there are still many attempts to capture or represent actual cause judgments via a mixture of verbal and partially formal proposals. (For a recent example see Paul and Hall, 2013.) In this literature, the judgments to be captured are often described as "intuitions" that the writer has about various scenarios. For example, a scenario (EX1.1) may be constructed in which Suzy and Billy throw rocks at a bottle, Suzy's rock strikes the bottle first, the bottle shatters and Billy's rock passes through the empty space previously occupied by the bottle. The writer then announces that she has the intuition that the impact of Suzy's rock caused (where this is understood to mean "was an actual cause of") the shattering and Billy's rock did not. Some philosophers think of intuitions of this sort as potential sources of information about the underlying metaphysics of causation or about "causal reality," but whether or not they claim this, they at least try to develop accounts that reproduce such intuitive judgments, while perhaps satisfying other constraints which may be more metaphysical in nature. Often it is assumed if they can produce an account that captures a wide range of intuitive judgments (and perhaps additional constraints), this shows that the account in question is (in some sense) warranted or correct. Similar assumptions seem to be made in some treatments of actual causation developed by non-philosophers. For example, in Halpern's (2016) book-length treatment, the standard for correctness also seems to be largely agreement with intuitive judgment.

One obvious question raised by these various literatures (and accompanying research agendas) is how if at all, they might fit together. For example, how should we think about the relationship between normative models of actual cause judgment and descriptive facts about how people in fact judge? What is (or should be) the relationship between empirical investigations of the sort conducted by psychologists and experimental philosophers into people's patterns of judgments and the "intuitions" about causal relationships to which some philosophers appeal?

The rest of this chapter is organized as follows. Section 2 provides an overall framework for thinking about causation, including actual cause judgments. I argue that causal claims of all varieties should be understood in terms of the goals or functions that they serve. This framework has been fairly successful in characterizing so-called type causal claims but is less successful in dealing with actual causation, in part because the function or functions of such judgments remain controversial. More specifically, I argue that we have a somewhat plausible functional account of actual cause judgments that involve *causal selection* but this account does not seem to fit actual cause judgments that are apparently not influenced by selection considerations and instead involve a distinct notion that I call "actual causal contribution." At least some of the failures of current theorizing derive from attempts to provide a single unified account of what may be rather different varieties of actual cause judgments with different functions. Section 3 argues, contrary to what some metaphysicians seem to assume, that actual causation (however this is understood) is not a foundation or ground for all other sorts of causal judgments. Instead, judgments of actual causation have a number of distinctive, even idiosyncratic features not shared by other varieties of causal judgment. Section 5 describes a standard account of actual causation that draws on the resources of structural equations and directed graphs. Section 6 describes several counterexamples to this standard account and an alternative more recent treatment, due to Halpern (2016), that attempts to accommodate the counterexamples by incorporating "normality" considerations. I argue that Halpern's account tracks our practices of causal selection fairly well but is less successful in characterizing non-selective judgments of the actual contribution variety. Sections 7–9 attempt to flesh out this actual contribution notion in more detail. Section 10 contains some methodological reflections concerning the distinctions described earlier and also regarding the use of verbal probes to explore people's actual cause judgments. Section 11 speculates on a possible function for actual contribution judgments and Section 12 concludes.

2 Framework and background

Actual cause judgment is, in my view, just one possible variety of causal judgment among many (in fact, as we shall see, a kind of causal judgment with some rather idiosyncratic features). Like other forms of causal judgment, actual causal judgments are best approached from a "functional" standpoint (Woodward, 2014, forthcoming). What I mean by this is that causal judgments of any variety should be understood in terms of their function, goal or point—what people are trying to do or accomplish when they make such judgments. This focus on function in understanding causal cognition is now fairly widely, although by no means universally, accepted—see, for example, Icard, Kominsky, and Knobe (2017). As an interventionist about causation (see Woodward, 2003), I take one of the most distinctive and important functions of causal thinking to have to do with discovery and use of information relevant to manipulation and control. However, there are many different kinds of manipulation-related questions and different sorts of causal judgment can be thought of as answers to such different questions. For example, a so-called type-causal claim such as "smoking causes lung cancer" suggests that intervening on whether people smoke will change the incidence of lung cancer—type-causal claims can be thought of as having the goal or function of providing information relevant to questions of this sort. As we shall see, actual cause judgments can also be thought of as answers to rather different but nonetheless manipulation-related questions.

Although functional treatments of type-causal claims have been fairly successful, I think it fair to say that similar treatments of actual cause judgment have so far been less illuminating. This is at least in part because it is a disputed issue what the goal(s) or point of actual cause might be or whether this is even an appropriate question to ask about such judgments. It may also be the case, as I will suggest below, that actual cause judgments are a heterogenous class, with different judgments having different goals or functions. One candidate for such a function, advanced by several researchers (e.g., Hitchcock and Knobe, 2009, Icard, Kominsky, and Knobe, 2017), is that it has to do with the identification of the most effective targets of intervention in some specific actual situation, given that one wants to change some effect. That is, c is judged to be an actual cause of e when intervening on c is thought to be an effective way of changing e (or a more effective way of changing e than other possible intervention targets), given the actual situation in which c and e obtain. I will explore this suggestion below, suggesting that it fits some sorts of actual cause judgments better than others.

Above, I distinguished between normative and descriptive treatments of causal judgment. One obvious normative standard (and the one assumed in this essay) comes from the notion of function just described: one shows that some account of causal reasoning, judgment, learning etc. is normatively good (correct etc.) by showing that proceeding in accord with the account contributes to or promotes (is an efficient means to) various goals associated with causal thinking. Applied to actual cause judgment this means that if we are to develop an account that tells us which such judgments are "correct" or "warranted" we should proceed by identifying goals or functions associated with such judgments and then use these to distinguish judgments that contribute to these goals from those that do not.

Of course, even given this understanding of "ought," how people ought to judge and how in fact they judge are two different matters, but the normative and descriptive can be brought into closer contact if an additional assumption holds: that people are, at least a significant portion of the time, "rational" or behave in a normatively appropriate way in the causal judgments they make. ("Rational" here should be understood in purely in terms of means/ends—some pattern of judgments is "rational" to the extent that it contributes to rather than frustrating ends that the judgers have, where these have to with, for example, identifying relations relevant to manipulation and control, among other possibilities.) To the extent that this is so we can use normative models to capture and explain features of judgments that, as an empirical matter, people make. At the same time, if we find that people's causal judgments exhibit, as an empirical matter, certain features and not others this can suggest (*suggest*, not by itself conclusively establish) various hypotheses about their ends or goals, and the ways in which their judgments are effective means to these.

As an illustration, one aspect of actual cause judgment (although arguably not all that is involved in such judgments—see below) concerns *causal selection*. Suppose that two events—c_1 and c_2—must both be present for e to occur (the causes act "conjunctively") and that together they are in some relevant sense causally sufficient for e, as when striking a match (c_1) in the presence of oxygen (c_2) is followed by ignition e. In such cases, when subjects are asked what caused e they tend to select the "abnormal" event c_1 rather than the more normal event c_2, and when they are asked to make "causal strength" judgments they assign higher ratings to c_1 than to c_2. A number of different verbal probes have been used to elicit such judgments. Knobe and Fraser (2008) and Icard, Kominsky, and Knobe (2017) ask subjects to rate on a seven-point scale whether they agree with descriptions of the form "c caused e." In the former study, assignment of a higher rating to c_1 than to c_2 is taken to indicate "selection" of c_1. In the latter study, stronger agreement is taken correspond to a judgment of greater causal strength. Vasilyeva, Blanchard, and Lombrozo (2018) use a somewhat different probe to measure causal strength: "how appropriate is it to describe this relation as causal?" As noted below, variations in wording can make a difference to the judgments elicited in ways that are not fully understood.[2]

Assignment of higher causal strength to abnormal causes in the conjunctive case makes sense if (as suggested earlier) one of the functions of such causal selection judgments (or one of the goals subjects have in making such judgments) is to identify the events or factors that are effective targets of intervention in the actually obtaining situation. As a standard example, described but not tested in Icard (2017), oxygen is almost always present on the earth's surface (as reflected in the judgment that its presence is normal) and in most cases it is difficult or impossible for people to change whether it is present. By contrast, match strikings are comparatively unusual statistically speaking (abnormal) and relatively easy to control. If one wishes to bring about or prevent a match ignition, in most circumstances it makes sense to focus on whether the match is struck or not, rather than whether oxygen is present. This is not to say that the effectiveness of intervention rationale applies to all cases of actual cause judgment, but it does illustrate one possible version of functional approach to actual causal judgment.

Next some remarks about the role of appeals to "intuition" which, as I have said, is ubiquitous in discussions of actual causation. As argued elsewhere (Woodward, forthcoming), I think it is implausible to view intuitive judgment as a kind of rationalistic grasping of underlying metaphysical truths or anything similar. Instead, to the extent that there is genuine information in reports of intuition these should be understood as claims about how the intuiter and others judge—in other words, such reports are simply empirical claims (or evidence for empirical claims) about practices of causal judgment. Consider the episode (EX1.1). When we have the "intuition" that the impact of Suzy's rock caused the bottle to shatter, this simply reflects our judgment about the case with (in most cases, if the intuition is of any interest) the further claim that others will judge similarly. It is, of course, an empirical question whether this further claim is true, although it is very plausible that it is.[3] If we think of the significance of intuitive reports in this way, the information they potentially provide is broadly similar to the information provided by experimental investigations into patterns of causal judgment conducted by psychologists and experimental philosophers. Insofar as philosophers' intuitions provide information of this sort, there is nothing special or unique about them.

Traditional "armchair" philosophers often dismiss the relevance of empirical studies of folk judgment to their projects, presumably in part because they expect (or fear) that the empirical studies will produce results in conflict with their intuitions. However, my assessment is that this expectation of conflict has largely turned out to be incorrect when the topic is causal judgment. That is, as an empirical matter, philosophers' intuitions (when construed as claims about how people will judge) often turn out to produce results that are consistent with more systematic empirical studies[4]—something that ought to be a source of satisfaction to the armchair oriented. This is not to say that the empirical studies are superfluous. For one thing, they can serve as additional checks on philosophers' reports of intuitions. More interestingly, there are many issues concerning causal cognition that can be explored by empirical methods employed by psychologists but not by armchair appeals to intuition.[5] The empirical methods can also yield information that might possibly be provided by armchair methods but which traditional philosophers have not tried to provide. For example, as observed above, it is standard in psychological research to ask subjects to make graded judgments of "causal strength" rather than binary judgments (did c cause e?). Philosophers' appeals to intuition tend to involve only the latter. Finally, there are patterns of judgment discovered in psychological experiments that are at least somewhat surprising and that have not been uncovered by armchair methods—one example is "abnormal deflation" in disjunctive causal systems (e.g., Icard, Kominsky, and Knobe, 2017).[6]

Given this continuity (in many cases) between philosopher's intuitions and experimental results, I will draw on both in what follows. To the extent that philosophical intuition is empirically accurate as a characterization of people's judgments, it is obvious why it has a role to play in descriptive accounts of such judgments. However, following the program outlined above, intuitive judgments can also play a legitimate role in normative inquiry. To the extent that we can assume people reason and judge in normatively appropriate ways, empirical results about how they do reason can *suggest* hypotheses about how one ought to reason and judge and functions and goals of such reasoning. I write "suggest" because in this view, agreement with intuitive judgment is not by itself *sufficient* to establish normative correctness. Instead, establishing normative correctness requires the kind of means/ends analysis and reference to function described earlier. For example, if it is correct or warranted to select the occurrence of the short circuit rather than the presence of oxygen as "the cause" of the fire, this is so not because most people judge in accord with this selection but rather because, assuming the effectiveness of intervention goal or function, intervening on the short circuit better conduces to this goal. In fact, assuming the effectiveness of intervention rationale, a number of actual cause judgments that people regularly make seem, if not mistaken, highly suboptimal. For example, in making actual cause judgments about causes of disease and industrial accidents, most people focus on "proximate" causes, such as infection or operator error, even though the most effective targets of intervention are often more distal, having to do with social organization.

There are many other reasons why assessing theories of causal judgment merely by fit with intuitive judgments (without attention to function) is unlikely to produce fully satisfactory results, either from a normative or descriptive perspective. In connection with actual cause judgment, I will mention just two. As Glymour et al. (2010) note, the examples of actual cause judgments explored by philosophers represent a tiny subset of the possible cases. Even for these known cases it is far from clear that any of the extant formal models fully capture our intuitive judgments (again, Glymour et al., 2010). Moreover, even if we were to find a model that captures our judgments in all of the examples considered so far, this by itself provides no assurance that there will not be other examples, perhaps many, for which the model fails. Adding functional constraints can help with this problem: If we specify a function for actual cause judgments and a formal model characterizing how actual cause judgments meeting the conditions of the model achieve this function *and* if we find that the model captures the judgments people actually make (or some substantial subset of these) this may help to assure us that there are not a large number of unexplored counterexamples lurking around the corner or, if there are, that these need to be understood in terms of some other function.

3 The place of actual causation

I turn next to some general remarks about the place of actual cause judgment in the overall panoply of practices of human causal judgment. My overall picture is that there are structures or patterns of counterfactual-supporting dependency relations that are "out there" in the world. These are present at different levels of organization, from the behavior of elementary particles to cells to people and so on. Various sciences—physics, chemistry, biology, economics—provide information about these structures and this information allows us to answer questions about what would happen if various interventions were to be performed. Causal models and structural equations of the sort described below encode portions of this dependency information.

Different kinds of causal judgment attempt to report on different features of this underlying structure—they attempt to provide answers to different kinds of queries we may make concerning this structure. What is distinctive about actual cause judgments is the kind of questions they attempt to answer and the information they draw on in doing so.

To spell this out, let us return to the often-invoked contrast between actual cause and so-called type level claims. Although I have employed this terminology it is potentially misleading. It is not plausible to interpret (3.1) "Smoking causes lung cancer" as asserting that some uninstantiated abstract type or property ("smoking") stands in a causal relation to some other abstract property ("lung cancer"). Instead, (3.1) is best understood as the claim that when particular individuals smoke this can or will cause those individuals to develop lung cancer. Both in the case of (3.1) and (3.2) "Jones' smoking caused his lung cancer," any causation that goes on is at the token level—in both cases the units, so to speak, are individual episodes of smoking and lung cancer, co-attributed to particular people. (3.2) differs from (3.1) in that it purports to answer a different question about this underlying structure—among other things, (3.2) picks out or refers to a particular (extended) episode of smoking causing lung cancer while (3.1) does not.

Another important difference between (3.1) and (3.2), noted by a number of writers, is this: In assessing a claim like "Smoking causes lung cancer," one begins with a putative cause—smoking—and reasons "forward" from this to determine whether it has some effect (e.g., lung cancer). The reasoning is thus from causes to possible effects. Although it would of course be highly unethical to conduct an experiment in which subjects are randomly assigned to either a treatment group in which they are forced to smoke or, alternatively, to a control group in which they are prevented doing so, the results of such an experiment would provide us with very good evidence for whether claim (3.1) is true. Similarly, we might establish that (3.1) is true by applying some appropriate causal modeling technique to statistical information about patterns of covariation involving the incidence of smoking, lung cancer, and other variables in a population.

Actual cause judgments are associated with a very different question and present us with a different inferential task, requiring different evidence. Typically, when one makes such judgments one is presented with a known effect such as the occurrence of lung cancer in a particular individual, Jones. It is assumed that this effect has some cause or causes. The task is to reason "backwards" from this effect to what caused it—was it Jones' smoking or something else such as his exposure to asbestos or radon? Or was this perhaps a case of overdetermination involving two independently acting causes each of which was sufficient for the effect? In this case, the direction of reasoning is the opposite from what it is in connection with (3.1). Although experimental evidence can certainly be relevant in various ways to (3.2) one can't settle whether (3.2) is true by doing an experiment, however well-designed. Similarly, population level statistics and causal modeling will not by themselves provide information sufficient to determine whether (3.2) is true.

In cases in which several different candidates for the cause of the effect of interest are present (Jones both smokes and was exposed to asbestos), determining which of these was the actual cause typically requires further specific information about the system of interest (in addition to generic causal information relating smoking to lung cancer and asbestos exposure to lung cancer). In a number of cases, this takes the form of information about the presence of a "mechanism of action." The idea here is that when a cause is not merely present but efficacious in causing an effect (that is, an actual cause of the effect), there may be independent evidence (that is, evidence in addition to the occurrence of the cause and the effect) that this is the case or, alternatively, evidence that despite being present the cause did not produce the effect. This can take the form of evidence about mediating variables (a "connecting process") that must be present if the cause is to produce the effect, evidence about the presence of other effects (but not mediating variables) that will be present if the cause is efficacious and information about the spatio-temporal relations between the candidate cause and effect. One sometimes speaks in such cases of finding a "signature" or "fingerprint" that one candidate actual cause and not another was operative in producing an effect. In rocks-thrown-at-bottles scenarios, unless something very unusual is going on, even if a number of rocks are "present," the rock that is the actual cause of the shattering is the one that comes into spatial contact with the intact bottle. If Jones is shot in the head and dumped in the river, forensic analysis may be able to determine (e.g., based on the presence or not of water in his lungs) whether the actual cause of his death was drowning or the gunshot.

My claim is *not* that that such information about mechanisms of action can be used to define or characterize what it is for one event to be an actual cause of another—I see little promise in such a project. Rather, my point is that actual cause judgments are answers to different questions than those to which other sorts of causal claims are directed and also rely on different sorts of information. As noted below, this has implications for whether information contained in actual cause claims will fix the truth values for other sorts of causal claims (or conversely).

In this connection it is also worth remarking that some of the standard examples used to illustrate actual cause claims in the philosophical literature suggest a misleading picture about how easy it is to establish such claims. When Suzy's rock comes in contact with the bottle before Billy's it is straightforward to use this information to establish the actual cause of the shattering, but many actual cause judgments in which we are interested are not like this. Establishing that global warming was an actual cause of some particular weather event, like a hurricane, although arguably not impossible, is highly non-trivial. Similarly, it can be very difficult to establish that it was exposure to asbestos rather than smoking that caused Jones' lung cancer—something exploited by lawyers for industries using asbestos in tort actions.

A great deal of theorizing in science does not aim at the explanation of particular events via actual cause claims but rather at accounting for more generic explananda—patterns or phenomena in the sense of Bogen and Woodward (1988). For example, General Relativity provides explanations of such phenomena as the deflection of light by massive bodies, the Hodgkin Huxley model explains the generic shape of the action potential and so on. In such cases, it may be assumed that all particular episodes of light deflection etc. have the same explanation so that in discovering the correct explanation we are again faced with a rather different inferential problem than that of choosing among different candidates for the actual cause of some particular outcome. Even when different possible causes of an outcome may be operative, in scientific investigation the interest is often in whether there is a pattern of outcomes that suggest a generic causal relation, rather than identifying the actual causes of particular outcomes. For example, in a randomized controlled trial that tests the efficacy of a drug in causing recovery from an illness, what is of interest is usually whether there is a higher incidence of recovery in the treatment group than in the control group. If there is, this implies that some individuals in the treatment group were caused to recover by the drug, but the experiment as described does not identify these individuals and it may be difficult or impossible to do so. Moreover, there may be little point in doing so if what is of interest is a generic claim concerning whether the drug causes recovery.

This is not to say that scientific investigation is never concerned with establishing actual cause claims. Scientific investigations into particular historical episodes such as the Cretaceous-Tertiary extinction of the dinosaurs are naturally viewed as concerned with establishing actual cause claims. Moreover, actual cause claims are of central interest in many other contexts and disciplines—not just in common sense contexts but in law, in diagnosing the causes of failure in engineering contexts (what caused the challenger disaster?) and in history more generally. My point is simply that actual cause claims play a much less central role in science than many suppose.

I stress this because there is a tendency among some philosophers—particularly those with a metaphysical orientation—to think that actual cause claims, largely as revealed in our ordinary practices of intuitive judgment, provide us with a notion of causation that is a foundation for *all* causal judgments.[7] This may be thought to follow from a metaphysical thesis according to which other sorts of causal claims are "grounded" in actual causation. I will not try to engage with this metaphysical claim but the considerations described above (as well as others discussed below) suggest that it is a mistake to think that all of the features present in actual cause judgments will also be present in other forms of causal judgment. In other words, the common philosophical practice of undertaking to discuss "causation" and then discussing only actual cause claims as though these will have all of the features possessed by other kinds of causal claims is misguided.

4 Causal selection

One of many issues about actual causation raised by both the philosophical and psychological literature concerns the role of causal selection in such judgments. Philosophers with an interest in actual causation have had very different attitudes toward causal selection. Hall (2004), after noting the existence of such practices, says that his target is what he calls an "egalitarian" notion of (actual) causation. According to this notion, in the match ignition example, both the striking and the presence of oxygen are among the actual causes of the ignition and an account of actual causation should capture this fact. This egalitarian notion is seen as capturing an objective causal structure while selection of particular factors from this structure is seen as reflecting "subjective" and likely unsystematic factors having to do with our interests. Causal selection is thus a potential source of error or distortion in dealing with actual causation. This of course assumes that we possess (or can isolate) a notion of actual causation in which selection practices play no role and that we can recognize when our judgments track such a notion. I suggest below that it is an open question whether this assumption is correct.

More recently, there has been a great deal of interest in the details of how causal selection influences actual cause judgments, both among philosophers and psychologists. Indeed, to a considerable extent, current theories of "actual causation" now aspire to capture causal selection practices, often within formal frameworks. In other words, "actual causation" and "causal selection" are not distinguished in the way that Hall advocates but are rather seen as a single topic which should be given a unified treatment.

If this is the most appropriate way of approaching the topic of actual causation important consequences follow. As noted earlier, a number of empirical investigations have shown that judgments of "normality" vs. "abnormality" play an important role in causal selection. In "conjunctive" structures like the match example, the statistically abnormal cause (the striking) tends to be selected as the cause and also receives a higher causal strength rating than the more normal cause. Moreover, this pattern extends to causes that involve norm violation vs norm conformity. In a scenario described in Knobe and Fraser (2008), staff are permitted to take pens from the secretary's desk while faculty members are prohibited. Both a staff and faculty member take pens from the desk with the result that the secretary is unable to take an important message. Here the norm-violating action of the faculty member receives a higher causal strength rating than the action of the staff member.

Presumably, no one thinks that causal selection judgments that reflect norm violations are tracking some fundamental objective structure in the world. At least in many cases generic causal claims in the physical sciences (such as those mentioned above) do not appear to exhibit this sort of norm sensitivity. Somewhat more subtly, according to many normative theories, whether a generic causal relation like "C causes E" holds and how "strong" it is or whether it is appropriately described as causal should not depend on how frequently C occurs.[8] Moreover, as a descriptive matter, at least in many cases, when we are dealing with generic causal relations judgments of causal strength are *not* influenced by the frequency with which C occurs or at least not influenced in the way in which actual cause judgments are. Here again, the factors that influence such causal judgment appear to be rather different from those that influence causal selection in actual cause judgments.

If causal selection judgments are viewed as a legitimate aspect of actual cause judgments or if it is not possible to separate out the selection aspect from a more egalitarian core to such judgments in the manner Hall suggests, this strengthens the case that such judgments are not metaphysically fundamental (or fundamental to understanding causation in science) in the way some have supposed, given the differences between selection judgments and other, more generic causal judgments just described. However, the issues here are complicated. Returning to some of the actual cause judgment discussed above, it is not clear all of them involve the kind of causal selection effects that are present in the short circuit/oxygen or pen example. For what it is worth, my own intuitive judgment (and what I assume will be the similar judgment of others) in EX1.1 that the impact of Suzy's rock caused the shattering and Billy's did not does not seem to be sensitive to normality considerations in the way in which causal selection judgments are. If Suzy's throw was very normal and Billy's very abnormal (Suzy frequently throws rocks at bottles and Billy does not, Suzy is permitted to do this and Billy is not) or vice-versa, this does not make me any more or less willing to judge that Billy's throw was the actual cause if Suzy's rock came into physical contact with the bottle and Billy's did not.[9] (I acknowledge, though, that my judgment may be eccentric—more systematic investigation is needed.) A similar assessment may be warranted for a number of the other examples described above, such as those involving disease causation—e.g., the normality or not of Jones' asbestos exposure does not seem to influence our judgment about whether this was an actual cause of his lung cancer.

Considerations of this sort may seem to suggest that there is, after all, a notion of actual causation and actual cause judgment that is distinct from and independent of whatever is involved in causal selection judgments and thus that it is a mistake to try to construct a single unified theory of both kinds of judgment. Instead we have two kinds of judgments, one reflecting something more like Hall's egalitarian notion and the other reflecting selection effects. I tentatively endorse this claim below, describing the non-selective notion as involving "actual causal contribution." On the other hand, as we shall see, several theorists, proceeding on the assumption that we should look for a single unified theory of actual causation, argue instead that various examples force formal theories of actual causation to incorporate normality considerations (and hence what appear to be selection effects) into our understanding of *all* actual cause judgments. These theorists implicitly reject the idea that there are two (or more) different varieties of actual cause judgment. Moreover, there are cases in which it is by no means clear whether we are dealing with causal selection judgments or some non-selective more egalitarian notion. So, the idea that there is a sharp separation between actual cause judgments that involve normality influenced causal selection and those that do not, although intuitive, may not prove to be sustainable.

5 Structural equations and formal models of actual causation

To explore these issues in more detail, I turn to more detailed remarks about some formal theories of actual causation and the confrontation of these with experimental results and philosopher's intuitions. One currently popular form such models take makes use of structural equations and directed graphs (e.g., Halpern, 2016). For reasons of space and because I assume that such models are familiar to many readers, my exposition of these will be brief and not rigorous. In structural models, generic causal relations are represented by equations relating variables (or more pedantically, whatever in the world corresponds to variables) with, by convention, variables representing effects occurring on the left-hand side of such equations and variables representing the direct causes of those effects occurring on the right-hand side. A natural way of understanding such equations is that they encode information about what would happen if various interventions were to be performed. Thus

$$Y = 2X_1 + 3X_2 \tag{5.1}$$

is interpreted as claiming that an intervention that changes the value of X_1 by dx_1 (while leaving the other right-hand side variable X_2 unchanged) will be associated with a change in the value of Y of $2dx_1$. The most straightforward way of representing actual cause claims within such a framework (and the one that I will adopt for purposes of this chapter) is to take them to relate *values* of variables, where the variables themselves stand in relationships specified by the structural equations. For example, in connection with a structure like (5.1) one might ask whether, in some specific situation, X1 taking the value = 1 is an actual cause of Y= 2. (I will say more shortly about how this might work.) We can also associate a *directed graph* with such systems of structural equations, where the rule is that each equation corresponds to a structure in which there is a directed edge from each of the right-side variables into the left-hand side variable.

The use of the structural equations in the form described commits us to the claim that the generic causal relations modeled are deterministic. It is also generally assumed that the systems modeled do not contain causal cycles. I will adopt both assumptions in what follows. It is also worth noting that structural equations and graphical models were originally developed to represent generic causal relations; their extension to actual causation is a relatively recent development, apparently beginning with Halpern and Pearl (2000 and 2005). The extent to which these frameworks are suitable for this latter purpose ought to be regarded as an open question.

In most early versions of structural equation treatments of actual causation, the issue was approached in the following way. Suppose we are given (5.2) the full or complete set of structural equations governing the system of interest (that is, we proceed on the assumption that these are correct, so that these give us the ground truth about the relevant generic causal relations) and we are given (5.3) the actual values taken by all variables in the system of interest. The task was then taken to be this: to specify an algorithm or set of rules that takes the information in (5.2) and (5.3) and outputs (5.4) the actual cause relations that hold in the system. As noted above, the test for whether the output (5.4) is correct was commonly taken to be agreement with the intuitive judgments of the researcher or perhaps others, although more function-based standards of assessment are also possible.

The idea that there should be such an algorithm might seem to have considerable antecedent plausibility. First, in a considerable range of cases (although arguably not all, as we shall see) people do seem to have firm judgments about actual cause relations, suggesting some stable target to be captured. Moreover, if we think of (5.2) as specifying something like the "laws" or dependency relations governing the system of interest, it may seem very plausible that these, in connection with (5.3) the actual values taken by the variables characterizing in the system, should be sufficient to "fix" all of the actual cause relations in the system. That is, the thought is that (5.2) and (5.3) together specify all of the information relevant to the actual cause relations in the system—all of the information that goes into people's intuitions—so that there must be some mapping from (5.2) and (5.3) to people's intuitive judgments.

Philosophers (e.g., Lewis, 1986; Paul and Hall, 2013) who use so-called "neuron diagrams" to investigate actual cause judgment employ a somewhat different representational framework but (I think it fair to say) have broadly similar expectations. These diagrams represent connections or dependency relations between nodes and also the values of the nodes (whether they are "on" or "off")—information that parallels the information about dependency relations between variables and their values in the structural equations framework. As in the structural equations representation, the goal of the neuron diagrammers is to specify rules that allow one to go from this information to the intuitive actual cause judgments one makes about such systems.

In what follows I will focus on the structural equations framework both because I am more familiar with it and because it is more widely used in current discussion. My guess is that much of what I say about this framework will transfer to (have analogues in) neuron diagram treatments, but I will not try to show this.

Having set the common problem up in this way, I can now come to an important punchline: it is, at the very least, extremely difficult to fully carry out the program just described. Although there are a number of proposals relying on the information described above (dependency relations plus actual values) that successfully capture a number of our intuitive actual cause judgments, none seem to capture the full range of our judgments. Of course, one possible reaction is that if we just try harder and explore more possibilities, we will find an account that works. Another possible reaction—which I'm inclined to think must be closer to the truth—is that actual cause judgments (or at least some of them—see below) are influenced by other inputs besides those just described and that is the reason why the proposals fail.[10] In fact, as we shall see, several more recent modeling proposals in a broadly structural equations framework seem to acknowledge this.

To develop this theme, I turn to a very partial exploration of several modeling proposals beginning with one in the spirit of Halpern and Pearl. (See also Hitchcock (2001) for a similar proposal.) As before my goal is not precision but conveying an underlying intuition. First some terminology. Given a directed graph G with variables V representing the system of interest, with X1 and Y in V, P is a *directed path* from X1 to Y if there is a set of additional variables X2, X3,..,Xn also in V such that X1→X2, X2→ X3,...Xn→Y. An *off-path variable* with respect to path P is any variable in G that is not on P. Then the proposal is

(**AC**) X1=x is an actual cause of Y=y if the following conditions hold:

(**AC1**) X1= x and Y=y—i. e., these events actually occur

(**AC2**) There is a directed path P from X 1 to Y in G such that for some allowable setting or "contingency" (see below) of values of variables that are off P, an intervention that changes the value of X=x1 to some alternative value X1= x1* would change the value of Y=y1 to some alternative value Y=y*1

The specification of what counts as an allowable setting is a matter of some delicacy, with a number of different proposals in the literature. However, the intuitive idea or at least part of it is that the allowable off-path settings (contingencies) in **AC2** are those that do not change the value of Y or any other variable on the path P.

To illustrate how this is intended to work, consider several examples:
If Suzy throws, her rock will shatter the bottle, Billy will not throw if Suzy does, but if Suzy does not throw, Billy will throw and his rock will shatter the bottle. Suppose that Suzy throws. With C1 representing whether or not Suzy throws, C2 representing

whether or not Billy throws and E representing whether or not the bottle shatters, we have the following equations and associated graph.

$E = C1 \vee C2$
$C2 = \text{not } C1$
Actual values: $C1=1, C2=0, E=1$

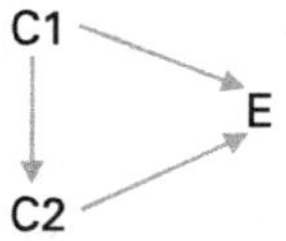

```
C1 ─────┐
 │       ↘
 │         E
 ↓       ↗
C2 ─────┘
```

Figure 2.1 Simple Pre-emption: (EX5.1).

$C1 \rightarrow E$ is a path P from C1 to E. C2 is an off-path variable with respect to P. Set C2 to its actual value = 0—setting a variable to its actual value is always allowable because this does not change the values of variables on P. Under this setting an intervention that changes the value of C1 from 1 to 0 would change E from 1 to 0. Hence, in accord with intuitive judgment, $C1=1$ is an actual cause of $E=1$. $C2=0$ is not an actual cause of $E=1$ because under the setting $C1=1$, changes in the value of C2 make no difference to the value of E and, the alternative possible setting of C1 ($C1=0$) is not permissible, since that would change the value of E.

Equation: $D = S1 \vee S2$
Actual values $S1=1, S2=1, D=1$.

Graph:

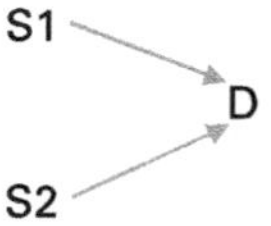

```
S1 ─────┐
         ↘
           D
         ↗
S2 ─────┘
```

Figure 2.2 Over determination: (EX5.2). Two riflemen simultaneously shoot (S1, S2) and hit victim. Either hit is sufficient for death (D)

Consider whether S1 is an actual cause of D. AC 1 is satisfied. AC2 is also satisfied: There is a path P from S1 to D. S2 is an off-path variable with respect to P. Setting $S2=0$ is an allowable setting since setting S2 to that value will not change the value of D (D is still = 1). Under the setting $S2=0$, intervening to change the value of S1 will change the value of E, so $S1=1$ is an actual cause of $D=1$. Parallel reasoning shows that S2 is also an actual cause of $D=1$. Although there is some dispute, this seems to be in accord with the intuitive judgments of most people; both shooters are actual causes of death.

Note that although AC succeeds on the examples above it plainly fails to capture judgments that reflect what we naively think of as causal selection. In the match/oxygen example, the structural equation is:

$F = M \cdot O$

where O, M, and F take values {1,0} according to whether oxygen is present, the match is struck and the fire occurs, with actual values, F, M, O= 1.

O is an off-path variable with respect to the path from M to F. Setting O at its actual value=1, the value of M makes a difference to whether F=1 so M=1 is an actual cause of F=1. But similar reasoning shows that O=1 is an actual cause of F=1, so that there is no asymmetry between the roles of S and O. This is not surprising if causal selection reflects normality judgments, since normality plays no role in **AC**. **AC** captures a notion of actual causation that looks more like Hall's egalitarian notion.

Why does **AC** seem to work (to the extent that it does)? Here is one way of understanding the underlying rationale. (I introduce it now because I will make use of it later.) Suppose that causes (of any variety) are difference-makers, under some appropriate understanding of that notion—that is, when c causes e, we expect that there is some change in c that in some circumstances will be followed by a change in e so that in this sense e depends on c. However, the difference-making aspect of a cause can be "hidden" when it is embedded in a larger causal structure, which is what happens in EX5.1 and EX5.2. In EX5.1 the difference making role of Suzy's throw is masked by the fact that Billy will shatter the bottle if she does not. We can uncover Suzy's role if we "control for" or remove the elements that hide it. Obviously, though, we don't want to change the values of variables lying on the candidate path by which c has a difference-making impact on e, since this will alter or disrupt that path. So we consider whether c has a difference-making impact on e, given settings of variables that are off the path under consideration. However, there needs to a limit on which off-path contingencies are allowed. In particular, when we consider whether there will be changes in e under changes in c for possible settings of the off-path variables we don't want those change in e to be due to the settings of the off-path variables rather than the changes in c. The requirement in **AC2** that the off-path settings do not change the value of e or other variables on P from what they are in the actual situation attempts to accomplish this.

Let me note for future reference that the rationale just described is most compelling when a kind of invariance or robustness assumption holds regarding the $c \rightarrow e$ relation. That is, it is when we can assume that c's difference-making role with respect to e can hold somewhat uniformly across a range of different situations (corresponding to settings of off-path variables), that the strategy of making that role appear by setting those variables to different values appears most plausible. Such an invariance assumption seems to be satisfied in EX5.1 and EX5.2: Rock impacts have a shattering effect on bottles across a range of difference circumstances and we think that they can continue to have such an effect even when back-up causes like Billy's throw are present, although in this case the difference-making role of the impact of Suzy's rock is hidden. In other words, the causal role that the impact that Suzy's rock would have if Billy were absent remains the same when Billy is present. In EX5.2, if each shot is sufficient for death, and there is no interaction between the shots, it is extremely natural to think of the causal contribution of S1 to D as the same whether or not S2 is also present, which motivates bringing out the difference-making role of S1 by considering a situation in which S2 is absent. Thus the application of **AC** to the example again relies on some such invariance/robustness assumption. At least some of the limitations of **AC** that are

6 Problems with AC: Normality, elections and other scenarios

Although proposals along the lines of **AC** successfully capture a range of intuitive judgments, more recent discussion has uncovered a number of examples in which this is apparently not the case. Among other possible deficiencies, it appears that **AC** is overly permissive in the sense that it counts events as actual causes when they are not. (I write "appears" because whether this assessment is correct depends in part on issues having to do with the place of causal selection in a theory of actual causation. It would perhaps be more accurate to say that **AC** counts events as actual causes that would not readily be selected in a causal selection task.) I will describe two illustrations, due to Livengood (2013) and discussed in Halpern (2018).

Suppose Jack and Jill are potential voters in an area that votes heavily Republican. Jack leans strongly Republican but does not vote because he thinks that the Republican candidate will win without his vote. Jill would vote Democrat if she were to vote but decides not to vote because she is disgusted with the process. As expected, the Republican candidate wins overwhelmingly. With $V1 \ldots Vn$, representing the decisions of eligible voters (which can take values = R, D or abstain) and O the outcome, the graph consists of edges from each of $V1, \ldots Vn$ into O. (We thus assume that the voters don't influence one another's votes.)

According to **AC** the abstentions of both Jack and Jill are actual causes of the outcome. This is because among the permissible settings of off-path variables are those that switch a number of the Republican votes to Democrat, as long as this is consistent with the Republican winning. Suppose there are $2n+1$ eligible voters, $2n-1$ of whom vote either R or D, with only Jack and Jill abstaining. Switch votes among those who vote so that there are n R votes and n-1 D votes. Then if Jack had voted Democrat there would have been a tie and the Republican would not have won. On the other hand, if Jack had voted R the Republican would have won. Under this contingency, Jack's choice is difference-making. So, Jack's choice = abstention is an actual cause of the Republican winning. A parallel argument shows that Jill's abstention is an actual cause of the Republican winning. Halpern claims that our intuitive judgment, though, is that although Jill's abstention is such an actual cause, Jack's is not. It is not clear to me that this is correct but it does seem wrong to treat Jack and Jill's abstentions in exactly the same way (as **AC** requires), given the different ways they would have voted had they voted.

A second example, a slight variant on one also suggested by Livengood, is described by Halpern (2018) as follows:

> consider a vote where everyone can either vote for one of three candidates. Suppose that the actual vote is 17-2-0 (i.e., 17 votes for candidate A, 2 for candidate B, and none for candidate C). Then not only is every vote for candidate A a cause of A winning, every vote for B is also a cause of A winning. To see this,

consider a contingency where 8 of the voters for A switch to C. Then if one of the voters for B votes for C, the result is a tie; if that voter switches back to B, then A wins (even if some subset of the voters who switch from A to C switch back to A).

As Halpern observes, this may seem particularly unreasonable because if option C (which received no votes) had not been present, then votes for B would not be causes of A's winning.

What these cases may seem to suggest is that at least some actual cause judgments are influenced by assessments of how likely (or perhaps "normal") various alternatives to the actual situation are and that this in turn influences which settings of off-path variables are permissible, assuming that we continue to think in terms of a proposal that is broadly like **AC**. In particular, it is likely that if Jill had voted, she would have voted Democrat, so a scenario in which that happened seems or may seem relevant to our causal assessments. By contrast, if Jack had voted, it is extremely unlikely he would have voted Democrat, so considering a contingency in which that happens seems less appropriate than a contingency in which Jill votes Democrat. In addition, if the area is heavily Republican, a possibility in which a large number of voters switch from Republican to Democrat seems very unlikely. In the second example, given that C received 0 votes, an alternative in C receives 8 is naturally viewed as very unlikely. Again, one might think it follows that this an inappropriate or relatively inappropriate contingency for the purposes of applying **AC**.

Halpern's proposal for capturing the role of these considerations is to add a "normality ordering" to a model along the lines of **AC**. This is a partial order which ranks alternatives to the actual situation in accord with how "normal" they are—e.g., Jill's voting Democrat is more normal than Jack's so voting. In Halpern's proposal, the normality ordering incorporates information about the probability of various variable values but it can also incorporate information about other sorts of norms, such as prescriptive norms or institutional rules. In this case, contingencies including actions that are more in accord with prevailing norms are viewed as more normal than those that violate such norms. This allows him to capture cases like Knobe's pen example.

Given this ordering, normality considerations can be incorporated into causal judgment in at least two ways. One possibility is to add to **AC** the following restriction on permissible settings of off-path variables: alternative settings which change actual values to more abnormal values are not permitted while changes in the direction of greater normality are, with actual causation being assessed accordingly. (This might be expanded to prohibit other sorts of normal to abnormal changes—for example, in the governing equations themselves—but I will not consider such possibilities here.) This proposal leads to categorical judgments according to which some c either is or is not judged an actual cause.

Another possibility is this: As noted above, in research on the empirical psychology of causal cognition, it is very common to ask subjects to make graded judgments of causal strength. Thus a theory of actual causation might itself take a graded form and be assessed in terms of how well it captures such strength judgments. That is, the theory would say that c is an actual cause of e to a greater or lesser extent (or an actual cause of greater or lesser strength), depending on how abnormal the contingencies have to be to reveal the dependence of e on c. There is an obvious sense in which this second, graded alternative seems more natural, since normality itself is a graded notion. Many recent discussions, including Halpern's (2016, 2018) as well as Hitchcock and Knobe (2009) have taken such a graded notion of actual cause judgment to be the target to be captured. Adopting this graded notion, both Jack and Jill are relatively weak (non-strong) causes of the Republican victory since a contingency in which their votes make a difference to the victory would be "abnormal."[11] Nonetheless, Jack's abstention is an even weaker (albeit only slightly) cause of the Republican victory than Jill's abstention since a contingency in which Jack votes Democrat is more abnormal than Jill's so voting. (The proposal thus captures the intuition that Jill's role is in some way different from Jack's.)

To the best of my knowledge, there have been no empirical studies of ordinary subject's actual cause judgments in the specific election scenarios described above.[12] (Researchers have instead relied on their own intuitive judgments.) For what it is worth, my guess is that to the extent that we have in mind a dichotomous notion of actual causation, according to which the only alternatives are that c caused e or that it did not, many people would be reluctant to agree with the claim that Jack's or Jill's abstention "caused" the Republican victory. Turning to the graded notion, it is also not clear to me whether or not most people would agree that Jack or Jill's abstentions were even "weak" causes of the Republican victory. It does seem plausible that if "weak cause" is interpreted to mean something like "small causal contribution" many might agree that each individual Republican vote made some such a contribution to the Republican victory and perhaps that Jill's abstention also did so. However, for reasons to be discussed below, it is not clear that the normality-based account adequately captures this "causal contribution" idea.

In this connection, it is also worth emphasizing that when one talks about the actual causes of election outcomes with large electorates, it is usually substantial blocs of voters who are regarded as candidates for such causes—e.g., Obama to Trump voters in 2016 in states like Wisconsin and Michigan—rather than individual voters. If a shift in a substantial bloc of voters is regarded as, so to speak, a single step in the direction of abnormality or normality (rather than many steps corresponding to changes in individual votes), one can recover, within a framework like Halpern's, the judgment, endorsed by many, that it was the Obama to Trump votes rather than the votes of those who always vote Republican that caused Trump's victory or at least that the former was a "stronger" actual cause than the latter. So, the normality-based account does seem to capture at least some causal judgments about blocs of voters.

7 Normality, causal selection and actual causal contribution

I turn now to some more general comments on Halpern's proposal and others like it. First, to the extent that the proposal captures a set of considerations that influence actual cause judgment, it helps to explain the puzzle raised earlier. It suggests that the reason why it is so hard to write down a rule which takes us from (i) a specification of the laws or structural equations governing a system and (ii) the actual values of the variables characterizing the system to a conclusion about actual cause judgments is that such judgments depend on information in addition to (i) and (ii)—in particular, information about normality. To express the point slightly differently, say that a factor is "intrinsic" to the causal connection between c and e if and only if it has to do with whether or not c and e occur or with whether there is a law or causal generalization linking c to e. Then to the extent that normality considerations play a legitimate role in actual cause judgments, such judgments will incorporate the influence of non-intrinsic (extrinsic) factors. Moreover, to repeat a point made earlier if actual cause judgments incorporate normality considerations, this is a reason (in addition to others described above) to think that such judgments are not a foundation for all other causal judgments, assuming that the latter will not incorporate normality considerations, at least in the same way.

Halpern's theory aims to cover all actual cause judgments and incorporates a potential role for normality in all such judgments. Assuming that normality tracks selection effects, Halpern's theory thus seems committed to rejecting the idea that we can distinguish two categories of actual cause judgment, one that reflects selection effects and another, presumably more like Hall's egalitarian notion (reflecting what I call "actual contribution" below) that does not reflect selection effects. Moreover, regardless of whether Halpern's theory is accepted, it seems clear from the examples above that many of our intuitive actual cause judgments are influenced by factors associated with selection effects. It may not always be easy to recognize and remove the influence of such factors, in a way that allows us to get at some underlying egalitarian notion just by consulting ordinary intuitive responses. For example, to the extent that we judge that Jill's abstention was an actual cause of the Republican victory or a stronger such cause than Jack's abstention, it is arguable that we are making a causal selection judgment, even though this may not be immediately obvious. Thus, even if there is an underlying egalitarian notion that philosophers should reconstruct, reliance on "intuition" or ordinary folk judgment as a way of getting at that notion may be problematic if many intuitive judgments are "infected" by normality type considerations in a way that may not be easy to recognize. At the very least, if there is a more egalitarian notion of actual causation, we need criteria for recognizing when our judgments reflect it and when they do not.

8 Actual causal contribution

Let me now turn to some remarks exploring this more egalitarian, non-selective notion, beginning with the election scenarios. There seems to be an obvious sense in which each person who voted Republican in Wisconsin in 2016 made exactly the same "actual causal contribution" to the Republican victory. "Actual causal contribution" here is intended to contrast with more generic causal claims that make no reference to actual circumstances or to what actually happened—instead the actual contribution claim is that the votes were causally operative in producing a particular effect (victory) in the specified actual circumstances. This makes it arguable that this actual contribution notion has a serious claim to be considered *a* notion of "actual" causation," even if it is not the only such notion. To enlarge on this: Assuming the absence of fraud, every Republican vote counts exactly as much as every other vote. The mechanism for aggregating votes is straightforwardly additive, each vote has equal weight, and it is not as though some votes make more of a contribution depending on how others have voted. To be sure, we may also find it natural to describe the Obama to Trump voters as causing Trump's victory and the votes of regular Republican voters as having a different causal status vis à vis this outcome. However (it might be argued), this seems to involve a practice of causal judgment (one rooted in causal selection considerations) that is different from the actual contribution notion just described. It is not as though the Obama to Trump voters did something that is causally different from the regular Republican voters who voted for Trump. The votes of the former did not have more causal power or "umph" than the votes of the latter—to that extent, thinking of them as having more "causal strength" (as reflected in verbal probes that are interpreted as measuring causal strength) is potentially misleading. Indeed, the reason we find it natural to describe our practice of singling out the Obama to Trump voters as a causal selection practice is exactly because this involves singling out a subset from a larger set of causes (all of the Republican votes), where the latter corresponds to the actual causal contribution notion.

To this we may add the kind of reasoning that we appealed to in support of the original **AC** account of actual causation. Consider first an election between two candidates and just one voter V1. Here no one doubts that V1's vote for A is an actual cause of A's victory, that if V1 abstains, this is an actual cause of A's failure to win and so on. If we assume that as we add voters to the electorate there are no interaction effects of their votes (the votes combine additively) then it seems reasonable to think that each continues to make the same contribution as they would make in the case in which each was the only voter. Thus using an invariance or robustness assumption of the sort described in Section 5 in combination with a symmetry assumption according to which each vote contributes equally leads us from the presence of an actual cause relation in the only one voter case to the presence of such a relation for each voter in the n voter case, even if n voters are far more than are required for a Republican victory.

9 Features distinguishing actual causal contribution and some additional illustrations

I will say more about the possible applicability of this actual contribution notion to other sorts of cases below, but before doing this, it will be worthwhile to spell out explicitly some of the ways in which this notion differs from the notion captured by Halpern's normality-based account.

9.1. Assuming (as we have throughout) that we are not dealing with cases in which different candidate causes have different probabilistic propensities to produce their effects, the actual contribution notion is not graded and does not come in degrees—either c is an actual cause (in the contribution sense) of e or it is not. By contrast, as we have seen the normality-based notion does come in degrees.

9.2. To the extent we are dealing with a notion of actual causation that incorporates normality considerations, the associated judgments will be influenced by variations in these. The corresponding claim will not be true to the extent that we are dealing with judgments that involve the actual contribution notion.

9.3. Consider the suggestion made earlier about the (or a) goal or function of actual cause judgments—that these track the effectiveness of possible interventions. This function fits well with a notion that incorporates normality-based considerations. Often an abnormal factor (among all those relevant to some outcome) will be a particular good target for intervention. If one wanted to prevent Trump's victory in 2016 it would have been a better strategy to try to persuade Obama to Trump voters to change their votes (this would be more likely to be successful) than to target life-long Republicans. By contrast the effectiveness of interventions story fits less comfortably with the actual contribution notion. As the election scenarios illustrate, the actual contribution notion treats each voter symmetrically.

I have used 9.1–9.3 to contrast normality-based actual cause judgments with a conjectural actual causal contribution notion that behaves somewhat differently, but we can also use 9.1–9.3 and some of my other remarks above as empirical diagnostic tools. If there is a notion of actual causation in use that looks like the actual contribution notion and not so much like a normality-based notion, perhaps we may be able to use considerations like 9.1–9.3 to identify instances.

With this possibility in mind, consider again the pre-emption case (EX1.1). If your "intuitive judgments" are like mine, you are likely to regard this as a case in which categorical yes/no rather than a graded judgment seems most natural. That is, the intuitive judgment is that the impact of Suzy's rock was the actual cause of the shattering and Billy's rock was not an actual cause at all, rather than an actual cause of less strength than Suzy's. Note that the "actual causal contribution" notion of actual causation seems to fit this case very well: It was the impact of Suzy's rock that made an actual causal contribution to the shattering, Billy's throw made no such contribution. If this is in fact how people judge, one might expect that when presented with such a scenario, subjects would assign a very high causal rating to Suzy's throw (a rating at ceiling or nearly so) and a very low rating to Billy's throw, where this is interpretable as "not a cause at all"). In contrast, if Billy's throw were to receive some more intermediate score, this would indicate that, contrary to what I have suggested, subjects are willing to make graded judgments in this sort of case. As far as I know, examples of this sort have not been studied empirically. Such investigations might help to determine whether there are cases in which people judge in accord with an ungraded causal contribution notion rather than a more graded notion.

Next consider whether normality manipulations affect actual cause judgments in various scenarios. Suppose it is extremely common and not at all statistically abnormal for Suzy to throw rocks at bottles and to shatter them and extremely rare (abnormal) for Billy to do this, although both are equally efficacious when they do throw. Or suppose that the rules permit Suzy to shatter bottles but prohibit Billy from doing so. Or suppose Suzy and Billy have the opposite abnormality/ normality profiles. Would variation of any of these factors make a difference for most people's actual cause judgments in a pre-emption case concerning which events involving rock impacts were the actual causes of a bottle shattering? Although there is some contrary evidence from somewhat similar experiments,[13] my guess is that such normality manipulations would have little effect on people's actual cause judgments in scenarios of the sort described involving collisions and event causation. If so, this again may be evidence that we are dealing with a kind of actual cause judgment that is somewhat different than the notion involved in normality-based selection judgments.

Finally, consider the effectiveness of intervention account of the function of actual cause judgments. We noted above that this seems to fit many actual cause judgments that are influenced by normality considerations/causal selection rather well. By contrast, this account provides a less satisfying treatment of the pre-emption example. If our goal is to identify the intervention that would be most effective in preventing the shattering of the bottle, it isn't clear why we should distinguish so sharply between Suzy's and Billy's throw. Given the stipulations of the example, even if we had prevented Suzy from throwing or deflected her rock, the bottle still would have shattered because of Billy's throw. Even if we think that in any realistic case, there would be some non-trivial probability that Billy would have missed, had Suzy not shattered the bottle, one would expect, on the effectiveness of intervention account, for this to result in graded judgments of actual causation, with a slightly higher causal strength judgment for Suzy than for Billy. (We know that Suzy's rock hit the bottle, so that preventing her throw while not preventing Billy's would replace a situation in which shattering occurs with one in which it is merely probable that shattering occurs.) In this connection, we may note that asking subjects how effective they think various interventions would be, might be another way of tracking whether we are dealing with different varieties of actual cause judgments: if subjects agree that preventing Suzy's throw would not be a particularly effective way of preventing bottle shattering, while agreeing that Suzy's throw was an actual cause, this would suggest that the effectiveness of intervention rationale does not capture their judgments.

10 Some methodological reflections

The possibility just floated—that there may be at least two different varieties of actual cause judgments—raises several methodological issues. One obvious point is that to the extent this is the case, it is presumably a mistake to look for a single theory of actual causation that covers both kinds of judgment. Indeed, if we are dealing with two different kinds of judgments with sensitivities to different factors, this might help to explain why finding a single theory that covers everything that we may think of as an actual cause judgment has turned out to be so difficult.

However, if we take the route of supposing that there are several different sorts of actual cause judgments, requiring different theories, we face the issue of how to recognize cases of each sort of judgment. The criteria 9.1–9.3 above may help with this but as also suggested in Section 8 more fine-grained verbal probes (and use of a variety of these rather than a single probe) may prove fruitful. One motivation for this is that standard causal strength questions track or are sensitive to a number of distinct and apparently independent dimensions of causal assessment. For example, type-level causal relations that are more stable or robust in the sense of Woodward (2006) tend to receive higher strength judgments (Vasilyeva, Blanchard, and Lombrozo 2018) and when causal relations are probabilistic, causes that boost the probability of an effect more highly receive higher strength ratings (e.g., Cheng, 1997). All this is in addition to the fact that strength judgments are affected by normality considerations (which presumably are at least somewhat independent of robustness and probability raising considerations) in the case of actual cause judgments. Probes that are more sensitive to differences among actual cause judgments and between these and other sorts of judgments might help to ameliorate this limitation. For example, rather than only providing subjects with different actual cause claims to be rated according to strength, researchers might also describe scenarios and (i) ask subjects what "the" cause or causes of some effect are in the scenarios or, alternatively (ii) ask them to list "all" of the causes they can think of or anything that qualifies as "a cause." (In other words, subjects are asked to generate their own lists of causes rather than assessing causal claims provided by the researcher.) Possibly, if there are differences in answers to (i) and (ii) this might suggest that (i) tracks a selection-influenced notion of causal selection while (ii) tracks a notion that is less sensitive to selective considerations. As an illustration, suppose that in the pen case, when asked for "the" cause of the secretary's being unable to take the message, subjects tend to select the professor's taking the pen but when asked to list all of the causes, they also include the action of the member of staff, so that the answers to (i) and (ii) are different. By contrast, suppose that in a pre-emption scenario like EX5.1, subjects give the same answer to (i) and (ii)—in both cases only the pre-empting cause is cited. This might be taken to reflect a difference between what the subjects are doing in the two sorts of cases, a difference that might be less apparent if a generic causal strength probe is employed. More generally, given that there are many different verbal probes that might be employed, it would be very desirable to understand how they relate to one another—when they give concordant answers and when they do not. For example, when subjects give a higher causal strength rating (according to some standard probe) to (i) c caused e than to (ii) c^* caused e in some scenario, do they spontaneously cite (i) rather than (ii) when asked about "the cause" of e in the scenario?[14]

As another possibility, consider the target of intervention idea as an account of the function of actual cause judgment. If this is correct (or to the extent it is correct) one would expect that when subjects are asked what they would do to change some outcome in a scenario, the results would mirror their actual cause judgments as measured by some other verbal probe. If one were to find that in some cases actual cause judgments correlate closely with targets of intervention queries and in other cases do not, this again might suggest that we are dealing with two different kinds of judgments. For example, actual cause judgments in the election scenarios considered above might track intervention questions well but this might not be the case for scenarios like (EX5.1).

11 What might be the function of the actual contribution notion?

I suggested above that the target of intervention notion provides a fairly intuitive account of the function of some actual cause judgments in which selection seems to be operative but I have not suggested a function for the actual contribution notion (supposing that there is such a thing). What work does the latter do? One possibility is that the robustness features of this notion make it better adapted to generalization or transportability to other contexts than a notion in which selection figures more centrally. In particular, suppose that we think of "actual contribution" in the following way: If c makes such and such an actual causal contribution x to e in one set of circumstances then insofar as c makes an actual contribution to e in other circumstances, we expect it to make the same contribution x, at least for a range of such circumstances, so that a kind of invariance or robustness of this contribution is present. This is the sense in which a vote for a candidate makes the same actual causal contribution regardless of how others vote. Similarly, when asked whether a drug is an actual cause of some effect in a patient, we tend to frame this as an actual contribution question because we proceed on the assumption that if the drug is efficacious at all, it will be an actual cause of broadly the same effect in many others. (We think of a vaccine as making the same contribution to immunity in different people, regardless of whether administration of the vaccine is "normal.") By contrast, since selection effects are sensitive to such "extrinsic" factors as the frequency with which a cause occurs in a population or how likely it is that a cause will assume some alternative value if it does not take its actual value, causal selection judgments will tend not to exhibit this sort of robustness. Since generalizability is among the considerations we care about in making causal judgments, this suggests one kind of rationale or function for actual causal contribution judgments—a rationale that seems somewhat independent of the target of intervention considerations that influence causal selection.

To this we may add the observation that to the extent that responsibility and credit and blame judgments are influenced by causal judgments, the actual contribution notion seems to play an important role (of course as illustrated earlier, normality-based considerations can also matter). In the overdetermination case EX5.2 we hold both shooters responsible for the death because we think of them as making the same actual contribution to the death. In the rock throwing example, Suzy's throw and not Billy's is blamed or credited with the destruction of the bottle because it is her throw that made the actual contribution. Billy is guilty of something else—e.g., attempted bottle destruction.

12 Conclusion

If the arguments in this chapter are defensible then, whatever else might be said about actual causation, it turns out to be complicated. There appears to be some reason to think that actual causation is somewhat heterogenous, incorporating at least two different notions or elements, one more closely linked to causal selection and the other to a notion that tracks something more like actual contribution. However, in some cases the line between these two notions is rather indistinct as a number of the examples above illustrate. Given the complexities of the notion, it seems a bad strategy to take actual causation (at least as this is reflected in our intuitive judgments) as metaphysically fundamental or as a kind of stand-in for causation in general.

Notes

1. The terminology of "actual causation" seems to be becoming increasingly standard. In the not very recent past in philosophy the judgments in question were commonly described as involving "token causation," as opposed to "type causation"—see below for discussion of this terminology. Another term that is sometimes employed to characterize the claims/judgments in question is "singular causation."
2. Woodward (2021) discusses a number of additional examples in which the wording of the verbal probe used in eliciting causal judgments makes a difference to the reported results. Other papers (among many) showing how variation in wording affects results include Samland and Waldman (2016) and Sytsma and Livengood (2020).
3. Put differently, we need to distinguish what the having of the intuition is evidence for from whether the claim reported in the intuition is true. The having of the intuition can be evidence for how people judge but the having per se is not evidence that the claim reported in the intuition is true—the latter has to do with such worldly facts as the ability of rocks to break bottles, the fact that Suzy's rock came in to contact with the bottle and so on. If matters are as reported in the scenario, it is likely that the reported causal claim is true but that is not because having the intuition is a way of establishing that it is true.
4. For discussion of a number of examples in which this has turned out to be the case, see Woodward (2021).
5. Again, see Woodward (2021) for examples.
6. In a disjunctive causal system multiple events are each sufficient to produce an outcome. "Abnormal deflation" refers to the tendency of people to judge such events in disjunctive systems as more causal to the extent that they are less rare.
7. This is often implicit, but it is hard to make sense of the nearly exclusive focus on actual cause judgments in writers like Paul and Hall (2013) unless they are assuming that there is something fundamental about such claims or that the interesting features of other kinds of causal claims are already present in actual cause claims. Strevens (2008) is one writer who explicitly takes actual causation as his starting point.
8. For example, this is so for the Cheng's (1997) causal power theory. Woodward (2021) argues that is a deep feature of many causal generalizations and laws that they are expected to be invariant across change in the frequency with which the independent variables are instantiated.
9. The impact of normality on causal judgment will depend both on (i) the way in which the scenario is modeled and (ii) the details of the account of actual causation adopted and on the way in which normality figures in that account (see below). However, as an empirical matter, normality has some influence on causal selection in both conjunctive and disjunctive structures and formal theories like those due to Icard, Kominsky, and J. Knobe (2017) and Halpern (2016, 2018) predict such influences. So, if it is correct to

assimilate the rock throwing example to other cases of causal selection one would expect some influence of normality on the former.

10 Another way of putting this issue is in terms of function. Full information about the equations or dependency relations governing a system and the actual values taken by variables enables one to answer a range R of counterfactual questions about how the system would behave under various settings of the variables. If this information is not enough to fully answer queries about the actual cause relations in the system, such queries must correspond to different questions than those in R. This suggests that the point or function of actual cause claims is not to answer questions like those in R.

11 Halpern has confirmed this assessment in recent correspondence.

12 I am grateful to Alex Wiegmann for drawing my attention to Gerstenberg et al. (2015) which reports the results of a study of ordinary subject judgments of *responsibility* for various election outcomes. Assuming that subject's actual cause judgments are related to (although perhaps not identical with) their responsibility judgments, it is arguable this chapter provides information about the former. In the election scenarios studied by Gerstenberg et al., a number of distinguishable factors seem to influence responsibility judgments—these include the extent to which a vote is pivotal, and what the authors call dispositional and situational normality. Perhaps one might think of all of these as having to do with normality in some extended sense, but if so, normality will be a complex and apparently multidimensional notion.

13 Icard, Kominsky, and J. Knobe (2017) report evidence of what they call "abnormal deflation" according to which if E depends disjunctively on both A and C, both occurring, people will be more inclined to say that C caused E if C is normal rather than abnormal. These, of course, are overdetermination rather than pre-emption scenarios. Moreover, the verbal probe asks about the causal role of agents (Billy and Suzy) rather than events, which may well make an important difference, as shown in Samland and Waldmann (2016)—questions about agents seem more likely to be interpreted as questions about blame. In addition, the scenarios themselves did not involve collision events such as rock throwing. Still, I acknowledge that the results are surprising: if a similar pattern holds in a scenario in which two simultaneous impacts are each sufficient for bottle shattering, people will assign the impact of Suzy's rock a higher causal strength rating than Billy's to the extent that Suzy's rock throwing is more normal—a pattern of judgment which I at least would not have expected. In any case, one wonders whether similar effects would be present in pre-emption scenarios. Interestingly the normality or abnormality of A in disjunctive structures does not seem to affect judgments about the causal status of C.

14 These issues about different verbal probes and their interrelation also have implications for the common philosophical practice of appealing to intuitions about cases. When different philosophers do this, they may be asking themselves different questions or failing to recognize ambiguities in the questions that they ask themselves. If so, the "same" case may elicit different responses for reasons that are unrecognized. Again, see Woodward (forthcoming).

References

Bogen, J. and J. Woodward (1988). "Saving the phenomena." *Philosophical Review* 97: 303–52.

Cheng, P.W. (1997). "From covariation to causation: A causal power theory." *Psychological Review 104*: 367–405.
Gerstenberg, T., J. Halpern, and J. Tenebaum (2015). "Responsibility judgments in voting scenarios." web.mit.edu.tger/www/papers
Glymour, C., D. Danks, B. Glymour, F. Eberhardt, J. Ramsey, R. Scheines, P. Spirtes, C.M. Teng, and J. Zhang (2010). "Actual causation: a stone soup essay." *Synthese 175*: 169–92.
Hall, N. (2004). "Two concepts of causation." In J. Collins, N. Hall, and L.A. Paul (eds.), *Counterfactuals and Causation* (225–76). Cambridge, MA: MIT Press.
Halpern, J. (2016). *Actual Causality*. Cambridge, MA: MIT Press.
Halpern, J. (2018). "Appropriate causal models and the stability of causation." asXiv:1412.3518. pdf
Halpern, J. and C. Hitchcock (2015). "Graded causation and defaults." *British Journal for the Philosophy of Science 66*: 413–57.
Halpern, J. and J. Pearl (2005). "Causes and explanations: A structural-model approach. Part I: Causes." *British Journal for Philosophy of Science 56*: 843–87.
Hitchcock, C. (2001). "The intransitivity of causation revealed in equations and graphs." *Journal of Philosophy* XCVIII: 273–99.
Hitchcock, C. and J. Knobe (2009). "Cause and norm." *Journal of Philosophy 106*: 587–612.
Icard, T., J. Kominsky, and J. Knobe (2017). "Normality and Actual Causal Strength." *Cognition 161*: 80–93.
Knobe, J. and B. Fraser (2008). "Causal judgment and moral judgment: Two experiments." In W. Sinnott-Armstrong, *Moral Psychology* (441–8). Cambridge, MA: MIT Press.
Lewis, D. (1986). "Causation." In *Philosophical Papers*, Vol. II (159–213). New York: Oxford University Press.
Livengood, J. (2013). "Actual causation in simple voting scenarios." *Noûs 47*: 316–45.
Paul, L. and N. Hall (2013). *Causation: A Users Guide*. Oxford: Oxford University Press.
Pearl, J. (2000). *Causality: Methods, Reasoning and Inference*. Cambridge: Cambridge University Press.
Samland, J. and M. Waldman (2016). "How prescriptive norms influence causal inferences." *Congnition 156*: 164–76
Strevens, M. (2008). *Depth: An Account of Scientific Explanation*. Cambridge, MA: Harvard University Press.
Sytsma, J. and J. Livengood (2020). "Actual causation and compositionality." *Philosophy of Science 87*: 43–69.
Vasilyeva, N., T. Blanchard, and T. Lombrozo (2018). "Stable causal relationships are better causal relationships." *Cognitive Science*, 42(4): 1265–96.
Woodward, J. (2003). *Making Things Happen: A Theory of Causal Explanation*. New York: Oxford University Press.
Woodward, J. (2006). Sensitive and insensitive causation." *The Philosophical Review 115*: 1–50.
Woodward, J. (2014). "A functional account of causation." *Philosophy of Science 81*: 691–713.
Woodward, J. (2020). "Causal attribution, counterfactuals, and disease interventions." In N. Eyal, S.A. Hurst, C.J.L. Murray, S.A. Schroeder, and D. Wikler (eds.), *Measuring the Global Burden of Disease: Philosophical Dimensions*. Oxford: Oxford University Press
Woodward, J. (2021). *Causation with a Human Face: Normative Theory and Descriptive Psychology*. New York: Oxford University Press.

3

Juggling Intuitions about Causation and Omissions

Carolina Sartorio[*]

1 Introduction

Intuitions are central to philosophical theorizing about causation, but there are different kinds of intuitions, which can play different kinds of roles. In this chapter, I focus on the following four types:

Causal intuitions: Intuitions to the effect that something is/isn't a cause of a given outcome.

Explanatory intuitions: Intuitions to the effect that something is/isn't part of the explanation of something else—where the relevant notion of explanation tracks something potentially broader than just causation.

Responsibility intuitions: Intuitions to the effect that agents are/aren't morally responsible for a given outcome.

Grounding intuitions: Intuitions to the effect that agents are/aren't morally responsible for a given outcome *because*, or *to the extent that*, they are/aren't a cause of (or part of the explanation of) that outcome. These intuitions track grounding relations between causation (or explanation) and moral responsibility.

I focus on these four types of intuitions because I believe that they are particularly relevant to philosophical theorizing about causation. (I don't mean to suggest that these are the *only* sets of intuitions to be deserving of consideration, but just that they are some central ones.) In particular, my main focus here will be, not these intuitions taken in isolation from each other, but the *interplay* between them. I'll be examining questions such as these: In what ways do these different intuitions interact with one another? How should these interactions inform our theorizing about causation? What should we do when there's a conflict between intuitions of different kinds? And so on. The main examples I'll work with are cases of *omission* (failures to act). The reason for this is that, as we will see, in cases of omission the interaction between intuitions of different kinds is particularly significant for the purposes of theorizing about causation. Hence, they make for an interesting case study.

Causation theorists typically focus on intuitions of the first kind, *causal intuitions*, insofar as these can be directly used to motivate philosophical theories of causation or to critically evaluate them. However, intuitions of the other kinds are also relevant to philosophical theorizing about causation, in a more indirect but still important way. Causation is not an isolated concept but one that is connected with other theoretically useful concepts, including, in particular, the concept of explanation and the concept of moral responsibility.[1] As a result, it can be illuminating to look at the broader picture that includes these other concepts and the interrelations among them. As we will see, this is particularly important in cases where our causal intuitions themselves aren't particularly clear, such as cases of omission. (Another example of this that I will discuss in this chapter is cases of causal overdetermination.)

Interestingly, this perspective is rarely taken in the literature on causation. This chapter is an attempt to remedy this. I believe that an investigation of the concept of cause won't be exhaustive unless we think about the way causation fits with those other key concepts. Accordingly, one of the main goals in this chapter is to raise awareness about the centrality of this issue.

Some preliminaries are in order before we start.

First of all, I must note that, as a metaphysician, the concept of cause which I'm interested in is a *natural* concept. That is, it's a concept that picks out a certain relation between events or states of affairs, one that exists "out there in the world." This is a concept that is importantly connected to some normative concepts, such as the concept of moral responsibility, but it's not itself a normative concept. In particular, being causally responsible doesn't require being morally responsible for something. Natural events such as tornadoes are causally responsible for outcomes, but they are not morally responsible for anything. The same goes for moral agents like us: we can be causally responsible for outcomes without being in any way morally responsible for them, as when we trip over someone accidentally and faultlessly cause them harm.

Second, I see intuitions the way I think many other theorists do, as starting points or as data that should be taken into account in our theorizing, but almost never as the last word. In my view, intuitions about causation are important to the extent that they help us latch on to the relevant relation in the world (the one that we're trying to pick out with our concepts and language). However, given, in particular, the connections that exist between causation and other concepts such as responsibility and explanation, it can be hard to know how to "juggle" all the different kinds of intuitions at once, and how to strike the best balance among them. Such a process of *reflective equilibrium* can result in our paying more attention to some intuitions rather than to others, and even to jettison some altogether, when we formulate our theories.[2]

Third, here I won't be relying on empirical studies, but mostly on what I consider to be "educated guesses" about commonly shared intuitions about causation and the other connected concepts. My belief is that most of these educated guesses would quite reliably track lay people's intuitions. Others may not, at least not as reliably—but not because they would necessarily clash with them, but simply because raising the issues in an intelligible matter requires a bit more philosophical sophistication or training. I think it could be interesting, and to some extent illuminating, to run empirical studies on some of these educated guesses, especially those involving a certain kind of scenario of omission that I'll focus on later, but I'll leave that task to others.

More generally, and despite my mainly theoretical focus, I hope this chapter will be of interest to those working on empirical debates about our concept of causation, given, in particular, the new questions it raises about the interactions among the different kinds of intuitions, and the special challenges to which those interactions give rise. I believe that paying attention to those unexplored challenges can be fruitful when theorizing about causation, both from a purely theoretical perspective and from an empirically informed one.

Again, I predict that the majority of readers will share my intuitions about the cases presented in this chapter, but even if you don't, some of those same challenges are still likely to arise. I'll walk you what I take to be the most common intuitions about cases, and the particular questions that those intuitions provoke. Even if you don't share some of these intuitions, similar questions may arise for you as you attempt to juggle your own intuitions. We all tend to have intuitions of the four kinds above, and it isn't always clear what the best way to accommodate them is.

2 Introducing cases of omission and overdetermination

I'll start with some relatively "easy" cases—cases where causation theorists are mostly in agreement about the role played by the relevant intuitions. We will then consider more complex scenarios in which there is more disagreement: cases of omission and cases of overdetermination.

As mentioned above, causation theorists typically focus on intuitions of the first kind, *causal intuitions*, to formulate or confirm their theories. Sometimes these intuitions are so pervasive and powerful that they can settle important theoretical questions pretty much on their own. These "bedrock" intuitions are the basis on which much theorizing about causation is done. A good example of this is intuitions about **preemption cases**. For instance, philosophers typically focus on scenarios of this kind:

> **Fast and Slow:** Two agents, Fast and Slow, throw rocks at a fragile and valuable vase. Fast's rock reaches its target and breaks the vase right before Slow's rock, which sails through empty space. If Fast's rock hadn't broken the vase, the vase would have broken anyway, and in a very similar way, as a result of Slow's rock hitting it.[3]

What caused the vase to shatter? The answer seems obvious: it was Fast's throw, not Slow's throw, but it's notoriously hard to accommodate this simple fact within a general theory of causation. In particular, some popular views that attempt to analyze causation in terms of the notion of counterfactual dependence face the challenge of explaining why it is that Fast's throw caused the vase's shattering, when the shattering doesn't counterfactually depend on Fast's throw.[4] Much philosophical work in this tradition has acknowledged the force of these bedrock causal intuitions, and has focused on finding solutions to problems of this kind.[5]

Incidentally, note that cases like **Fast and Slow** can also be used to illustrate the force of some *grounding intuitions*. Imagine that we know that only one of the rocks hit the vase, but we don't know which one that was. Imagine, also, that both agents acted intentionally, freely, etc. In that case, we can still be in a position to know that whoever broke the vase is *morally responsible for its shattering*, and the other agent isn't. This is based on a grounding intuition: the intuition that an agent's moral responsibility for the broken vase is grounded, among other things, in having caused that outcome. As a result, the agent who didn't cause the outcome cannot be morally responsible for it[6] (although, of course, she can still be responsible for other things, such as for trying to break the vase, for acting with a malevolent intention, and so on). For the purposes of this chapter (given our focus on causation and the causal upshots of our behavior), this is the type of responsibility that we're mainly interested in: responsibility for *outcomes*, or a moral assessment of agents in light of the upshots of their behavior. When we ask about who is morally responsible for the outcome in this case, it's only natural to look at who is causally responsible.

Of course, in this example there are certain empirical facts of which we are unaware, and this is what results in the uncertainty about the causes of the outcome. That uncertainty can be eliminated simply by coming to know the relevant empirical facts (whose rock hit the target on that occasion). This could easily lead to the impression that, to the extent that we are aware of all the relevant empirical facts about particular cases, the corresponding causal intuitions will always be sufficiently clear. However, this is actually far from the truth, for causal intuitions can fail to be fully clear or universal *even in cases where we know all the relevant empirical facts*. These are the kinds of cases that are of particular interest to us here, because they point to a genuine unclarity about how to theorize about causation itself (assuming the empirical facts are settled). Not coincidentally, they are also the kinds of cases for which the interaction between the different types of intuitions mentioned above becomes particularly relevant. In what follows, I'll draw attention to two examples of this phenomenon.

The first example, which will be our main focus here, is cases of **omission** (or absences in general) and the lively philosophical debate concerning whether omissions can be causes.[7] This debate is typically fueled by a more basic debate about the nature of the *causal relata* (the "terms" of the causal relation, or the kinds of things that the causal relation relates). Some think that only "positive" things like ordinary events can be causal relata, and this seems to rule out omissions and other absences; others, however, disagree. In the context of this debate, we could know all the relevant facts about agents' omissions (including everything that agents haven't done but could have done, and all the facts concerning what would have happened if they had done those things, etc.), and this still wouldn't come close to settling the basic philosophical issue of whether omissions can be causes, or what the causal relata in general are.

Of course, there are some powerful intuitions to the effect that agents *can* cause outcomes by omission. For example, philosophers have focused on scenarios of this kind:

Dead plants: I hired a gardener who committed to caring for the plants in my backyard. He failed to tend to my plants (e.g., he didn't water them), and my plants died. They would have lived otherwise.

In this case, it seems very natural to regard the gardener as a cause of the plants' death. In response, however, some argue that intuitions about causation involving omissions are still not as clear or forceful as intuitions about causation involving positive events. If a thunderstorm uproots all the plants in my backyard, the thunderstorm seems to be more clearly a cause of my plants' demise than any omission by the gardener that would have prevented that outcome (imagine, for example, that the plants would have been spared if he had protected them with thick cloth coverings). Dowe (2001) calls this "the intuition of difference." He then goes on to argue that omissions lack causal efficacy, partly on the basis of the intuition of difference.[8]

Another potential reason to discount the significance of causal intuitions involving omissions, such as the intuition concerning **Dead plants**, is that it's notoriously difficult, or even impossible, to accommodate all those causal intuitions within a general theory of causation. For intuitions about causation by omission tend to be infused by normative considerations that are in tension with the aspirations of a philosophical account of causation conceived of as a *natural* concept (and this concept, recall, is my focus here).[9] As a result, no general account of this concept is likely to be able to capture the whole range of causal intuitions involving omissions.

We can illustrate this point with the same example from before. Notice that, although the gardener appears to be a cause of my plants' death in **Dead plants**, Tucson's mayor (Regina Romero) doesn't, but we can imagine that Regina Romero bears all the same natural relations to my plants' death as my gardener (in particular, she could have dropped by my home in Tucson and watered my plants, and the plants would have survived if she had watered them). The main difference is that it was *the gardener's job* to water them (and not Regina Romero's); hence, only the gardener is morally responsible for the plants' death. In other words, our responses in these cases seem to be tracking, at bottom, *moral responsibility intuitions*. However, again these judgments about moral responsibility are tracking normative considerations that don't bear on the natural concept of cause. As a result, an account of that concept will have to ignore some of the causal intuitions about omissions.

Finally, imagine that, as some philosophers believe, omissions cannot be causes. Still, it is surely possible to account for the significance of the gardener's omission in other terms, without appealing to causation. On this alternative "fallback" view, the gardener's failure to care for my plants is *part of what explains* why they died, even if it's not a cause of the plants' death. Notice that this is what's captured by the third kind of intuitions mentioned above: *explanatory intuitions*. Many authors who reject the causal efficacy of omissions in fact embrace the idea that omissions can be part of the full explanation of events (see for example, Dowe, 2001; Beebee, 2004; and Varzi, 2007). This idea can be put to use to account for the agents' moral responsibility in those cases, in accordance with the corresponding *grounding intuitions* (by claiming that moral responsibility is grounded in, if not the causal powers of omissions, at least their explanatory power).

What could be meant by "explanatory power," you may ask, if not a causal power? Without giving a precise account of this concept, the idea is that, if omissions and other absences cannot be causes, they can still contribute to the full explanation of events in that those events still happen, at least partly, *because* of those absences. For example, the plant died, at least partly, because it wasn't watered. (After all, if somebody had watered it, it wouldn't have died.) It is also common to suggest—and the authors mentioned above do suggest—that, if omissions cannot be causes, we can still capture the explanatory power of omissions in terms of a form of causation. This time it's not *actual* causation, but *counterfactual* causation, however. That is, we can say that omissions help explain events, not because of the causal relations that actually obtain, but because of the causal relations that *would have* obtained if the omissions hadn't taken place. In terms of possible worlds, this is the idea that omissions are explanatorily powerful by virtue of causal relations that obtain in possible worlds relevantly similar to the actual world. For example, the non-watering of a plant can help to explain why it died in that, in close possible worlds where the plant is watered, it survives.

So far, we have identified cases of omission as one main set of examples where causal intuitions aren't fully clear or pervasive, even when we are aware of all the relevant empirical facts. In those cases, as we have seen, there is a lack of clarity about causation itself. We also noted the relevance, in those cases, of the intuitions of the other types (responsibility intuitions, explanatory intuitions, and grounding intuitions) and the relations among them. As we have seen, looking at the causal intuitions as part of a larger net of intuitions can help us get a better perspective on things, from which we can see the different options that open up when theorizing about causation.

Another example of the same type of phenomenon is **symmetric overdetermination cases**. These cases have also been the subject of lively philosophical debates. I'll go through these a bit more quickly.

Philosophers have illustrated the phenomenon of symmetric overdetermination with examples of the following kind:

> **Two Rocks:** Imagine that two agents throw rocks at a vase, but this time the rocks hit the vase simultaneously. Imagine, also, that each rock would have been sufficient on its own for the vase to break (in roughly the same way, and at roughly the same time).[10]

An important difference between a symmetric overdetermination scenario like **Two Rocks** and the **Fast and Slow** scenario described above (a preemption case) is that in **Two Rocks** the potential causes (the two rocks, or the two rock-throwing events) are fully on a par—hence the label "symmetric." Thus, it is not the case that one of them is a cause while the other one isn't, or that one "preempts" the other.

Plus, although it's clear that the vase broke, somehow, thanks to the two throwers' actions, this doesn't fully settle how we should think about the causal structure of the case. For consider: Should we say that each of the rocks or rock-throwing events was an individual cause of the vase breaking? (Some argue for this position. But note that this results in more causes than is needed to explain the effect, which some people find objectionable.) Or should we say, instead, that the cause is a fact that is more "proportionate" to the effect—perhaps the fact that *somebody* threw a rock at the vase? Or some "collective" event? (However, what kinds of facts or events are these? How can they be causes without the individual events being causes?) Again, the precise causal structure of a scenario like **Two Rocks** remains unclear even if we know all the relevant empirical facts about the case.[11]

Notice that, here too, we have an explanatory claim to fall back on, in case we conclude that the best way to make sense of the causal structure of the case is to say that overdeterminers aren't individual causes. For, surely, even if overdeterminers aren't individual causes, they *help explain* the outcome, in some important sense, considering the collective contribution they make to it. In other words, the full explanation of the vase's shattering will have to appeal, in some way or other, to the contribution made by the two rocks. The vase didn't just break for no reason!

In any case, here I'll understand the term "explanatory" in this very broad way, as an umbrella term that captures contributions of different kinds—including, in particular, some non-causal contributions as well as some collective contributions. If we're looking for a real "fallback" option to explain what happened, and to potentially ground the moral responsibility of the agents involved, this broad notion seems to be the best candidate.

To sum up: in this section, we have identified two types of case where causal intuitions tend to be particularly less clear or pervasive than in other (more ordinary) cases, and where this is due to a genuine uncertainty about causation, or about the conceptual tools needed to make sense of certain causal scenarios (and not about the underlying empirical facts). In the next section, I look more closely at the interplay of intuitions of different kinds that takes place in those cases, and I offer a diagnosis.

3 The resilience of moral responsibility and the flexibility of grounding intuitions

The scenarios discussed in the previous section can help bring out the *flexibility of grounding intuitions* in our theorizing about causation. So far, we have alluded to purely *causal* grounding intuitions, when discussing the **Fast and Slow** preemption scenario. In that case, I pointed out, it's very natural to take moral responsibility to be straightforwardly grounded in, among other things, causation. On the basis of that causal grounding intuition (and other things, such as the fact that the agents in question were acting freely, with a bad intention, etc.), we tend to conclude that whoever broke the vase (the preemptor) is also, thereby, morally responsible for the vase's breaking. This is so even if we might not know who that is, or who preempted whom, but must grounding intuitions *always* play this same kind of role? Must they all be *causal* grounding intuitions?

Presumably not. For consider, again, cases of omission and cases of symmetric overdetermination. Imagine that we come to believe that our best theories of causation imply that omissions and overdeterminers are never causes. Would we be tempted to conclude, on that basis, that the agents in those cases simply lack any moral responsibility for the outcome (because they didn't cause those outcomes)? Again, presumably not. Instead, we'd be willing to *relax* the relevant grounding claim, in a way that would allow for the agents' moral responsibility in those cases to be grounded in something other than individual causal relations.

In the previous section we noted that, in both kinds of cases, we have some explanatory intuitions to fall back on. In **Dead plants**, we could still blame the gardener for the death of my plants, for his omission would still be part of the explanation of my plants' death (in the broad sense described above) even if it were not a cause. In **Two Rocks**, we could still blame the two agents who threw the rocks at the vase and broke it simultaneously, because their behavior would still be part of the explanation of the vase's breaking (again, in the broad sense described above), even if they were not individual causes of that outcome. I take it that most of us would be ready to appeal to that fallback option, rather than letting intuitively culpable agents off the hook.

To clarify, when I say that agents seem clearly responsible in these cases and that it would be a mistake to let them off the hook, I simply mean that it's clear that they bear *some* moral responsibility for the outcome. This is consistent with claiming, for example, that agents are less blameworthy in virtue of their omissions than by virtue of their actions.[12] It's also consistent with claiming that agents involved in symmetric overdetermination cases are less blameworthy than if they had been the only agents involved.[13] I won't take a stand on these issues. All I'm interested in here is the claim that the agents would not simply be off the hook, in that they would still bear some moral responsibility for what happens. I take this to be a non-negotiable intuition.

Now, why is it that not letting the agents off the hook seems like the right reaction to have about these cases? I propose the following diagnosis. Judgments about moral responsibility are, to some important extent, resistant to certain philosophical—in particular, metaphysical—discoveries, such as discoveries about the true nature of causation. This includes the discovery that omissions or overdeterminers aren't causes. Let's give this idea a label:

The resilience of moral responsibility: Many judgments about responsibility are "resilient" in that they would survive certain metaphysical discoveries about the nature of causation.[14]

My suggestion, then, is that the resilience of moral responsibility is what results in the flexibility of the corresponding grounding claim. The flexibility of the grounding claim is the idea that we (most of us, anyway) are prepared to, if needed, relax the purely causal grounding intuition and instead rely on a substitute or surrogate intuition of the following kind:

Relaxed grounding intuition: Moral responsibility for outcomes is grounded in, if not causation, then, more broadly, *explanation* (in the broad sense of explanation described above).

The readiness to switch from the purely causal version to this relaxed version of the grounding claim seems to strike the best balance between the different types of intuitions that we have about these cases. For it allows us to preserve resilient judgments about moral responsibility while holding on to a close analog of the causal grounding claim: the claim that moral responsibility is grounded in, more broadly than just causation, explanatory power.

I would in fact push for a slightly revised (and, I believe, improved) version of the relaxed grounding claim. This is the claim that moral responsibility for outcomes is grounded in, a bit more precisely, *moral responsibility* for some explanatory factors. I believe that this modification helps account for cases where some agents contribute to the full explanation of an outcome, but where they are still not responsible for the outcome because they are not responsible for the explanatory factors themselves. I have argued for this in earlier work and I won't go into any of the details here.[15] For present purposes, we can sidestep this complication for the most part, so I'll only make reference to it when needed.

Let me take stock of what we have so far. I started by distinguishing four different kinds of intuitions that can contribute to our theorizing about causation (in potentially different ways): causal intuitions, explanatory intuitions, responsibility intuitions, and grounding intuitions. As part of the discussion of *causal intuitions*, I described cases where those intuitions are so clear and pervasive that they tend to act as bedrock intuitions (my example of this was preemption cases). I then contrasted these scenarios with cases where the causal intuitions are much less clear (my examples were omission cases and symmetric overdetermination cases), and I discussed the interaction that takes place in those cases between intuitions of the four different kinds. I argued that, in those cases, where the judgments about moral responsibility tend to be quite resilient, and thus where the *responsibility intuitions* are particularly strong, the relevant *explanatory intuitions* act as a fallback resource that can be put to use (if needed) in accounting for the agents' moral responsibility. This, in turn, can be accomplished by relaxing the causal grounding claim, in a way that respects the substance of the relevant *grounding intuitions*.

In the next section, I will consider more complex scenarios involving omissions that raise special and more difficult challenges. In these cases, as we will see, the interplay between the different types of intuitions seems to come apart from what I have described in this section.

4 A special challenge: asymmetric omission cases

The case of omission discussed above, **Dead plants**, is a "simple" omission case where an agent fails to do something he was supposed to do and the outcome happened, apparently, as a result of that omission. But there are other omission cases that are much more complex. These cases can resist an easy treatment. In this section, I explain how I see the interaction between the intuitions of different types in these interesting cases.

One way to think about a *slightly* more complex omission case is to incorporate the features of the other type of scenario discussed above, the one involving symmetric overdetermination. This yields a **symmetric overdetermination case** involving omissions. Consider, for example, the following scenario:

Symmetric flooded room: Some valuable art pieces are kept inside a room. They are located in an area where heavy rains are common. When it rains heavily, the flooding of the room can be prevented by simultaneously closing *two doors*, door 1 and door 2 (a single door is not enough to stop the rainwater's flow). Two agents, A and B, are in charge of operating those doors (one door each, because the switches are in different locations). When the alarm sounds at time T, letting the agents know that they must pull their switches, both of them simultaneously fail to do this, purely out of laziness (neither agent is aware of what the other agent intended to do at T). The art pieces are ruined.[16]

This case is an omission case which is otherwise similar to **Two Rocks**, our earlier example of symmetric overdetermination. Since both doors needed to be shut to prevent the flood, each agent's omission is *sufficient by itself* to guarantee the occurrence of the flood and the destruction of the art pieces. Plus, the agents' contributions are perfectly symmetric or on a par (in particular, the relevant omissions are failures to close the doors *at exactly the same time*), so this means that there cannot be preemption of one omission by the other. For these reasons, this is a symmetric overdetermination case, albeit one involving omissions.

Now, in this case, the responsibility judgments seem to be just as resilient as those about **Two Rocks**: each agent seems to bear at least some moral responsibility for what happened. After all, the flood wouldn't have occurred had it not been for the behavior of the two agents, and that behavior was blameworthy (each of them should have done their part, and they had no good excuse for not doing so—in particular, they had no reason to believe that the other agent would *also* fail to do their part).[17] Notice also that, here too, we can use the relaxed grounding claim and the relevant explanatory claim to account for the agents' responsibility, if needed (if omissions or overdeterminers aren't causes). For we can say that what each of them did (or, in this case, *failed* to do) is part of the full explanation of what happened, and this explanatory role can be used to ground their responsibility.

Let's now see what happens when we turn it into a different kind of case: an ***asymmetric* overdetermination case**. This is a case where one of the two omissions precedes the other. That is, the relevant omissions are failures to behave in certain ways at *different* times (an earlier time and a later time).[18] For example, consider the following asymmetric variant of the flooded room case:

Asymmetric flooded room: The setup is similar to that of the symmetric case, except that door 1 can only be closed at time T1 and, door 2, at a later time T2. Imagine that A is supposed to close door 1 at T1, and B is supposed to close door 2 at T2. Again, neither agent is aware of what the other agent intends to do, since they are in separate rooms. And, again, imagine that both agents independently fail to do their job, purely out of laziness. As a result, they each independently fail to close their doors, and the art pieces are ruined.[19]

This type of case raises some unique problems.

There is still *a* judgment about moral responsibility that seems resilient in this case, but it's not the claim that both agents are responsible. Rather, it's the claim that *somebody* is responsible (either A or B, or both). Somebody must be responsible, for, again, the art pieces wouldn't have been ruined if it hadn't been for the blameworthy behavior of two agents. So, we can't just excuse both agents. This is, arguably, a non-negotiable intuition. But what's interesting about this case is that now it's no longer perfectly clear *who* is responsible: if one, or the other, or both. (In symmetric cases, it was clear that it was both, in light of the perfect symmetry of the case.) As a result, the more specific judgments about moral responsibility are less clear in this case: we're not as sure who to blame.

Why is this, exactly? One main reason is that, given that the case is no longer perfectly symmetric, preemption reappears as a live option: given the temporal asymmetry, A could be preempting B, or B could be preempting A (or the equivalent of that for non-causal explanatory relevance, if omissions turned out not to be causes: A could be explanatorily relevant instead of B, or B instead of A). Or it could be that, despite the temporal asymmetry, this is still a case of symmetric overdetermination (or, again, the equivalent of that for non-causal explanatory relevance: both are equally explanatorily relevant).[20]

This uncertainty exists even though we know all the relevant empirical facts. This means that it's an uncertainty about the causal or explanatory power of omissions; in particular, it's an uncertainty about the conditions under which causal or explanatory preemption happens, *for omissions*. For notice that cases involving ordinary ("positive") events and causal connections don't raise equally difficult challenges. In those cases, we have physical causal processes to look at. If two rocks are thrown at a vase, for example, we can follow the rocks' paths and we know that there is preemption if one rocks get to the target and breaks it first. But in omission cases there are no such physical processes, but *absences of* physical processes. As a result, there is nothing to trace.

Also, asymmetric cases of overdetermination involving omissions are especially challenging because in these cases one could potentially argue that the two behaviors "cancel each other out"—that is, one could argue that the first omission isn't causally or explanatorily relevant because the second omission renders it irrelevant, and vice-versa. Thus, in **Asymmetric flooded room**, one could argue as follows: "B was going to fail to close door 2 later (at T2) regardless. So, the fact that A failed to close door 1 *earlier*, at T1, is simply irrelevant: closing that door wouldn't have made any difference to the outcome." However, in a parallel fashion, one could argue as follows: "A had *already* failed to close door 1 (at T1). So, the fact that B failed to close door 2 *later*, at T2, is simply irrelevant: closing that door wouldn't have made any difference to the outcome." Of course, when we combine these two pieces of reasoning, we're led to the conclusion that neither behavior was causally or explanatorily relevant. However, this is unbelievable: on the basis of this, and the relevant grounding intuition, we would be able to conclude that neither agent is morally responsible for what happened, but as noted above, this seems unacceptable. So, something went wrong in this reasoning, but it's hard to say what it is.

Finally, another thing that makes these cases puzzling is that the responsibility judgments are likely to change significantly when we imagine variants on the cases where one of the agents is replaced by a mechanism or a non-agential, natural phenomenon. Imagine, for example, that there is no agent B, and that in its place door 2 was going to be closed automatically at time 2. Imagine, however, that the mechanism fails, or that lightning strikes at that precise moment and destroys it before it's activated. In that case, doesn't agent A seem less responsible for the art pieces being ruined? After all, they were bound to be ruined as a result of an "act of God" (the legal terminology that is typically used for this kind of thing), and not as a result of two agents failing to do their job. But, how can we explain the difference in responsibility between this "natural" variant on the case and the original version? The contribution that agent A herself makes seems to be the same in both cases. In both cases, A fails to close door 1 when door 2 was not going to be closed for independent reasons; whether those reasons concern another agent or a natural phenomenon is arguably irrelevant to the causal contribution that A herself makes.[21]

So, let me return to what I think we do know for sure about a case like **Asymmetric flooded room**: we know that someone is responsible for what happened. What we do not know is who is responsible. Now, what could possibly determine who is responsible? At this point, it seems that knowing what the *actual* causal or explanatory structure of the case is could help. For it would tell us whose behavior was *in fact* relevant to what happened.

In other work, I have explained what I take the causal (explanatory) structure to be, and the implications for the responsibility of the agents involved. The answer isn't simple, but it's not important for our purposes in this chapter.[22] Here I'm only interested in the general issue concerning the special kind of interplay that takes place between the different types of intuitions in these cases. I think it's clear that it's quite unusual; in particular, it seems to be different from what we have seen in the previous section.

How does the interaction between intuitions work, in these cases? What general lessons can we learn from this?

One thing that these cases seem to show is that the **resilience of moral responsibility**, despite being an important and widespread phenomenon, may only be *limited*. That is to say, sometimes we can be *genuinely uncertain* about who is responsible and who is not, even when we know all the relevant empirical facts. The answer in those cases seems to hinge on who is a cause, or who is explanatorily relevant (or—I would say—on who is morally responsible for the cause or explanatorily relevant factors), and we must do some heavy-duty philosophical work to figure this out.[23]

This is unlike what happens in the simpler cases, where we know who is responsible (assuming we know all the relevant empirical facts), and the philosophy we need to do consists in figuring out the best way to conceptualize this—if in terms of causation, or a non-causal form of explanatory relevance. With the asymmetric cases, in contrast, we must start from scratch, in a way. For we have to figure out, *at once*, and presumably by means of a delicate exercise of reflective equilibrium, who is responsible and who is explanatorily relevant (or responsible for the explanatorily relevant factors). As a result, given that we have to do everything at once, it's hard to know where to start.[24]

Let me end by commenting on the potential value of doing empirical research on these cases. To the best of my knowledge, there are no empirical studies on cases of this kind.[25] This is a shame. It would be interesting to know what people's intuitions are about these cases, but it's important to realize that these scenarios are challenging, not just for purely theoretical purposes, but also for the purposes of running empirical studies. For their structure is quite complex, in that they combine special features of different kinds: they are *omission* cases; plus, they involve *overdetermination*; plus, they are *asymmetric*. This combination of features is what results in their being such an interesting case study, but it's also what results in inevitable complexities at the time of surveying people's intuitions.

I think it would be interesting to know, in particular, what people think about the agents' *moral responsibility* in these kinds of cases: Am I right in thinking that we're not ready to let both agents off the hook for what happened? Would people tend to blame both agents, or just one of them? If only one of them, then which one?

Here it's important to recall the important distinction between being responsible for one's *behavior* and being responsible for the *outcomes* of one's behavior. The outcome, not the behavior, is what's overdetermined in scenarios like **Asymmetric flooded room**. Thus, what we're interested in finding out about these cases is who is morally responsible for the outcome (the flood, or the art pieces being ruined), not who is morally responsible for their own behavior. However, this is a distinction that it might be easy for the ordinary person to overlook, or to underestimate, when thinking about complex cases like this. Sometimes we just want to blame blameworthy people, and we don't pay close attention to whether we're blaming them for what they did or for the results of what they did. After all, this is a subtle philosophical distinction that might take some time getting used to. So, this is a challenge that would have to be overcome in running these studies.

It would also be interesting to know what people think about the *causal or explanatory structure* of these kinds of cases: Who caused the flood? Or, whose behavior was explanatorily relevant to the flood's occurrence?

Here it's important to bear in mind the phenomenon alluded to before, in section 2: ordinary causal judgments about omissions tend to be normatively loaded. (This might be true more generally too, but, as noted above, it's *especially* true in the case of omissions.) Due to this effect, it's natural to expect that people's causal or explanatory judgments will tend to go hand in hand with their moral responsibility judgments. However, these results would have to be taken with a grain of salt, if what we're interested in is the natural concept of cause that is the main focus of metaphysical investigations.

To sum up: in this section, we have considered some complex scenarios involving omissions, asymmetric overdetermination cases, which raise special and more difficult challenges. I have argued that here the interplay between the different types of intuitions is unlike what we see in more ordinary omission cases. Correspondingly, these scenarios give rise to new theoretical questions about causation, as well as to some unique challenges for doing empirical research on the subject.

5 Conclusions

In this chapter, I have discussed the interface between intuitions of different kinds as it bears on our theorizing about causation. I focused mostly on scenarios of omission as a distinctive case-study.

Omissions are interesting to philosophers for many reasons, one of which is that they raise special puzzles about the nature of causation. I have suggested that some of those puzzles are reflected in the interaction that takes place between different *kinds* of intuitions: intuitions about causation, explanation, moral responsibility, and intuitions to the effect that moral responsibility is grounded in causation or explanatory power. As we have seen, perhaps surprisingly, that interaction isn't always clearly the same, for all omission cases; instead, it can take different forms depending on the particular type of case at issue. This makes the study of omissions (and of different kinds of scenarios involving omissions) especially challenging, but at the same time especially interesting.

Notes

* For helpful comments, thanks to Shaun Nichols, Alex Wiegmann, Pascale Willemsen, and an anonymous reviewer for this volume.
1. Some argue that there is more than one concept of cause (see for example, Hitchcock, 2007). I don't want to take a stand on this issue, and the existence of more than one concept of cause is in fact compatible with everything I say in this chapter. What the chapter assumes is only that there exists *some* concept of cause (a natural concept—as I explain next) that is connected with moral responsibility in important ways. For a discussion of this assumption in the context of the problem of free will and moral responsibility, see Sartorio (2016), especially chapter 2.
2. For a more extended discussion of this perspective, see Paul and Hall (2013), especially pp. 2–4 and 41–2. There intuitions are described as "defeasible guides to potentially interesting and important features of our causal concept or a causal relation" (p. 2). This is how I see them too. However, Paul and Hall don't discuss the role played by the interplay between the different types of intuition I focus on in this chapter (they work mostly with causal intuitions).
3. This is a classical "late preemption" case (see Lewis, 1986, postscript E).
4. An event Y counterfactually depends on another event X when the counterfactual conditional "If X hadn't occurred, then Y wouldn't have occurred" is true (X and Y are both actual events). In **Fast and Slow**, the vase's shattering doesn't counterfactually depend on Fast's throw because it would still have occurred (as a result of Slow's throw) if Fast's throw hadn't occurred.
5. See for example, the papers collected in Collins, Paul, and Hall (2004).
6. This is what gives rise to the interesting phenomenon of resultant moral luck. I offer an analysis of this concept in Sartorio (2012a).
7. For example, see the debate between Dowe and Schaffer in Hitchcock (2004). See also Bernstein (2015) for a general overview.
8. Of course, there are other ways of accounting for the intuition of difference. For example, one could claim that causation comes in degrees and that omissions and other absences are causes to a lesser degree than positive events. (However, the view that causation is a scalar notion is quite unpopular among causation theorists—for an overview of the relevant literature, see Kaiserman, 2018. I have argued against the intelligibility of degrees of causation in Sartorio, 2020.) One could also account for the intuition of difference without appealing to a metaphysical difference between actions and omissions, but only to a pragmatic difference. For example, one could argue that omissions tend to be much less salient causes than actions, although both of them are causes.
9. See my comment on this in section 1 above. There has been much discussion of the influence that normative considerations have on causal judgments about omissions;

see for example, Beebee, (2004); McGrath (2005); Livengood and Machery (2007); Clarke et al. (2015); Willemsen (2016); Henne, Pinillos, and De Brigard (2017); Henne, et al. (2019); and Willemsen (2019). For an overview of how normative considerations affect causal judgments more generally, see Willemsen and Kirfel (2018).

10 For a classical discussion of symmetric overdetermination cases, see Lewis (1986), postscript E.

11 For a discussion of these two positions on the problem of symmetric overdetermination, see Schaffer (2003). Schaffer calls the two views "individualism" and "collectivism." He himself defends the individualist position.

12 This is usually connected with the idea that there is a moral difference between doing and allowing harm (for an overview of the doing/allowing harm debate, see Woollard and Howard-Snyder, 2016). For empirical research on asymmetries in moral judgments concerning actions and omissions, see for example, Cushman and Young (2011).

13 Zimmerman (1985) discusses this view and argues against it.

14 I discuss this thesis in Sartorio (2021). There I also discuss the contrast between these kinds of metaphysical discoveries and others that could potentially be relevant to moral responsibility judgments, such as finding out that determinism is true. (*Incompatibilists* about the determinism and free will problem believe that the truth of determinism would, in fact, undermine our free will and moral responsibility.)

15 See Sartorio (2004, 2012b, 2015a, and 2017).

16 I discussed a case with a similar structure, the "Two Buttons" case, in Sartorio (2004).

17 For a dissenting opinion about this kind of case, see Moore (2009; chapters 5, 6, and 18). I respond to this aspect of Moore's view in Sartorio (2012b). There I discuss the best interpretation of the slogan "Two wrongs don't make a right," and I argue that it yields the consequence that both agents are blameworthy for the outcome in this type of scenario.

18 Most real-life cases, I take it, are asymmetric in this sense, given the artificiality of the symmetric cases (where, recall, the two agents needed to act at precisely the same time in order to prevent the occurrence of the outcome). Real-life cases typically involve *windows of time* during which the agents could have acted, and those windows won't perfectly overlap. For example, imagine that Joe had part of the day to work on his contribution to a project, and Mary had another part of the day (maybe partially overlapping Joe's); each contribution was essential to the success of the project, and both independently failed to do their part; as a result, the project failed. **Asymmetric flooded room** is a "cleaner" case, artificially designed to avoid these complications, in order to keep things as simple as possible.

19 Similar cases have been discussed in the causation literature. Most of them don't directly involve omissions, though, but actions that have some relevant absences as results, which raise similar puzzles. See for example, McDermott (1995) and Collins (2000) on "preemptive prevention" cases. See also the puzzle of the "desert traveler" case from the literature on causation in the law (see for example, McLaughlin, 1925–6, and Hart and Honore, 1985). Briefly, the puzzle is the following: A man takes a trip into the desert, carrying his water canteen. The man has two enemies, A and B, who want him to die and who independently come up with a criminal plan to make sure that happens. A first drains the water out of the canteen, and then, not noticing that the canteen is empty, B steals it. The man dies of thirst in the desert. Who killed the desert traveler?

20 See Metz (forthcoming) for an argument that the first agent preempts the second in a case of this kind. (See also Zimmerman, 1985 for a similar claim about responsibility.)

In the literature on the desert traveler puzzle (the puzzle mentioned in n. 19 above), each of the different possible positions has been defended by at least one theorist, which goes to show how much disagreement there is on this issue. (I discuss the puzzle and my own solution to it in Sartorio, 2015a.)

21 I argue that this type of reasoning gives rise to a new form of moral luck in Sartorio (2015b).
22 Spoiler alert! My view is that A is the one who's morally responsible for the outcome, and B is not. In fact, this is not because A is explanatorily relevant and B isn't, but because A is *morally responsible* for the explanatorily relevant factors and B isn't. (See my modification of the relaxed grounding claim alluded to in the previous section.) However, I admit that not everybody would agree with this solution to the puzzle; after all, it's really hard to know what the best solution is. I discuss puzzles of this kind in Sartorio (2015a and 2017).
23 Notice that, if I am right and the answer depends on who's morally responsible for the explanatorily relevant factors (as explained in section 3), then the answer will depend on another judgment about moral responsibility. But notice that such a judgment is just as uncertain: it is also not clear, at least initially, who's responsible for the explanatorily relevant factors. This is what makes the puzzle particularly hard, in my view.
24 Notice that one intuition that does seem indefeasible, even in these challenging cases, is the *relaxed grounding intuition*. If one has in mind a very broad sense of explanatory relevance, as I do here, then the claim that responsibility for an outcome requires being explanatorily relevant to the outcome (in some way or other) seems simply undeniable. Personally, I can't imagine circumstances that would lead me to reject it.
25 Reuter et al. (2014) contains interesting empirical research on the effect that temporal differences have on the phenomenon of causal selection. But their studies involve actions, not omissions—and joint causation, not overdetermination.

References

Beebee, H. (2004). "Causing and nothingness." In J. Collins, N. Hall, and L.A. Paul (eds.), *Causation and Counterfactuals* (291–308). Cambridge, MA: MIT Press,

Bernstein, S. (2015). "The metaphysics of omissions." *Philosophy Compass* 10(3): 208.

Clarke, R., J. Shepherd, J. Stigall, R. Repko Waller, and C. Zarpentine (2015). "Causation, norms, and omissions: A study of causal judgements." *Philosophical Psychology* 28: 279–93.

Collins, J. (2000). "Preemptive prevention." *Journal of Philosophy* 97(4): 223.

Collins, J., N. Hall, and L.A. Paul (eds.) (2004). *Causation and Counterfactuals*. Cambridge, MA: MIT Press.

Cushman, F. and L. Young (2011). "Patterns of moral judgment derive from nonmoral psychological representations." *Cognitive Science* 35: 1052–75.

Dowe, P. (2001). "A counterfactual theory of prevention and 'causation' by omission." *Australasian Journal of Philosophy* 79(2): 216–26.

Hart, H.L.A. and T. Honore (1985). *Causation in the Law,* 2nd ed. Oxford: Oxford University Press.

Henne, P., A. Pinillos, and P. De Brigard (2017). "Cause by omission and norm: Not watering plants." *Australasian Journal of Philosophy* 95(2): 270–83.

Henne, P., L. Niemi, A. Pinillos, F. De Brigard, and J. Knobe (2019). "A counterfactual explanation for the action effect in causal judgment." *Cognition* 190: 157–64.

Hitchcock, C. (ed.) (2004). *Contemporary Debates in Philosophy of Science*. Malden, MA: Blackwell.
Hitchcock, C. (2007). "Three concepts of causation." *Philosophy Compass* 2(3): 508–16.
Kaiserman, A. (2018). "'More of a cause': Recent work on degrees of causation and responsibility." *Philosophy Compass* 13(7).
Lewis, D. (1986). "Causation." In *Philosophical Papers*, Vol. II (159–213). New York: Oxford University Press.
Livengood, J. and E. Machery (2007). "The folk probably don't think what you think they think: Experiments on causation by absence." *Midwest Studies in Philosophy XXXI*: 107–28.
McDermott, M. (1995). "Redundant causation." *British Journal for the Philosophy of Science* 46: 523–44.
McGrath, S. (2005). "Causation by omission: A dilemma." *Philosophical Studies* 123/1: 125–48.
McLaughlin, J.A. (1925–6). "Proximate cause." *Harvard Law Review* 39: 149.
Metz, J. (forthcoming). "Preemptive omissions." *Erkenntnis*.
Moore, M. (2009). *Causation and Responsibility*. Oxford: Oxford University Press.
Paul, L.A., N. Hall and E.J. Hall (2013). *Causation: A User's Guide*. Oxford: Oxford University Press.
Reuter, K., L. Kirfel, R. van Riel, and L. Barlassina (2014). "The good, the bad, and the timely: How temporal order and moral judgment influence causal selection." *Frontiers in Psychology* 5(5): 1336.
Sartorio, C. (2004). "How to be responsible for something without causing it." *Philosophical Perspectives* 18(1): 315–36.
Sartorio, C. (2012a). "Resultant luck." *Philosophy and Phenomenological Research* 84(1): 63–86.
Sartorio, C. (2012b). "Two wrongs don't make a right: Responsibility and overdetermination." *Legal Theory* 18: 473–90.
Sartorio, C. (2015a). "Resultant luck and the thirsty traveler." *Methode* 4(6): 153–72.
Sartorio, C. (2015b). "A new form of moral luck?" In A. Buckareff, C. Moya, and S. Rossell (eds.), *Agency, Freedom, and Moral Responsibility* (134–49). Palgrave-Macmillan.
Sartorio, C. (2016). *Causation and Free Will*. Oxford: Oxford University Press.
Sartorio, C. (2017). "The puzzle(s) of Frankfurt-style omission cases." In D. Nelkin and S. Rickless (eds.), *The Ethics and Law of Omissions* (133–47). New York: Oxford University Press.
Sartorio, C. (2020). "More of a cause?" *Journal of Applied Philosophy* 37(3): 346–63.
Sartorio, C. (2021). "Responsibility and the metaphysics of omissions." In S. Bernstein and T. Goldschmidt (eds.), *Non-Being: New Essays on Non-Existence* (294–309). New York: Oxford University Press.
Schaffer, J. (2003). "Overdetermining causes." *Philosophical Studies*, Vol. 114 (1/2): 23.
Varzi, A. (2007). "Omissions and causal explanations." In F. Castellani and J. Quitterer (eds.), *Agency and Causation in the Human Sciences* (155–67). Paderborn: Mentis Verlag.
Willemsen, P. (2016). "Omissions and expectations: a new approach to the things we failed to do." *Synthese* 195: 1587–614.
Willemsen, P. (2019). *Omissions and their Moral Relevance: Assessing Causal and Moral Responsibility for the Things We Fail to Do*. Paderborn: Mentis Verlag.
Willemsen, P. and L. Kirfel (2018). "Recent empirical work on the relationship between causal judgments and norms." *Philosophy Compass* 14: 1.

Woollard, F. and F. Howard-Snyder (2016). "Doing and allowing harm." *The Stanford Encyclopedia of Philosophy* (Winter 2016 Edition), Edward N. Zalta (ed.), https://plato.stanford.edu/archives/win2016/entries/doing-allowing/

Zimmerman, M. (1985). "Sharing responsibility." *American Philosophical Quarterly 22*: 115–22.

4

Causal Perception and Causal Inference: An Integrated Account

David Danks and Phuong (Phoebe) Ngoc Dinh

Much has been written about whether causation is a genuine feature of the world (for an overview, see Beebee, Hitchcock, and Menzies, 2009), but it seems undisputed that causation mediates much of human understanding and experience of the world. Causal knowledge enables us to predict future instances, explain past events, design interventions, categorize entities, reason about counterfactuals, and more (Sloman and Lagnado, 2015). As such, causation has been of longstanding interest to psychologists and philosophers alike. One prominent feature of causation is its variability: causal events exhibit diverse observable features, time courses, and necessary or sufficient conditions across domains. There is no single way that causation appears in our experience, no single phenomenological property that (seemingly) occurs for all causation. For example, imagine a rolling ball hitting a stationary ball, after which the latter immediately begins to move. Most adults would discern—easily, immediately, without prompting, and typically in one instance—that the former caused the latter to move (i.e., causal perception, Hubbard, 2013a, 2013b; Michotte, 1946/1963). In contrast, consider the case of determining whether smoking causes lung cancer. Here, learning appears effortful and explicit, requires multiple observations, and is amenable to top-down influences such as knowledge of other risk factors of lung cancer (i.e., causal inference, Cheng, 1997; Sloman and Lagnado, 2015).

In light of the seemingly distinct ways that humans learn and reason about causal events, as well as the diversity of events in the world that appear to involve causation, the idea of *causal pluralism*—the theory that there is a plurality of causal concepts and learning modes—has been repeatedly proposed in philosophy (Anscombe, 1971; Cartwright, 2004; Godfrey-Smith, 2010; Hall, 2004; Hitchcock, 2007, 2012; Psillos, 2010). Causal pluralism has also been suggested, though to a lesser extent, in psychology (Lombrozo, 2010; Waldmann and Mayrhofer, 2016). Even when psychologists do not explicitly endorse causal pluralism, they often tacitly assume it in their research programs: research on one kind of causal learning rarely incorporates insights from research on others, and efforts to investigate potential overlaps between (ostensibly different) causal concepts have largely been absent (with a few notable exceptions, such as Schlottmann and Shanks, 1992).

Despite the allure of causal pluralism, we contend that it stands on shaky empirical grounds. First, the apparent empirical distinction between different notions of causation discovered in psychological research is systematically confounded by methodological differences. Second, even if one concedes that there are truly different clusters of causal learning behaviors, there is research, albeit piecemeal and preliminary, to suggest that the corresponding conceptual boundary must be quite blurry. Even if causal pluralism provides a useful first approximation of human behavioral data, close inspection reveals the need for either substantial modifications or theoretical alternatives. Nonetheless, causal pluralism has remained a prominent view in both philosophy and psychology of causation, partly because extant monist theories all suffer from their own significant shortcomings.

In this chapter, we attempt to remedy this latter issue. We propose a new monist account of people's concept of causation and provide a computational model of cognitive processes involving it. In particular, our monist account shows how a single kind of casual concept can nonetheless support multiple forms of causal learning and reasoning. This monist concept does not privilege any specific type of information *a priori*, but rather it can be inferred from spatiotemporal, statistical, and mechanism information. We posit that causal learners opportunistically use any-and-all features to which they have epistemic access in order to infer causal connections, and then use those inferred connections to explain, predict, and reason about the world around them. We show that the new monist concept is capable of explaining existing empirical data on human causal learning, including data to suggest interactions between input of different modalities. We additionally aim to show that our proposal is not empirically vacuous, but rather makes novel predictions that have not previously been explored.

Before turning to our new account, though, we first survey the data that purportedly support causal pluralism. We then show that methodological confounds in experimental paradigms, measures, and explanatory foci undermine the conceptual boundaries proposed in causal pluralism. We also briefly discuss extant data that make a unitary causal concept seem plausible. We consider two existing monist proposals, each of which uses one of the proposed causal concepts to ground the other. We then introduce the basic tenets of our proposed monist causal theory and provide a high-level explanation of how it can be computationally implemented. We show that this account makes testable predictions and outline some preliminary investigations. We conclude with observations and lessons for both philosophy and psychology of causation as well as other domains.

A brief argument for causal pluralism

The most common form of causal pluralism in psychology posits two concepts and learning modes of causation: causal perception and causal inference. The first mode of learning—causal perception—is characteristically found in collisions or other direct physical causation. This mode hinges on signature perceptual features of dynamic events, such as the spatiotemporal contiguity between agents and recipients during launching (Michotte, 1946/1963; Yela, 1952), or the synchrony between the motion onsets of different objects in a chain of events (Hubbard and Ruppel, 2013; White and Milne, 1997). More recent research suggests that humans distinguish between some categories of causal interactions (e.g., launching vs. entraining) even in "low-level" vision (Kominsky and Scholl, 2020). Furthermore, causal perception appears impervious to top-down influences such as goals and prior knowledge, similar to some visual illusions (Firestone and Scholl, 2016). In most studies of causal perception, adults only need one exposure to determine the causal nature of the event. Notably, causal perception appears irresistible and phenomenologically salient (Michotte, 1946/1963) even if learners "know" otherwise given statistical dependency information (Schlottmann and Shanks, 1992). Infants develop the ability to perceive simple launches as causal between six-and-a-half and ten months of age (Leslie and Keeble, 1987; Oakes and Cohen, 1990), and as early as four-and-a-half months of age with experience of self-generated action (Rakison and Krogh, 2012).

In contrast, the second mode of learning—causal inference—is characteristically found in learning from repeated experiences, as when one learns that aspirin relieves headaches (or red wine can produce them). Causal inference is sometimes subdivided into learning causal strength and learning causal structure, though these are not necessarily distinct cognitive processes (Griffiths and Tenenbaum, 2005). Spatiotemporal contiguity plays little-to-no role in causal inference. Instead, adults typically use contingency information between categorical variables (Rottman and Keil, 2012), covariation information between continuous factors (Marsh and Ahn, 2009; Soo and Rottman, 2018), deviations from base rates (Perales and Shanks, 2003), and other forms of statistical information. In experiments, participants extract statistical data from observation (Steyvers et al., 2003) or generate the data themselves (Hagmayer and Waldmann, 2007), and then draw conclusions about the existence, strength, and direction of causation. Causal inference is typically thought to be more effortful and explicit, and less phenomenologically salient, than causal perception. Top-down prior knowledge can readily guide causal inference (Hagmayer et al., 2011); for example, it can direct attention to causally relevant aspects of an event, or to potential interventions (Kushnir, Wellman, and Gelman, 2009). The earliest convincing evidence for children's causal inference was found in nineteen-month-old toddlers (Sobel and Kirkham, 2006). Causal inference becomes more sophisticated with development (McCormack et al., 2013; Waismeyer and Meltzoff, 2017).

Causal perception and causal inference present as strikingly different cognitive processes and behavioral patterns, and so some psychologists have argued that each learning mode requires a different kind of causal concept. For example, causal perception has been said to hinge on a perceptual concept in which causation is characterized by signature perceptual features that indicate a causal connection, such as spatiotemporal contiguity (White, 2014), or causal perception may be grounded in a concept of causation as a mechanistic process that transfers power or a conserved quantity from one object to another in ways that yield perceivable signals (Wolff, 2014). These psychological proposals align nicely with process- or production-centric theories in philosophy, where causation is defined by either a conservation or invariance of some quantity through state changes (Dowe, 1992, 2000) or the propagation of causal influence through a chain of spatiotemporally contiguous events (Salmon, 1984, 1994).

In contrast, causal inference seems to be grounded in a concept of causation that emphasizes statistical information, interventions, and explicit prior knowledge. That is, causation for this type of learning is thought to be the statistical relations between causal variables (Cheng and Buehner, 2012; Tenenbaum et al., 2011) or post-intervention probabilities or counterfactuals (Sloman and Lagnado, 2005; Waldmann and Hagmayer, 2005). The statistical concept echoes several difference-making proposals in the philosophy of causation, including those in which a cause is statistically correlated with its purported effect (Good, 1961a, 1961b), counterfactually related to the effect such that if it had not occurred then the effect would not have (counterfactual, Lewis, 1974), or manipulable to produce changes in the effect (interventionism, Menzies and Price, 1993; Woodward, 2005, 2011).

The ample (apparent) evidence for different types of causal learning, as well as different concepts and paradigmatic features, seems to support causal pluralism in psychology, one causation from causal perception and one from causal inference (for a more extensive synthesis, see Dinh, Danks, and Rakison, under review). This conclusion is reinforced by philosophical arguments for a similar position (Hall, 2004; Hitchcock, 2007). Causal pluralism has received explicit endorsement in the field (e.g., Lombrozo, 2010; or Waldmann and Mayrhofer, 2016 for a modified causal pluralism). Even when psychologists do not explicitly endorse causal pluralism, the field evolves as if causal perception and causal inference are indeed distinct clusters: many studies in causal inference exclude factors of causal inference that might be at play, and vice versa. Both in theory and practice, causal pluralism is arguably the default.

Methodological challenges to causal pluralism

Although the main advance of this chapter is the proposal of a novel monist theory, we must first address the extensive body of work seemingly in support of causal pluralism. Our core response is that there is a natural alternative explanation (besides causal pluralism) for these behavioral and phenomenological data: namely, the systematic methodological differences between the two research areas. That is, we contend that the differences between causal perception and causal inference can potentially be explained by methodological confounds, rather than distinct concepts. Of course, this argument does not thereby establish causal monism, but by undermining the main argument in favor of causal pluralism, we open the door for consideration of novel theories. We focus here on three methodological confounds (but see Dinh and Danks, 2021, for more systematic consideration of this challenge to causal pluralism).

One source of methodological divergence lies in the typical experimental paradigms for causal perception and causal inference. In causal perception research, participants usually judge individual events of bivariate causation (e.g., launching between two objects). The use of one-shot presentations in which the cause may or may not be efficacious means that events in causal perception paradigms often appear fully deterministic. In contrast, studies of causal inference usually encourage (if not require) that participants integrate data from multiple data points, whether presented as a table of summary statistics, a matrix of individual trials, or a sequential presentation of trials. Causal inference studies can involve both simple and complex causal relations, ranging from bivariate relations to causal webs with multiple causal mediators.

Additionally, the causal relations studied in causal inference are often nondeterministic (with the probabilities provided through the statistical information conveyed to participants).

Another difference between causal perception and causal inference research is their measures. In causal perception research, adults typically answer questions about the power of the cause, whether through free-form responses, forced choices, or continuous rating scales. Alternately, implicit measures such as perception of overlap or expectations of the distance that the causal recipient should travel (i.e., representational momentum) are used in an effort to separate "low-level" causal percepts from the resulting "high-level," cognitively mediated inferences (Wagemans, van Lier, and Scholl, 2006). In contrast, measures in causal inference research span from predictions of future successes, to ratings of causal power on a continuous scale, to direct interventions on a causal system, and more. That is, measures of causal perception require that participants consider only the event they just watched (i.e., individual event, token), whereas those of causal inference often require that participants consider a group of trials or a causal type.

Yet another divergence between causal perception and causal inference research centers on the kinds of stimuli (and data) provided to participants. In causal perception, participants typically perceive dynamic events that unfold in space and time; temporal and spatial dimensions are explicitly presented in the stimuli. Other information about the kinematics of the event is also provided modally and directly (e.g., relative velocities, angle of approach). In contrast, the stimuli in causal inference research range widely in format, including dynamic events, diagrams of possible causal structures, static schematics of individual trials, or descriptions of events that accompany a summary table. In causal inference research, dynamic information such as space and time often need to be inferred, rather than being provided directly in the stimuli. It is even rarer for dynamic information to be presented modally in causal inference research.

The methods and measures of each research cluster are highly defensible if one starts with an appropriate understanding of the paradigmatic instances of causation for that research cluster. The methods and measures of causal perception research are tailored to phenomenological aspects of token events, while those of causal inference research are often cast at the level of causal types. As such, the theoretical perspectives that arise from one research cluster often struggle to account for information pertinent to the other research cluster. For example, many theories of causal perception have no formal account of how statistical information factors into the phenomenological salience of a launching event. Similarly, accounts of causal inference have difficulties in explaining or modeling how the experiential richness of causation arises from statistical data and top-down knowledge (cf. thick causation, Cartwright, 2004). To be clear, we are not suggesting that any causal perception or causal inference researchers (ourselves included!) have used incorrect or inappropriate methods. However, the significant differences in methods undermine our ability to draw strong inferences about differences in corresponding concepts, at least based on these empirical data. The argument for causal pluralism instead reduces to the intuitions with which we started this chapter. The methodologically splintered history of causal learning research makes it difficult to develop a principled investigation of the ways in which causal perception and causal inference might overlap.

The empirical case for a unitary account

Closer consideration of the empirical data actually provides some suggestive evidence that people might have a *unitary* concept of causation. In one direction, causal perception can exhibit traits typical of causal inference. For example, the perceptual triggers of experiences of causal perception, despite our previous characterizations, can be quite ambiguous and amenable to learning effects. With repeated exposure to delayed launches during experimental training, adults can perceive a delayed launch as causal, at least up to a point (Gruber, Fink, and Damm, 1957). Conversely, training with immediate launches narrows the temporal criterion for causal perception at test (Powesland, 1959). Adults misremember the order of event segments in a way that aligns with a causal interpretation if they perceived the entire event as causal (Bechlivanidis and Lagnado, 2016), and spatial criteria for causal perception are subject to similar effects: objects are judged as being spatially closer to each other when they are perceived as causally linked (Buehner and Humphreys, 2010). Relatedly, when a launch variant with spatial overlap between two objects is perceived as causal, adults underestimate the degree of overlap (Scholl and Nakayama, 2004). Interestingly, prior knowledge of typical features of causal actors (e.g., possession of dynamic parts, the ability to engage in self-propulsion) can constrain causal role assignment in a causal perception paradigm as early as twenty months of age (Rakison, 2006). These findings suggest that causal perception can be sensitive to top-down influences and training across trials, which are features more typically associated with causal inference.

In the other direction, causal inference is responsive to factors often associated with causal perception, particularly perceptual details about the dynamics of causal events. For example, young children struggle to discount misleading information about spatiotemporal contiguity when judging the outcome in a two-cause system. Compared to nine- and ten-year-olds, five-year-olds were more likely to predict that an effect would occur immediately even when the mechanism was known to be slow (Schlottmann, 1999). Similarly, three- to three-and-a-half-year-olds were less likely to succeed at the blicket detector task when the objects hovered above the machine rather than placed on it (Kushnir and Gopnik, 2007). Even though adults can resist the allure of spatiotemporal contiguity in their causal judgments, they need clear reasons to do so, such as knowledge of a delayed mechanism (Buehner and McGregor, 2009). More recent research suggests that adults use small differences in time windows during causal inference to select between different potential causal structures (Bramley et al., 2018). Overall, perceptual information (e.g., space, time) seems to be integrated with other kinds of information during causal inference, and such details are assumed by learners even in the absence of explicit bottom-up information or direct instruction (Hagmayer and Waldmann, 2002).

Alternatives to causal pluralism: two grounding accounts

Although causal pluralism has often functioned as the default position, alternative monist theories have started to emerge. Essentially all of these alternatives prioritize one of the two concepts (perceptual or statistical causality), and then explain the other concept in terms of the prioritized one. In one set of alternatives, the perceivable features of causation define the underlying concept and statistical features are based on that concept, so we refer to these monist accounts as *perceptual grounding theories*. When we look at causal perception, we find that cues such as spatiotemporal contiguity and self-propulsion signal agent and recipient roles in causal interactions, and thereby license the inference to a causal relation (Rips, 2011; White, 2014). Perceptual grounding theories often propose that learners become sensitive to these cues through lifelong experience with causal events that begin in their own experience of exerting change on their surroundings. Alternatively, causation might correspond to a continuous chain of events of the right, force-transmitting kind or mechanism (Ahn and Kalish, 2000; Wolff, 2014). Or learners may hold intuitive theories about momentum and physical causality that are made imprecise by perceptual noise, other prior beliefs, or even assumed uncertainty (Gerstenberg and Tenenbaum, 2017). Regardless of the exact story, all perceptual grounding accounts give perceptual features content beyond their perceivability, and thereby attempt to explain learning in contexts previously thought to be outside of the scope of causal perception. For example, perceptual grounding accounts have been offered to explain counterfactual simulations of launching (Gerstenberg, Halpern, and Tenenbaum, 2015) or the (context-appropriate) downweighting of spatiotemporal contiguity during causal judgments in cognitive development (Schlottmann, 1999).

Perceptual grounding accounts have some intuitive appeal and potential explanatory power, but also have a number of open questions. For example, even an extended or generalized concept of perceptual causation does not seem capable of representing events with few or no immediately perceivable features, such as the causal connection between antidepressants and depressive symptoms. This causal relation has a noisy time course, many mediators or defeaters, and no clear perceptual signatures for the learner to use. Many other phenomena also escape ordinary human perception, and yet we clearly learn causal relations, such as the discovery of the general shape of planetary orbits and what forces govern such a shape. Perhaps most importantly, most accounts of perceptual grounding have no straightforward way of differentiating observation from intervention even though human learners do (Waldmann and Hagmayer, 2005).

In a different set of monist alternatives, researchers aim to prioritize a concept of causation based on statistical information, and then build other causal concepts (e.g., perceptual causality) on top of that concept (Kemp, Goodman, and Tenenbaum, 2010), and so we refer to these as *statistical grounding theories*. These statistical features can manifest as correlations (Good, 1961a, 1961b), contingencies (Perales and Shanks, 2003), interventions (Gebharter, 2017; Woodward, 2005), or counterfactuals (Lewis, 1974). Regardless of the types of statistical information represented in a causal concept, learners can use them to learn and reason about both token- and type-level claims: Smoking increases the chances of developing lung cancer at both the population and individual levels. On these accounts, the perceptual features of a causal event are only salient (if at all) in virtue of their statistics (Woodward, 2011). For example, spatiotemporal contiguity almost always predicts successful launching (given certain conditions e.g., the recipient is not too heavy for the agent), and so the reliance on perceptual cues is entirely reducible to the use of highly statistically significant cues. Notably, several statistical grounding accounts can differentiate between observation and intervention (e.g., the *do* operator in causal graphical models).

Despite their explanatory power, statistical grounding accounts also face open questions and challenges. First, these theories struggle with the phenomenological salience and richness of many daily causal experiences. There is a clear phenomenological difference between the causal perception of our dog chasing after the neighbor's cat and calculations (even if implicit) of the probability of the cat getting hurt. The perception and corresponding beliefs are richer than the statistical properties that underlie them, and so suggest that statistical grounding theories must provide additional explanations to account for the richness of causal perception. Causal perception can provide compelling impressions that diverge from (and cannot be extinguished by) statistically driven conclusions, even if those impressions do not dominate learning outcomes in the end (Schlottmann and Shanks, 1992). Statistical grounding theories also need a way to represent mechanistic information, as there is empirical evidence that people do not conceive of causal mechanisms in purely statistical terms (Ahn and Kalish, 2000). Although causal perception is not completely immune to top-down influences, it does seem to be significantly more resistant to such effects than explicitly statistical causal beliefs. As with perceptual grounding theories, these open questions do not thereby show that these theories are false, but they should temper our potential enthusiasm for these avenues towards a monist theory.

Causal monism: A new alternative to causal pluralism

Causal pluralism faces significant empirical challenges, and there are legitimate theoretical worries about the monist causal learning theories that privilege either causal perception or causal inference. Given these concerns, we develop a different type of monist theory of causal learning and reasoning in this section. We present this theory below, but we emphasize that our primary goal here is to broaden the theoretical space to include a novel, empirically testable possibility. Systematic experiments remain a subject for future work. While this theory may ultimately be empirically falsified, our understanding of the potential relationships between causal perception and causal inference is, we suggest, significantly advanced by our proposed theory.

At a high level, this monist theory posits that people have a single, relatively amodal representation of "unobservable causal connection." This theory further posits that people are opportunists: they use any-and-all clues accessible to them in their efforts to infer these unobservable causal connections, including perceptual cues, statistical information, and verbal instructions. Given an inferred causal connection, one can then reverse the information flow to predict or infer other, not-yet-observed clues. For example, if I infer a causal connection on the basis of statistical information, then I can thereby reason that there is probably some measure of spatial and/or temporal contiguity (which might not be observable) mediating that connection. Importantly, these different sources of evidence (and targets for prediction and reasoning) do not correspond to different underlying concepts of causation but are simply different pathways towards a single concept. This is analogous to the way that my concept of DOG can be activated by an image of a dog, the sound of a bark, or someone telling me about their dog (though see, e.g., Barsalou, 1999 or Machery, 2009 for arguments that no single, shared concept is activated in these different cases). That is, we are not proposing a monist "cluster concept" of causation where "C causes E" sometimes means X and sometimes means Y. Rather, this theory posits that there is a single coherent (overarching) concept of causal connection that underlies our representations of causal structure in the world, but we use many different types of information to infer its existence in particular token cases or types of events.

This high-level proposal can be made precise by formalizing the theory using graphical models. Importantly, we are here using graphical models to represent informational relations, not necessarily causal ones; there is no problematic circularity of people (implicitly) assuming that causal connections *cause* statistical patterns or spatiotemporally contiguous change. The graphical model instead represents the relevant evidential and informational relations. (Of course, as with any graphical model, inferences can occur in both directions along an edge; the directions provide the pattern of informational dependencies, not restrictions on permissible inferences.) We start by considering a single case or event, where that case might include any of the following information about two factors C and E:[1]

1. Spatiotemporally contiguous change in C and E (e.g., a launching event or linked changes in magnitude)
2. Co-occurrence of C and E (e.g., both are present or both are absent)
3. Control (e.g., via intervention) of one or both of C and E
4. Verbal content directly about C and/or E
5. Background experiences that determine prior expectations (discussed more below)

We can graphically represent the inferential relations as in Figure 4.1. Specifically, there is an unobserved variable "C is causally connected to E" (henceforth, CC) whose possible multidimensional values encode presence/absence, causal strength, and any mechanistic or spatiotemporal details. CC is an informational driver of the possibly-observed factors corresponding to the elements in this list.

Full specification of the (informational) graphical model requires the relevant likelihood functions of each observable factor given the presence/absence and strength

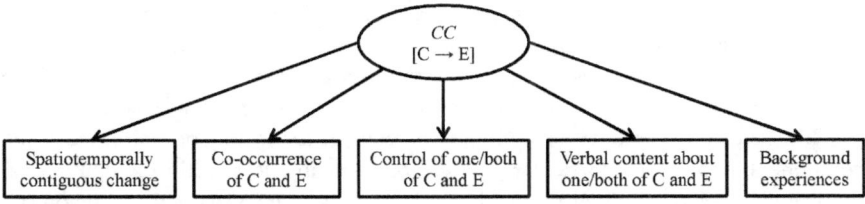

Figure 4.1 Graphical model for monist inference.

of an unobserved causal connection. Importantly, the graphical model structure implies that we do not need to consider direct factor-factor informational relations; everything is mediated through the unobserved causal connection. For example, the full graphical model includes $P(\text{co-occurrence} \mid CC)$, but not $P(\text{co-occurrence} \mid \text{verbal content})$. Put in different language, the state of CC "screens off" the different potential sources of causal information. As such, inferences to CC given some input enable subsequent learning and prediction of new input, whether of the same type or of a different type. The inference to CC need not be empirically accurate by some scientific standard; learners may infer CC mistakenly or hypothetically, given the data they observe. Most critically, inferences to the unobserved (or unobservable) variable CC are not an add-on feature, but rather are the unifying feature that binds together various instances of causal learning (similarly to the suggestion that abstraction to unobserved relations is key to human cognition, as argued by Penn, Holyoak, and Povinelli, 2008; Penn and Povinelli, 2007).

Given a single case or event, one can straightforwardly infer the probability of a causal connection of various types and strengths. Mathematically, this inference is simply standard Bayesian updating (though without requiring any of the usual metaphysical or normative baggage of Bayesianism). Some of the observable factors might not actually be observed, in which case they play no role in the inference. Everything that is observed, however, factors into the update about the probabilities of different values for CC. No type of observable evidence is privileged on theoretical or conceptual grounds for this inference, though they might have different informational values. If the probability distribution over CC changes due to the inferential update, then the informational impact of that change can "flow" back to the other factors (i.e., the ones that are observable, but not actually observed) in the usual way. That is, if I infer that there is probably a causal connection in this case because of factor A, then that change in my belief can also produce a revised expectation about factor B in this case (even if I have not yet observed B).

If we observe multiple cases of a type, then knowledge about the probabilities for CC can be transferred forward in standard ways.[2] Essentially, we are learning the "base rates" of causal connections with particular properties in instances of this type. Alternately, we might be explicitly told about type-level causal connections, which thereby set the relevant prior probabilities. Type-level information about different types could also exhibit structure; for example, if I know that dogs typically have a particular causal connection, then I might reasonably update my prior probabilities about this causal connection in wolves. These inferences can readily be captured through additional structure linking various CC variables (similarly to graphical model representations of between-concept relevance relations, as in Danks, 2014). The long-term result is that we can learn both whether a causal connection exists in a particular case (e.g., does this aspirin relieve this headache?) and also whether there are type-level causal connections (e.g., does aspirin generally relieve headaches?).

This sketch of a computational model can easily be made fully precise; none of the components or pieces are particularly esoteric or unusual (at least, within computational modeling). We have omitted the mathematics simply to help maintain focus on the conceptual and theoretical aspects of the proposal. That being said, we do need to provide here an account of the source of the likelihood functions, even if we skip the precise mathematical formulation. Adult humans clearly have various domain-dependent expectations about how causal connections manifest in the world, whether in terms of spatiotemporal, statistical, or manipulation relationships. For example, adults expect physical causation to be largely deterministic; psychological causation, not so much (Yeung and Griffiths, 2015; Strickland, Silver, and Keil, 2017). As another example, people plausibly expect that a causal connection in the realm of physical objects should (if it exists) exhibit spatiotemporally contiguous changes, while a causal connection in the realm of macroscale biological mechanisms should (if it exists) exhibit significant temporal gaps between the cause and effect. These expectations express exactly the information required for the likelihood functions. That is, people's intuitive (default) expectations about how causal connections might manifest in observable properties are precisely the relevant likelihoods (see Danks, 2018 for a complementary account of default expectations for statistical information).

This monist theory can straightforwardly explain the empirical findings in causal perception and causal inference. Given spatiotemporal information, the learner infers the possible existence of an unobserved causal connection in this token, and then uses that updated belief to provide ratings or answer other questions about the causal connection. Given covariation information summed over multiple instances, the learner infers the possible existence of a pattern of causal connections for the type, and then provides strength ratings, determines post-intervention probabilities, and so forth. In each case, the relevant cognitive processes are simply part of the inferences posited by the monist theory. Of course, the monist theory also predicts that people will draw a number of conclusions from these inferences that are not implied by either causal perception or causal inference in isolation; we return to those predictions shortly. The key observation here is that this monist theory subsumes the existing theories in the special case where our experimental methodologies consider only perceptual or only statistical inputs. The monist theory thus fits cleanly with our earlier critique of the evidence for pluralism, as it contends that the lack of (apparent) interaction between causal perception and causal inference is principally because we have not systematically looked for it (though recall the studies outlined earlier in "The Empirical Case for a Unitary Account").

This last observation about the monist theory suggests a potential fatal flaw: the theory might appear to be simply the concatenation of (the mathematics of) causal perception plus (the mathematics of) causal inference. Almost any set of non-contradictory theories can be "unified" by concatenating representations of them in a common mathematical language, but such a "unification" would tell us essentially nothing about the actual nature of the mind. There must be some content to the monist theory that goes beyond the union of the subsumed theories, otherwise we have not provided anything more than a mathematical parlor trick. We thus conclude this section by outlining three key empirical predictions that are, to the best of our knowledge, distinctive to this monist account (and not implied by the concatenation of causal perception and causal inference).

First, people should be able to make predictions symmetrically from one type of information to another. For example, when shown a canonically causal perception-evoking event, people should be able to make predictions about post-intervention probabilities for this type of event. Or when provided with covariational data, people should make some inferences about the likelihood of spatiotemporally realized mechanisms in various tokens (perhaps different mechanisms in different tokens). The standard pluralist picture implies that this type of cross-task information transfer should be difficult or noisy. Monist theories that ground perception in inference (or vice versa) predict that cross-task transfer should be asymmetric: easy when going from perceptual information to statistical, and hard in the other direction (or the opposite prediction if inference is grounded in perception). In contrast, our monist account proposes that this cross-task transfer should be straightforward and symmetric.

Second, information about one type of feature should inform future learning using other features. Probabilistic updates of CC not only inform reasoning and prediction, but also influence future learning. For example, recall that people judge objects to be closer together when they are believed to be causally related (Buehner and Humphreys, 2010). This effect was demonstrated entirely within the domain of causal perception (i.e., perceptions following actual launching or delayed launching events). This monist theory implies that a similar perceptual effect should occur if people are instead provided with covariational information indicating that a causal connection is almost certainly present in this token, even if people never see the actual collision event. There are clearly methodological challenges in testing this prediction; for example, one would want to minimize, or at least measure for later statistical control, any potential (perceptual) mental simulation by participants in response to the statistical information. Nonetheless, this prediction is distinctive to this monist theory.

Third, both of these effects—cross-task/evidence transfer in learning and in reasoning—are predicted to be entirely (or mostly) mediated by CC. In our proposed account, the information transfer happens because of updates to aspects of CC, rather than direct inference from one kind of observable content to another. This latter possibility is what one would expect if there were learned associations between different types of observable information. There are clearly correlations between the different observable signals of causation, so one might attempt to explain cross-task transfer in terms of direct learned associations between those signals. For example, spatiotemporally contiguous change might be directly associated with intervention counterfactuals since those two go together frequently in a learner's experience. In contrast, our proposed theory implies that this information flow is via CC, and so fixing the values of CC (either statistically or causally) should block the cross-task transfer. We are currently developing an experimental design to test this more subtle prediction.

We conclude our proposal by describing some initial data that suggest that perceptual and statistical cues to causation can interact flexibly to influence the outcome of causal learning (Dinh and Danks, under review). We describe only the qualitative phenomena in this chapter for space reasons.[3] This experiment was designed to challenge a version of causal pluralism in which the multiple concepts are relatively independent. As a result, the experiment cannot distinguish between monism and an interactive version of causal pluralism whereby different causal concepts can strongly influence and constrain one another during learning (Waldmann and Mayrhofer, 2016).[4] (For attempts at developing differential predictions for these latter two

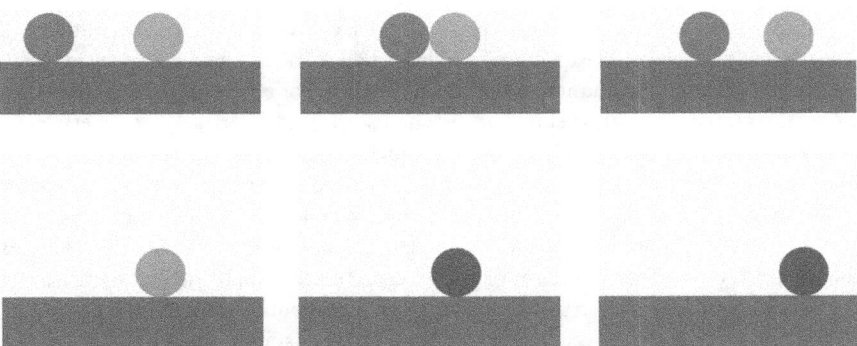

Figure 4.2 Screenshots of successful Launch (top row) and successful Blink (bottom row) events. In unsuccessful events, the recipient remained stationary.

theoretical possibilities, see Dinh, Danks, and Rakison, under review.) Nonetheless, the results point towards exactly the type of symmetry and flexibility between cue-types that is predicted primarily (though perhaps not exclusively) by our monist account. These experiments were all conducted with adults on Amazon Mechanical Turk, and all pitched perceptual and statistical cues against one another in a series of twelve animated, dynamic events. All events involved the motion onset of a stationary object, in response to either contact with a moving object (Launch event) or a rapid series of color changes between pink and purple in the stationary object before settling on purple (Blink event). These two types of events were chosen because we found a sharp divergence between expectations after a single successful instance: Launches were expected to be strong and reliable causes of motion, whereas Blinks were expected to be weak and unreliable.

The key experimental conditions contrasted these strong "perceptual" expectations against strong statistical evidence. For example, a participant might see a sequence of Launch events that were only 75 percent successful, or she might see a sequence of Blink events that were 100 percent successful. According to standard causal pluralism and perceptual grounding theories, participants should give relatively constant cumulative judgments across a sequence of Launch events, regardless of statistical information (since the perceptual cues should be overwhelming and automatic). In contrast, Blink events do not trigger causal perception, and so learning should proceed according to causal inference (and thereby produce a standard learning curve). Statistical grounding theories arguably predict that the statistical information should play a major role, though perhaps significantly attenuated in Launch sequences due to the strong prior expectation of a deterministic relationship. Our monist theory predicts a complex pattern of learning (details omitted) as the perceptual and statistical cues are all used opportunistically to learn about the type-level causal connections.

Results bore out the predictions of our monist theory with high congruence between our two different measures. The first question asked participants to rate the extent to which an apparent cause (Launch or Blink) made the stationary ball move

(–100 to +100). The second question asked participants to estimate the number of cases in which they would expect the stationary ball to move, given 100 cases in which the factor of that series (Launch or Blink) was present. For both questions, participants were asked to consider all events that they had seen in that series. When every event was successful (i.e., if determinism held), Launch sequences led to causal perception-like behavior but Blink sequences led to causal inference-like behavior (and cumulative causal judgments for Blink sequences never reached the levels of Launch sequences). When the sequence was nondeterministic, participant behavior was more complex than predicted by either pluralism or the grounding theories. If the first failure event happened on the very first trial, then participant judgments were low from the outset, regardless of whether it was a Launch or Blink event. A single failure at the very start was sufficient to largely eliminate the exclusive use of spatiotemporal cues. And if the first failure event occurred on a later trial, then participant judgments for Launch sequences dropped significantly more than for Blink sequences after that first failure. That is, the statistical information of a single failure (regardless of location in the sequence) had a significantly larger impact on the Launch sequence judgments, but those were supposed to be the judgments based on causal perception and so more resistant to statistical information! Similar findings occurred across a range of variations in timing of the first failure event, as well as pattern of failure events across the sequence. Our tentative conclusion is that people do not *a priori* privilege one type of information in causal learning. Rather, people opportunistically use and integrate information from diverse cues to infer aspects of the unobserved causal structure underlying their observations.

Conclusion

In this chapter, we briefly presented the central tenets and empirical support for causal pluralism, which is the proposal that human causal learning relies on two distinct kinds of causal concepts and modes of learning: causal perception and causal inference. We discussed methodological differences between the two research clusters and showed that they confound with claims of conceptual distinction between causal perception and causal inference. One alternative if we reject causal pluralism is to reduce one form of causal learning to the other, and so we reviewed two grounding accounts—perceptual grounding and statistical grounding. In contrast, we have proposed a third alternative, namely a monist account in which learners may use any and all cues accessible to them to infer the existence of an unobserved causal relation represented with a single, amodal causal concept. Once learners infer such causal connections, they can then make predictions about future occurrences or inferences about other, not-yet-observed, or unobservable features of the inferred relation. Finally, we provided three testable predictions of the monist account to distinguish it from a mere (mathematical) concatenation of existing theories. It remains to be seen whether our predictions will bear out with future empirical tests. Most importantly, we wish to call attention to a lack of systematic investigation into the ways in which causal perception and causal inference interact, despite extant results pointing to that possibility.

This chapter exemplifies an additional exercise relevant to philosophers and psychologists of causation and beyond. Any theory of empirical import must rely on findings that are discovered through particular research paradigms and methods. At the same time, theories provide the assumptions and constructs that guide and constrain their own experimental paradigms and methods. The interplay between theory and method can be a virtue: for example, theory-mediated measurements enable the precise quantification of key parameters relevant to a theory when done intentionally (Harper, 2007). Yet without that intentional design, methodological specifics can confound with and undermine inferences from data. We suspect this has been the case with research in causal learning. We recommend the incorporation of more diverse methods and measures in future research of causal concepts, as well as an investigation of the assumptions underlying those methods and how they might bear out in the data.

Acknowledgments

Thanks to the editors, Nick Ichien, and David Rakison for valuable comments and feedback on an earlier draft of this chapter. The empirical study reported in this chapter (Dinh and Danks, under review) was supported by Carnegie Mellon University's GSA/Provost GuSH Grant funding.

Notes

1 This list is not necessarily complete and exhaustive. One advantage of this monist account is that it is readily extensible if we discover that people employ some other type of cue or feature in causal learning: we simply add that type of feature as another "leaf node" that can be used opportunistically to infer an unobservable causal connection.
2 Multiple cases of a type can be represented mathematically using plate notation to capture the idea that these are all instances of the same class.
3 The raw data for the experiments described here can be found at https://osf.io/263x5/.
4 We thank Nick Ichien for this important observation.

References

Ahn, W.K. and C.W. Kalish (2000). "The role of mechanism beliefs in causal reasoning." In R. Wilson and F. Keil (eds.), *Explanation and Cognition* (199–225). Cambridge, MA: MIT Press.

Anscombe, G.E.M. (1971). "Causality and determination." Reprinted in E. Sosa and M. Tooley (eds.), *Causation* (1993) (88–104). Oxford: Oxford University Press.

Barsalou, L.W. (1999). "Perceptual symbol systems." *Behavioral and Brain Sciences*, 22: 577–660.

Bechlivanidis, C. and D.A. Lagnado (2016). "Time reordered: Causal perception guides the interpretation of temporal order." *Cognition*, 146: 58–66. https://doi.org/10.1016/j.cognition.2015.09.001

Beebee, H., C. Hitchcock, and P. Menzies (eds.) (2009). *The Oxford Handbook of Causation*. Oxford: Oxford University Press.

Bramley, N.R., T. Gerstenberg, R. Mayrhofer, and D.A. Lagnado (2018). "Time in causal structure learning." *Journal of Experimental Psychology: Learning, Memory, and Cognition*, 44 (12): 1880–1910. https://doi.org/10.1037/xlm0000548

Buehner, M.J. and G.R. Humphreys (2010). "Causal contraction: Spatial binding in the perception of collision events." *Psychological Science*, 21(1): 44–8. https://doi.org/10.1177/0956797609354735

Buehner, M. J. and S.J. McGregor (2009). "Contingency and contiguity trade-offs in causal induction." *International Journal of Comparative Psychology*, 22(1): 19–42. Retrieved from https://escholarship.org/uc/item/8tb8w6f1

Cartwright, N. (2004). "Causation: One word, many things." *Philosophy of Science*, 71(5): 805–19. https://doi.org/10.1086/426771

Cheng, P.W. (1997). "From covariation to causation: A causal power theory." *Psychological Review*, 104(2): 367–405. https://doi.org/10.1037/0033-295X.104.2.367

Cheng, P.W. and M.J. Buehner (2012). "Causal learning." In K.J. Holyoak and R.G. Morrison (eds.), *The Oxford Handbook of Thinking and Reasoning* (210–33). Oxford: Oxford University Press.

Danks, D. (2014). *Unifying the Mind: Cognitive Representations as Graphical Models*. Cambridge, MA: The MIT Press.

Danks, D. (2018). "Privileged (default) causal cognition: A mathematical analysis." *Frontiers in Psychology*, 9: 498. https://doi.org/10.3389/fpsyg.2018.00498

Dinh, P. and D. Danks (2021). Causal pluralism in philosophy: Empirical challenges and alternative proposals. *Philosophy of Science*, 88(5): 761–72. https://www.doi.org/10.1086/714878

Dinh, P.N. and D. Danks (under review). Expectations of Causal Determinism in Causal Learning. Department of Psychology, Carnegie Mellon University.

Dinh, P.N., D. Danks, and D.H. Rakison (under review). "Causal perception and causal inference: A methodological and theoretical synthesis." Department of Psychology, Carnegie Mellon University.

Dowe, P. (1992). "An empiricist defence of the causal account of explanation." *International Studies in the Philosophy of Science*, 6(2): 123–8. https://doi.org/10.1080/02698599208573420

Dowe, P. (2000). *Physical Causation*. Cambridge: Cambridge University Press.

Firestone, C. and B.J. Scholl (2016). "Cognition does not affect perception: Evaluating the evidence for 'top-down' effects." *Behavioral and Brain Sciences*, 39: e229. https://doi.org/10.1017/S0140525X15000965

Gebharter, A. (2017). "Causal exclusion and causal Bayes nets." *Philosophy and Phenomenological Research*, 95(2): 353–75. https://doi.org/10.1111/phpr.12247

Gerstenberg, T. and J.B. Tenenbaum (2017). "Intuitive theories." In M.R. Waldmann (ed.), *Oxford Handbook of Causal Reasoning* (515–48). Oxford: Oxford University Press.

Gerstenberg, T., J.Y. Halpern, and J.B. Tenenbaum (2015). "Responsibility judgments in voting scenarios." In D.C. Noelle et al. (eds.), *Proceedings of the 37th Annual Conference of the Cognitive Science Society* (788–93). Austin, TX: Cognitive Science Society.

Godfrey-Smith, P. (2010). "Causal pluralism." In H. Beebee, C. Hitchcock, and P. Menzies (eds.), *Oxford Handbook of Causation* (326–37). Oxford: Oxford University Press. https://doi.org/10.1093/oxfordhb/9780199279739.003.0017

Good, I.J. (1961a). "A causal calculus (I)." *The British Journal for the Philosophy of Science*, 11(44): 305–18.

Good, I. J. (1961b). "A causal calculus (II)." *The British Journal for the Philosophy of Science*, 12(45), 43–51.

Griffiths, T.L. and J.B. Tenenbaum (2005). "Structure and strength in causal induction." *Cognitive Psychology*, 51(4): 334–84. https://doi.org/10.1016/j.cogpsych.2005.05.004

Gruber, H.E., C.D. Fink, and V. Damm (1957). "Effects of experience on perception of causality." *Journal of Experimental Psychology*, 53(2), 89–93. https://doi.org/10.1037/h0048506

Hagmayer, Y. and M.R. Waldmann (2002). "How temporal assumptions influence causal judgments." *Memory & Cognition*, 30(7): 1128–37. https://doi.org/10.3758/BF03194330

Hagmayer, Y. and M.R. Waldmann (2007). "Inferences about unobserved causes in human contingency learning." *Quarterly Journal of Experimental Psychology*, 60(3): 330–55. https://doi.org/10.1080/17470210601002470

Hagmayer, Y., B. Meder, M. von Sydow, and M.R. Waldmann (2011). "Category transfer in sequential causal learning: The unbroken mechanism hypothesis." *Cognitive Science*, 35(5): 842–73. https://doi.org/10.1111/j.1551-6709.2011.01179.x

Hall, N. (2004). "Two concepts of causation." In J.D. Collins, E.J. Hall, and L.A. Paul (eds.), *Causation and Counterfactuals* (225–76). Cambridge, MA: MIT Press.

Harper, W. (2007). "Newton's methodology and Mercury's perihelion before and after Einstein." *Philosophy of Science*, 74(5): 932–42. https://doi.org/10.1086/525634

Hitchcock, C. (2007). "How to be a causal pluralist." In P. Machamer and G. Wolters (eds.), *Thinking About Causes: From Greek Philosophy to Modern Physics* (200–21). Pittsburgh, PA: University of Pittsburgh Press.

Hitchcock, C. (2012). "Portable causal dependence: A tale of consilience." *Philosophy of Science*, 79(5): 942–51. https://doi.org/10.1086/667899

Hubbard, T.L. (2013a). "Phenomenal causality I: Varieties and variables." *Axiomathes*, 23(1): 1–42. https://doi.org/10.1007/s10516-012-9198-8

Hubbard, T.L. (2013b). "Phenomenal causality II: Integration and implication." *Axiomathes*, 23(3): 485–524. https://doi.org/10.1007/s10516-012-9200-5

Hubbard, T.L. and S.E. Ruppel (2013). "Ratings of causality and force in launching and shattering." *Visual Cognition*, 21(8): 987–1009. https://doi.org/10.1080/13506285.2013.847883

Kemp, C., N.D. Goodman, and J.B. Tenenbaum (2010). "Learning to learn causal models." *Cognitive Science*, 34(7): 1185–243. https://doi.org/10.1111/j.1551-6709.2010.01128.x

Kominsky, J.F. and B.J. Scholl (2020). "Retinotopic adaptation reveals distinct categories of causal perception." *Cognition*, 203: 104339. https://doi.org/10.1016/j.cognition.2020.104339

Kushnir, T. and A. Gopnik (2007). "Conditional probability versus spatial contiguity in causal learning: Preschoolers use new contingency evidence to overcome prior spatial assumptions." *Developmental Psychology*, 43(1): 186–96. https://doi.org/10.1037/0012-1649.43.1.186

Kushnir, T., H.M. Wellman, and S.A. Gelman (2009). "A self-agency bias in preschoolers' causal inferences." *Developmental Psychology*, 45(2): 597–603. https://doi.org/10.1037/a0014727

Leslie, A.M. and S. Keeble (1987). "Do six-month-old infants perceive causality?" *Cognition*, 25(3): 265–88. https://doi.org/10.1016/S0010-0277(87)80006-9

Lewis, D. (1974). "Causation." *The Journal of Philosophy*, 70(17): 556–67. https://doi.org/10.2307/2025310

Lombrozo, T. (2010). "Causal-explanatory pluralism: How intentions, functions, and mechanisms influence causal ascriptions." *Cognitive Psychology*, 61(4): 303–32. https://doi.org/10.1016/j.cogpsych.2010.05.002

Machery, E. (2009). *Doing Without Concepts*. New York: Oxford University Press.
Marsh, J.K. and W.K. Ahn, (2009). "Spontaneous assimilation of continuous values and temporal information in causal induction." *Journal of Experimental Psychology: Learning, Memory, and Cognition*, 35(2): 334–52. https://doi.org/10.1037/a0014929
McCormack, T., V. Simms, J. McGourty, and T. Beckers (2013). "Blocking in children's causal learning depends on working memory and reasoning abilities." *Journal of Experimental Child Psychology*, 115 (3): 562–9. https://doi.org/10.1016/j.jecp.2012.11.016
Menzies, P. and H. Price (1993). "Causation as a secondary quality." *The British Journal for the Philosophy of Science*, 44(2): 187–203. https://doi.org/10.1093/bjps/44.2.187
Michotte, A. (1946). "La perception de la causalité." Louvain: Institut Superior de Philosophie, 1946. English translation of updated edition by T. Miles and E. Miles, *The Perception of Causality*. New York: Basic Books, 1963.
Oakes, L.M. and L.B. Cohen (1990). "Infant perception of a causal event." *Cognitive Development*, 5(2): 193–207. https://doi.org/10.1016/0885-2014(90)90026-P
Penn, D.C., K.J. Holyoak, and D.J. Povinelli (2008). "Darwin's mistake: Explaining the discontinuity between human and nonhuman minds." *Behavioral and Brain Sciences*, 31(2): 109–78. https://doi.org/10.1017/S0140525X08003543
Penn, D.C. and D.J. Povinelli (2007). "Causal cognition in human and nonhuman animals: A comparative, critical review." *Annual Review of Psychology*, 58: 97–118. https://doi.org/10.1146/annurev.psych.58.110405.085555
Perales, J.C. and D.R. Shanks (2003). "Normative and Descriptive Accounts of the Influence of Power and Contingency on Causal Judgement." *The Quarterly Journal of Experimental Psychology Section A*, 56(6): 977–1007. https://doi.org/10.1080/02724980244000738
Powesland, P.F. (1959). "The effect of practice upon the perception of causality." *Canadian Journal of Psychology/Revue Canadienne de Psychologie*, 13(3): 155–68. https://doi.org/10.1037/h0083773
Psillos, S. (2010). "Causal pluralism." In R. Vanderbeeken and B. D'Hooghe (eds.), *Worldviews, Science, and Us: Studies of Analytic Metaphysics: A Selection of Topics from a Methodological Perspective*. World Science Publishers. https://doi.org/10.1142/9789814299053_0009
Rakison, D.H. (2006). "Make the first move: How infants learn about self-propelled objects." *Developmental Psychology*, 42(5): 900–12. https://doi.org/10.1037/0012-1649.42.5.900
Rakison, D.H. and L. Krogh (2012). "Does causal action facilitate causal perception in infants younger than 6 months of age?" *Developmental Science*, 15 (1): 43–53. https://doi.org/10.1111/j.1467-7687.2011.01096.x
Rips, L.J. (2011). "Causation from perception." *Perspectives on Psychological Science*, 6(1): 77–97. https://doi.org/10.1177/1745691610393525
Rottman, B.M. and F.C. Keil (2012). "Causal structure learning over time: Observations and interventions." *Cognitive Psychology*, 64(1–2): 93–125. https://doi.org/10.1016/j.cogpsych.2011.10.003
Salmon, W.C. (1984). *Scientific Explanation and the Causal Structure of the World*. Princeton: Princeton University Press.
Salmon, W.C. (1994). "Causality without counterfactuals." *Philosophy of Science*, 61(2): 297–312.
Schlottmann, A. (1999). "Seeing it happen and knowing how it works: How children understand the relation between perceptual causality and underlying mechanism." *Developmental Psychology*, 35(1): 303–17. https://doi.org/10.1037/0012-1649.35.1.303
Schlottmann, A. and D.R. Shanks (1992). "Evidence for a distinction between judged and perceived causality." *The Quarterly Journal of Experimental Psychology*, 44(2): 321–42. https://doi.org/10.1080/02724989243000055

Scholl, B.J. and K. Nakayama (2004). "Illusory causal crescents: Misperceived spatial relations due to perceived causality." *Perception, 33*(4), 455–69. https://doi.org/10.1068/p5172

Sloman, S. A. and D.A. Lagnado (2005). "Do we 'do'?" *Cognitive Science, 29*: 5–39.

Sloman, S. A. and D.A. Lagnado (2015). "Causality in thought." *Annual Review of Psychology, 66*(1): 223–47. https://doi.org/10.1146/annurev-psych-010814-015135

Sobel, D.M. and N.Z. Kirkham (2006). "Blickets and babies: The development of causal reasoning in toddlers and infants." *Developmental Psychology, 42*(6): 1103–15. https://doi.org/10.1037/0012-1649.42.6.1103

Soo, K.W. and B.M. Rottman (2018). "Causal strength induction from time series data." *Journal of Experimental Psychology: General, 147*(4): 485–513. https://doi.org/10.1037/xge0000423

Steyvers, M., J.B. Tenenbaum, E.J., Wagenmakers, and B. Blum (2003). "Inferring causal networks from observations and interventions." *Cognitive Science, 27*(3): 453–89. https://doi.org/10.1207/s15516709cog2703_6

Strickland, B., I. Silver, and F.C. Keil (2017). "The texture of causal construals: Domain-specific biases shape causal inferences from discourse." *Memory & Cognition, 45*(3): 442–55. https://doi.org/10.3758/s13421-016-0668-x

Tenenbaum, J.B., C. Kemp, T.L. Griffiths, and N.D. Goodman (2011). "How to grow a mind: Statistics, structure, and abstraction." *Science, 331*(6022): 1279–85. https://doi.org/10.1126/science.1192788

Wagemans, J., R. Van Lier, and B.J. Scholl (2006). "Introduction to Michotte's heritage in perception and cognition research." *Acta Psychologica, 123*(1–2): 1–19. https://doi.org/10.1016/j.actpsy.2006.06.003

Waismeyer, A. and A.N. Meltzoff (2017). "Learning to make things happen: Infants' observational learning of social and physical causal events." *Journal of Experimental Child Psychology, 162*: 58–71. https://doi.org/10.1016/j.jecp.2017.04.018

Waldmann, M.R. and Y. Hagmayer (2005). "Seeing Versus Doing: Two Modes of Accessing Causal Knowledge." *Journal of Experimental Psychology: Learning, Memory, and Cognition, 31*(2): 216–27. https://doi.org/10.1037/0278-7393.31.2.216

Waldmann, M.R. and R. Mayrhofer (2016). "Hybrid causal representations." In *Psychology of Learning and Motivation*, Vol. 65 (85–127). Cambridge, MA: Academic Press.

White, P.A. (2014). "Singular clues to causality and their use in human causal judgment." *Cognitive Science, 38*(1): 38–75. https://doi.org/10.1111/cogs.12075

White, P.A. and A. Milne (1997). "Phenomenal causality: Impressions of pulling in the visual perception of objects in motion." *The American Journal of Psychology, 110* (4): 573–602. https://doi.org/10.2307/1423411

Wolff, P. (2014). "Causal pluralism and force dynamics." In B. Copley and F. Martin (eds.), *Causation in Grammatical Structures* (100–19). Oxford: Oxford University Press.

Woodward, J. (2005). *Making Things Happen: A Theory of Causal Explanation*. Oxford: Oxford University Press.

Woodward, J. (2011). "Causal perception and causal cognition." In J. Roessler, H. Lerman, and N. Eilan (eds.), *Perception, Causation, and Objectivity* (229–63). Oxford: Oxford University Press.

Yela, M. (1952). "Phenomenal causation at a distance." *Quarterly Journal of Experimental Psychology, 4*(4): 139–54. https://doi.org/10.1080/17470215208416612

Yeung, S. and T.L. Griffiths (2015). "Identifying expectations about the strength of causal relationships." *Cognitive Psychology, 76*: 1–29. https://doi.org/10.1016/j.cogpsych.2014.11.001

5

The Interplay between Covariation, Temporal, and Mechanism Information in Singular Causation Judgments

Simon Stephan and Michael R. Waldmann

Imagine you are taking a dose of a certain medication that causes stomach cramps as a side effect. Later that day you actually feel an unpleasant pain in your stomach. Did your taking the drug cause your stomach cramps, or did the two events merely co-occur coincidentally and your stomach cramps were actually caused by some alternative cause? Maybe instead of the drug it was your eating a salad for lunch that was spoiled?

The question being asked in the example is a singular causation question because it refers to a potential causal connection between events that actually occurred at a particular time in a particular place. Singular causation can be contrasted with general causation, which refers to causal relations obtaining between event types instead of event tokens. For example, the claim "Taking this type of medication causes stomach cramps" is a generic-level causal claim, whereas the claim that "My having taken this particular medication this morning was the cause of my stomach cramps at noon" is a singular-level causal claim. Singular causation queries are ubiquitous in our lives. Answers to singular causation queries often guide the goals we set and the actions we take to achieve them. For example, finding the cause of a disease in a specific patient guides treatment decisions for this patient. Finding the cause of environmental damage in a specific area may lead to specific interventions designed to reverse the situation.

Despite the prevalence of singular causation queries in our daily lives and their importance in professional disciplines such as medicine or law, answering the question of how we can know that two events were causally connected is far from trivial. The reason for this difficulty is, as has famously been noted by Hume (1748/1975), that causal connections between individual events are not directly perceivable (see also Cheng and Ichien, in this volume).

While the analysis of singular causation has kept philosophers busy for decades (see Beebee, Hitchcock, and Menzies, 2009) (see also Danks, 2017), most studies in psychology on causal cognition have focused on how people learn about general causal relationships (e.g., Cheng, 1997; Griffiths and Tenenbaum, 2005; Liljeholm and Cheng, 2007) (see Cheng and Buehner, 2012; Waldmann, 2017; Waldmann and Hagmayer, 2013, for overviews), how they use their general causation knowledge to make predictions (e.g., Rehder, 2014; Waldmann, 2000), or how they designate among a set of potential causes a specific one as the cause of that effect (i.e., causal selection) (see, e.g., Cheng and Novick, 1991; Kahneman and Miller, 1986; Kominsky et al., 2015; Samland et al. 2016; Samland and Waldmann, 2016).

We have recently begun to investigate how reasoners use their general causation knowledge to answer singular causation queries (Stephan, Mayrhofer, and Waldmann, 2020; Stephan and Waldmann, 2018, 2022). Building on the power PC model of causal attribution proposed by Cheng and Novick (2005), we have proposed the *generalized* power PC model of singular causation judgments. The model computes the probability that a particular target cause c actually caused a target effect e. The model combines information about the general strengths of the potential causes of the target effect, which can be induced based on covariational information, with information about temporal relations between causes and effects (Stephan, Mayrhofer, and Waldmann, 2020).

Apart from covariation and temporal properties, an important cue helping in the assessment of singular causation is information about the mechanisms linking causes and effects (see, e.g., Cartwright, 2015, 2017; Danks, 2005). Cartwright (2017) lists the discovery of intermediate steps in a causal chain as one of the crucial indicators of singular causation. Also, psychological studies (e.g., Ahn et al., 1995; Johnson and Keil, 2018) have shown that reasoners are sensitive to mechanism information when making causal judgments (see Johnson and Ahn, 2017, for an overview): when asked to determine the singular cause of an observed effect, reasoners tend to search for information about the status of known causal mechanism variables (Johnson and Keil, 2018).

What has been missing in the literature is a formal computational model explaining why causal mechanism information is helpful for the assessment of singular causation. We have recently (Stephan and Waldmann, 2022) proposed an extension of our generalized power PC model of singular causation judgments that incorporates causal mechanism information and thus provides an answer to this question.

In this chapter, we provide an overview of our latest work. The focus will be on our model, but we will also briefly summarize key empirical findings. Since our model is a generalization of Cheng and Novick's (2005) power PC model of causal attribution, we will start with a brief review of their model (which we henceforth refer to as the standard model) and show what the standard model gets right and where it fails. To foreshadow, a limitation of the standard model is that it solely focuses on the strengths of the potential causes of an effect (and their base rates if the causes are unobserved) and thus neglects the possibility of *causal preemption*. We will then summarize our generalized power PC model of singular causation judgments and demonstrate how it overcomes shortcomings of the standard model. Then, we will show that our model can also be used to provide a formal answer to the question under what conditions causal mechanism information is a valuable cue in the assessment of singular causation. We will end with a discussion of open questions and ideas for future studies.

The role of causal strength information in singular causation judgments—the standard power PC model of causal attribution

The standard power PC model of causal attribution (Cheng and Novick, 2005) is an application of Cheng's (1997) causal power PC theory to situations in which reasoners want to answer different types of causal attribution queries. For example, reasoners might observe an effect event (*e*) and want to know the probability that different candidate causes actually caused the observed effect. A different query might start with the observed co-occurrence of a potential cause and effect event (*c* and *e*) and ask about the probability that this co-occurrence is causal as opposed to coincidental. According to the standard model, to obtain this probability reasoners need to apply their knowledge about the general causal strength with which *C* generates *E*, as well as the strength of potential alternative causes *A* of the effect.

As has been shown by Cheng (1997), the strength (or power) of a target cause *C*, which is defined as the probability with which the target cause generates the effect independent of alternative causes (*A*), can be induced from observable patterns of covariation between a target cause and an effect given certain background conditions (see Liljeholm and Cheng, 2007; Novick and Cheng, 2004) by applying the following equation:

$$power_c = \frac{\Delta P}{1 - P(e|\neg c)}.$$

Under the causal Bayes net framework (Glymour, 2001; Gopnik et al., 2004; Pearl, 1988, 2000; Sloman, 2005) causal strength as defined by this equation corresponds to the parameter w_c of the causal arrow connecting *C* to *E* within a common-effect causal model in which the target cause *C* and an alternative cause *A* combine according to a *noisy-OR* gate (Glymour, 2003; Griffiths and Tenenbaum, 2005; Pearl, 1988). A graphical illustration of such a causal model is shown in Figure 5.1a. The additional parameters b_a and b_c represent the base rates of the alternative and the target cause, respectively. The parameter w_a denotes *A*'s causal strength (or power).

To illustrate how the standard power PC model of causal attribution applies knowledge about the causal strengths of the potential causes to attribute causality in a singular case, we will focus on a situation in which a reasoner has observed that *C*, *A*, and *E* have actually occurred in a specific situation (i.e., *C* = 1 or *c*, *A* = 1 or *a*, and *E* = 1 or *e*).

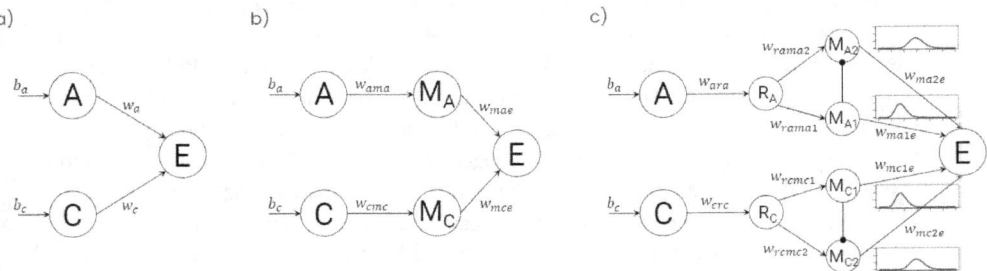

Figure 5.1 Different causal models in which C and A represent root causes of a common target effect E. Note: (a) a common-effect model with two causes, (b) an augmented version of that model with causal mechanism variables, (c) a model in which C and A generate E via different alternative mechanism paths. In this last model, the gray curves represent the causal latencies of the respective causal arrows. The causal link with the round head denotes an inhibitory link.

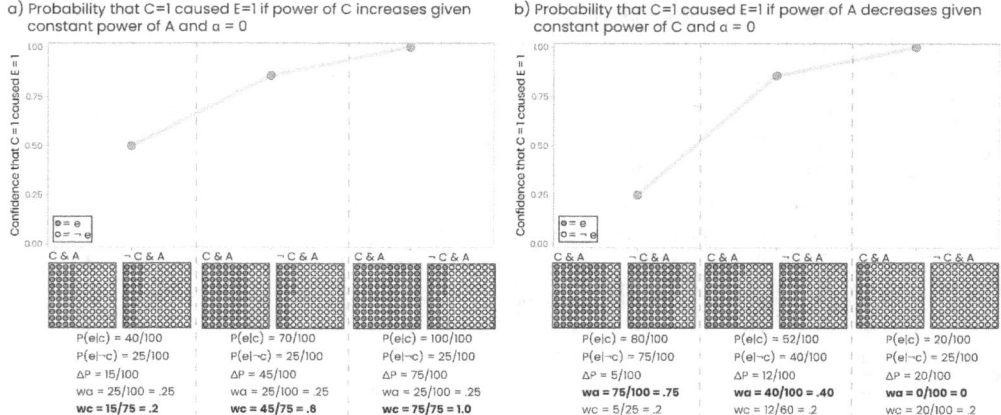

Figure 5.2 Predictions of the standard power PC model of causal attribution for different levels of w_c and w_a.

According to the standard model, the probability that c was the singular cause of e in this case is given by:

$$P(c \to e \mid c, a, e) = \frac{w_c}{w_c + w_a - w_c \cdot w_a} = \frac{w_c}{P(e \mid c, a)}. \tag{1}$$

The standard model thus predicts that in a situation in which C, A, and E are present, the probability that c caused e corresponds to C's general causal strength divided by the conditional probability of the effect given the presence of the two potential causes C and A. Situations in which one or both of the potential causes are unobserved can also be modeled. In this case, the causes' strength parameters need to be multiplied with their corresponding base rate parameters (b_c and b_a).

Equation 1 captures a number of intuitions about singular causation, which are summarized in Figure 5.2. The different pairs of panels below the graphs' x-axes show different contingency tables. In each pair, the right panel displays cases in which only the alternative cause is present while the target cause is absent ($\neg c, a$), and the left panel contains cases in which both potential causes are present (c, a). Cases in which the effect is present (e) are depicted as gray circles. $P(c \to e \mid c, a, e)$, as defined in Equation 1, can be understood as the relative frequency of gray circles in the left panel that were produced by the target cause C. In Figure 5.2a, the causal strength w_c of the target cause C increases from the left to the right contingency data set (from $w_c = 0.2$ to $w_c = 0.6$ to $w_c = 1.0$), while the strength w_a of the alternative cause remains constant ($w_a = 0.25$). The graph shows that the probability that c caused e increases when w_c increases. The model thus captures the intuition that we should be more confident that the target cause actually caused the target effect in a specific situation when this cause is generally more likely to produce the effect.

The right graph shows another plausible way of reasoning about singular causation that is captured by the model. This time the target cause's strength is constant ($w_c = 0.2$) while the strength of the alternative cause decreases (from $w_a = 0.75$ to $w_a = 0.40$ to $w_a = 0$). The graph shows that $P(c \rightarrow e|c,a,e)$ increases with decreasing strength of the alternative cause. The model captures the intuition that a candidate cause is more likely to be the singular cause of the effect if alternative causes are unlikely to produce the effect. In the case in which an alternative cause has a strength of zero, this event can be ruled out as the effect's singular cause. It therefore must have been the target cause that produced the effect, no matter how weak this cause generally is. This example shows that Equation 1 instantiates a reasoning principle that philosophers have called abductive reasoning, reasoning by elimination, or *Holmesian inference* (Bird, 2005, 2007, 2010). Later, when we address the role of mechanism information, we will show that mechanism information may allow reasoners to exclude alternative causes of a target effect even when these alternative causes have a general causal strength greater than zero.

Causal preemption—the generalized power PC model of singular causation judgments

In Stephan and Waldmann (2018) we have shown that a key problem of the standard model is that it solely focuses on the strengths of the potential causes of the target effect but neglects cases of potential preemption. Equation 1 predicts that the target cause is the singular cause of the target effect whenever the target cause is sufficiently strong to produce the effect. However, in the philosophical literature cases of redundant causation involving possible preemption have been discussed demonstrating that causal sufficiency of a target cause is itself not sufficient to conclude that a cause generated the effect in a singular case (see for example, Hitchcock, 2007; Paul and Hall, 2013). A cause that otherwise is sufficient to generate the effect might have been causally preempted in its efficacy on a singular occasion by an alternative cause that was simultaneously present and also sufficiently strong to generate the effect. A classic scenario in the philosophical literature illustrating the problem of causal preemption involves two rock throwers. Billy and Suzy are perfectly precise rock throwers, which means that neither of them ever fails to hit and destroy glass bottles when throwing stones at them. On a particular occasion, both protagonists end up throwing their rocks toward the same bottle. Both are throwing their rocks with identical force but Suzy manages to throw her rock a little bit earlier than Billy. Consequently, the bottle shatters. Intuitively, it was Suzy's and not Billy's throwing that was the singular cause of the bottle's shattering, even though we know that Billy's throwing was precise and strong enough to do the job. The problem of causal preemption can also occur in cases in which the potential causes are probabilistic, as we will show below.

To handle the problem of causal preemption, we (Stephan and Waldmann, 2018) have proposed the generalized power PC model of singular causation judgments, which is given by the following equation:

$$P(c \rightarrow e|c,a,e) = \frac{w_c - w_c \cdot w_a \cdot \alpha}{w_c + w_a - w_c \cdot w_a} = \frac{w_c \cdot (1 - w_a \cdot \alpha)}{P(e|c,a)}. \tag{2}$$

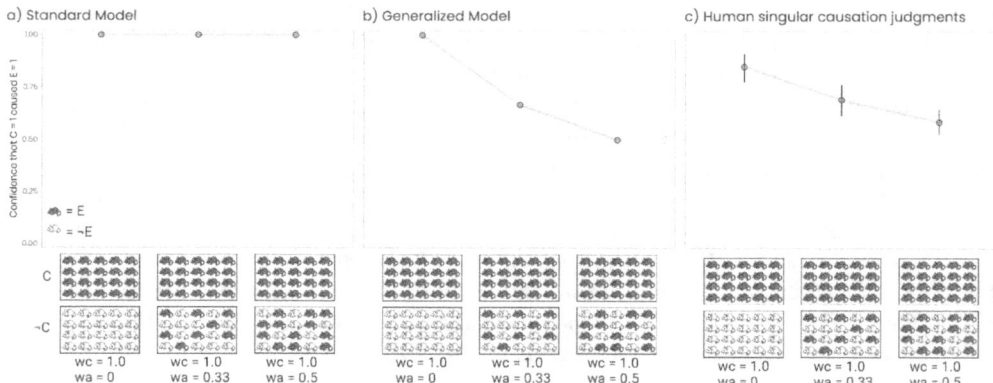

Figure 5.3 Model predictions and results of Experiment 1a from Stephan and Waldmann (2018). Results in c) show means and 95% CIs.

We now explain how the generalized model works by comparing Equations 2 and 1. As can be seen, the generalized model extends the numerator of Equation 1 by the product of the potential causes' causal strength and an additional weighting parameter α. The product $w_c \cdot w_a \cdot \alpha$ corresponds to the probability of causal preemption of the target cause c by the alternative cause a: the product of the causes' strength parameters, $w_c \cdot w_a$, is the probability that both causes are simultaneously strong enough to generate the effect. This product is relevant because the possibility of causal preemption only arises on occasions on which both potential causes have sufficient strength to produce the effect.

The product can be neglected in scenarios involving deterministic causes but it needs to be included in cases in which the potential causes have probabilistic strengths. On occasions on which causal preemption may occur (i.e., $w_c \cdot w_a$) it needs to be determined how likely it is that the target cause has indeed been preempted by the alternative cause. This probability is given by the α parameter of Equation 2. For example, an α value of 1.0 means that the target cause is always preempted by the alternative cause on occasions on which both a strong enough to produce the effect. An α value of 0.5 means that the target cause is preempted by its competitor on half of these occasions. Because $w_c \cdot w_a \cdot \alpha$ is the probability of causal preemption of the target cause by its competitor, it must be subtracted from the target cause's strength in the equation's numerator. Situations of "symmetric overdetermination" (see Paul and Hall, 2013) in which both potential causes are sufficiently strong to produce the effect and are acting absolutely synchronously, can also be handled. As no preemption occurs in situations of symmetric overdetermination α takes on a value of zero: the effect is caused by both c and a.

A relevant question is how the preemptive relation between the competing causes (i.e., the α parameter in our model) can be determined. In Stephan and Waldmann (2018) we suggested that this can be done based on *temporal* information about onsets and latencies of the competing causes.[1] We hypothesized that lay people intuitively incorporate assumptions about the causes' temporal relation in their singular causation judgments, even when temporal information is not explicitly mentioned in a situation. To test this hypothesis, we conducted an experiment (Experiment 1 in Stephan and Waldmann, 2018) in which we employed a standard causal induction paradigm (see, for example, Buehner, Cheng, and Clifford, 2003; Griffiths and Tenenbaum, 2005) as it is typically used in studies on how reasoners infer general causal relationships based on contingency data. We presented our participants with a fictitious scenario in which they were asked to take the perspective of biologists conducting an experiment to learn whether a particular chemical substance causes the expression of a particular gene in mice. The fictitious experiment was presented as a classical randomized control trial (RCT). The results were shown in summary format, similar to the panels shown on the x-axes in Figure 5.3. We tested three contingency data sets, which are shown in Figure 5.3. In each data set, all mice of the treatment group (C) were expressing the gene (i.e., $w_c = 1.0$), while the relative frequency of the control mice ($\neg C$) expressing the gene because of alternative causes varied between 0, 0.33, and 0.5. The test question was a singular causation test query referring to a specific mouse from the treatment group. Subjects were asked to indicate on a slider how confident they were that it was the treatment with the chemical substance that caused this mouse to express the gene (from "very certain that it was not the chemical" to "very certain that it was the chemical").

Since the target cause has a causal strength of $w_c = 1.0$ (i.e., it is always sufficiently strong to cause the effect) in all conditions, the standard model predicts that subjects should be maximally confident that the chemical treatment was the singular cause of the target mouse's expressing the gene, $P(c \rightarrow e|c,e) = 1.0$ (see Figure 5.3a). By contrast, we predicted that subjects would incorporate temporal assumptions about when the alternative causes produced their effects, and that this would lead to lower singular causation ratings with increasing strength of the alternative causes (w_a). We assumed that in a scenario about factors triggering the expression of a gene, it would be plausible to assume that factors determining gene expression in mice (i.e., alternative causes) were already in place and operating before the biologists conducted their study and treated some mice with the chemical substance (the target cause). Under this assumption, participants should conclude that the alternative causes preempted the target cause in all cases in which the target and alternative causes were simultaneously sufficiently strong to produce the effect (given by $w_c \cdot w_a$). We modeled this assumption by setting the α parameter of the generalized model to 1.0. The predictions of our generalized model are shown in Figure 5.3b. We found that subjects' mean singular causation judgments closely traced the predictions of the generalized model (see Figure 5.3c). Different additional control questions further corroborated the hypothesis that subjects incorporated temporal assumptions in their singular causation judgments. For example, we found that subjects assumed that the alternative causes had already exerted their influence before the target cause was introduced. We could also rule out that the observed decrease in the $P(c \rightarrow e|c)$ ratings resulted from increasing uncertainty about the existence of a general causal relationship between C and E. This was a possibility because lower values of Δ_p (which measures the degree of contingency) imply less support for the existence of a general causal link between the factors (Griffiths and Tenenbaum, 2005; Meder, Mayrhofer, and Waldmann, 2014). To address this problem, we used sample sizes for our contingency data that were large enough so that the posterior probability of the existence of a general causal link between C and E, as computed by the structure induction model (Meder, Mayrhofer, and Waldmann, 2014), was close to 1.0 even for the data set with the lowest contingency. Moreover, we asked subjects how strongly they believed that the chemical can generally cause the expression of the gene (which is a general causal structure query). Subjects reported high and almost identical confidence levels in all conditions.

The role of temporal relations

While our experiments in Stephan and Waldmann (2018) demonstrated that reasoners go beyond general causal strength knowledge and also incorporate temporal information when assessing singular causation relations, an open question was what exactly the relevant temporal factors are and how they need to be combined to determine the probability of causal preemption. In Stephan, Mayrhofer, and Waldmann (2020) we addressed this question by developing a theory of how the size of the model's α parameter might be determined.

Onset times

One relevant temporal factor we identified is the onset time difference between the competing causes. For example, in the philosophical preemption scenario about the two rock throwers our intuition that Billy's throwing was preempted by Suzy's is suggested by the information that Suzy's throwing occurred earlier than Billy's. Formally, if a target effect e could have been caused by either the target cause c or by one potential alternative cause a, the probability that c was preempted by a tends to be higher if a happened earlier than c. The onset time difference of two competing causes can be represented as $\Delta_t = t_a - t_c$, where t_a and t_c denote a's and c's onset times, respectively.

Causal latency

If two potential causes c and a are sufficiently strong to produce e but one occurred earlier, it is still not certain that the earlier cause actually preempted the other. A second temporal dimension that needs to be considered is *causal latency*, that is, the time it takes the causes to generate their effect. In the philosophical preemption scenario about Billy and Suzy, causal latency information is conveyed by saying that both protagonists are throwing their rocks with identical velocity. Thus, in this scenario identical causal latencies are assumed and the causes' preemptive relation depends only on their onset time difference. Generally, however, a potential cause occurring earlier than its competitor can still fail to preempt its competitor if the competing cause acts quicker than the target cause.

The causal latency of a cause C can formally be denoted as $t_{C \to E}$. Following previous research on general causal structure learning in dynamic contexts (e.g., Bramley et al., 2018) and queuing theory (Shortle et al., 2018), we used gamma distributions to model causal latency. The gamma distribution generalizes the exponential distribution and is defined by two parameters, a shape parameter $\kappa > 0$ and a scale parameter $\theta > 0$. A gamma distribution's expected value is given by $\kappa \cdot \theta$ and its variance by $\kappa \cdot \theta^2$. A cause's latency can be induced based on multiple observations tracking the onset differences between cause and effect. For example, in a context shielded from the influence of alternative causes, the expected value of a causal latency distribution can be estimated by the average of the observed cause-effect delays.

Having identified and formalized these two temporal dimensions we showed in Stephan, Mayrhofer, and Waldmann (2020) that α, that is, the probability that the target cause c was preempted by the competing cause a if both happen to be sufficiently strong to produce e, corresponds to the probability that the value of the target cause's latency is greater than the sum of the causes' onset time difference and the alternative cause's latency: $\alpha = P(t_{a \to e} + \Delta_t < t_{c \to e} | e, c, a)$. We also showed that $P(t_{a \to e} + \Delta_t < t_{c \to e} | e, c, a)$ can be approximated by a simple Monte Carlo (MC) algorithm that randomly draws causal latency samples from each cause's latency distribution.

An illustration showing how causal latency information determines the probability that c was the singular cause of e according to our generalized power PC model of singular causation judgments, and how causal latency information is integrated with causal strength information, is given in Figure 5.4. The figure shows five common-effect causal structures that differ with respect to the causal latency distributions assigned to C and A. For example, in the first causal structure C's causal latency distribution has a much smaller expected value than A's, and the two distributions almost do not overlap. Neglecting onset time differences ($\Delta_t = 0$), the resulting value of α is 0.001 in this case.

In Figure 5.4 the value of α increases from the first to fifth's structure because the causal latency distribution of A shifts to the left while the causal latency of C shifts to

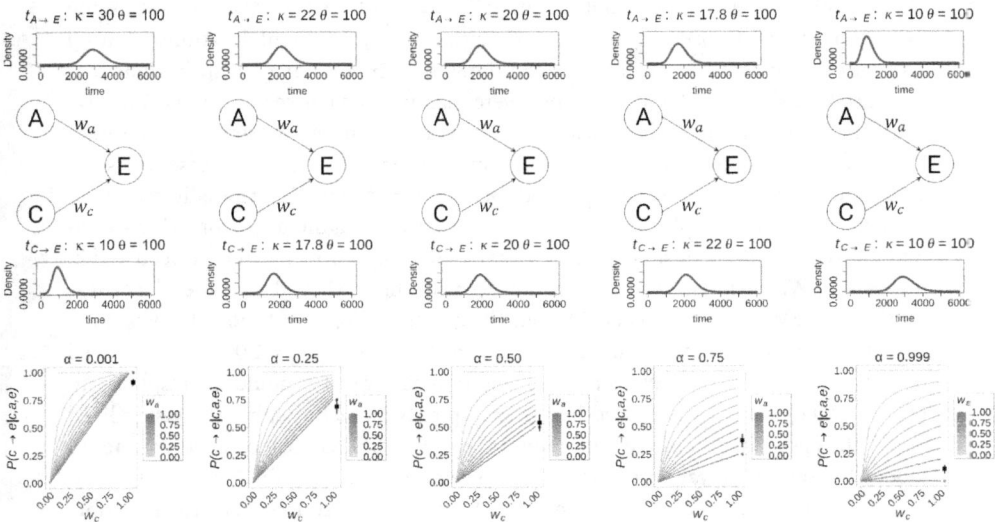

Figure 5.4 Illustration of how the causes' strengths and their causal latencies determine the predictions of the generalized power PC model of singular causation judgments. The black squares shown in the graphs of the last row show participants' mean singular causation ratings (error bars denote 95 percent CIs) as measured in Experiment 2 in Stephan, Mayrhofer, and Waldmann (2020). The gray points close to the means show the model predictions for the tested conditions.

the right. In the third causal structure, for example, both causes' latencies follow the same gamma distribution. In this case, the resulting α value is 0.5 because the chance that a randomly sampled single value from C's causal latency distribution is higher than a randomly sampled single value from A's causal latency distribution is fifty percent when the distributions fully overlap.

The five graphs in the last row of Figure 5.4 show how the value of α influences the predictions for $P(c \to e|c,a,e)$ made by the generalized power PC model of singular causation judgments for different combinations of causal strength values. In each graph, the causal strength of the target cause C is shown on the x-axis and different strengths of the alternative cause are represented by the different gray lines. Comparing the five graphs, it can be seen that increasing values of α tend to reduce the probability of a singular causal link between c and e. It can also be seen that the extent to which α diminishes $P(c \to e|c,a,e)$ tends to increase with increasing strengths of the alternative cause A. In the first graph, in which α is close to 0, the predictions of the generalized model correspond to those of the standard model.

In Stephan, Mayrhofer, and Waldmann (2020) we conducted several experiments testing the validity of the generalized model. The influence of causal latency information on singular causation judgments was tested in Experiment 2. A demo video of one of the study conditions can be found at https://osf.io/g6p72/. We presented subjects with a fictitious scenario about the emergency alarm system of a medieval kingdom. The scenario introduced soldiers located on two watchtowers, the Western and the Eastern tower. The task it was to look out for invading barbarians and to send out carrier pigeons to alarm the King's palace in case of an invasion. In two separate learning phases subjects first learned about the flight durations of the carrier pigeons from the two watchtowers by observing each tower multiple times. The flight durations followed a variant of the gamma distribution. The different pairs of latency distributions that were used are shown in Figure 5.4. They were manipulated between subjects. Since we were interested in the role of causal latency information on singular causation judgments in this experiment, we held the causal strengths of the two causes constant at $w_c = w_a = 1.0$. Thus, subjects observed that all carrier pigeons eventually arrived at the palace. In the test phase, subjects were asked to imagine a day on which both watchtowers simultaneously sent out a pigeon and on which an alarm later occurred in the palace. We then asked subjects how strongly they believed that the alarm was caused by the Western [or Eastern] tower. The graphs in Figure 5.4 show that when the potential causes, the pigeons, have causal strengths of $w_c = w_a = 1.0$, the generalized model predicts that subjects' singular causation judgments should corresponds to $P(c \to e|c,a,e) = 1 - \alpha$ (indicated by the gray points in each graph). The generalized model thus predicts a negative linear trend across the different test cases. The standard model, by contrast, always predicts that $P(c \to e|c,a,e) = 1.0$ when $w_c = w_a = 1.0$.

The mean singular causation ratings are shown as black squares (error bars denote 95 percent CIs) in Figure 5.4. As can be seen, the singular causation judgments followed the negative trend predicted by the generalized model, although ratings tended to be slightly less extreme than predicted by the model. In this experiment we also found that predictions that were based solely on the expected values of the latency distributions accounted less well for the ratings than predictions based on the full gamma distributions. This finding indicates that the singular causation ratings were not only sensitive to the expected values of the latency distributions but also to their variance.

This experiment successfully demonstrated that reasoners incorporate and integrate information about causal latency in their singular causation judgments, as predicted by the generalized model. In a further experiment in Stephan, Mayrhofer, and Waldmann (2020) we found that subjects also correctly incorporate onset time difference (Δ_t). Singular causation judgments thus were confirmed to be sensitive to both temporal dimensions considered by the generalized model. In a final study, we then crossed different causal latency distributions with probabilistic causal strengths of the competing causes. Since a crucial prediction of our model is that causal strength and temporal information should interact, this study provided an important further test of the model. The singular causation ratings were again predicted well by the generalized model.

The role of mechanism information

A further cue helping in the assessment of singular causation relations that has been discussed both in philosophy and psychology is knowledge about mechanisms. Cartwright (2017, p. 8) has, for example, included the "presence of expectable intermediate steps (mediator variables)" in a list of factors indicating singular causation. Different psychological studies have shown that people make use of mechanism information when asked to determine the singular cause of an effect (e.g., Ahn et al., 1995; Johnson & Keil, 2018). For example, in a recent study Johnson and Keil (2018) presented their participants with either generic (e.g., "eating polar bear liver causes a person to become dizzy") or singular (e.g., "eating polar bear liver caused Bill to become dizzy") causation statements and asked them to select the type of information that they consider most relevant to determine if the presented statement was true. Subjects could choose between anecdotal, statistical/covariational, and mechanistic information. Johnson and Keil (2018) found that subjects preferred mechanistic information over statistical information when asked to evaluate singular causation claims, while the reverse was found when subjects evaluated general causation statements. It is true that general causal relationships often are discovered without any knowledge about details of the underlying causal mechanisms. For example, the causal link between smoking and lung cancer had been established based on statistical evidence before anyone knew *how* smoking leads to lung cancer. The native people of Guyana knew that dipping the heads of their arrows into *wouralia*, a substance extracted from certain plants that today is known as *curare*, creates a deadly weapon, but nobody knew how the poison worked until French scientist Claude Bernard conducted first experiments in 1856 (see Craver and Darden, 2013). However, even when detailed mechanism knowledge is not available, in most cases people use *abstract* mechanism intuitions to select candidate causes and effects. It is more likely that smoking is viewed as a possible cause of lung cancer than watching TV because the inhalation of smoke makes it a more plausible candidate cause. Moreover, general causal knowledge induced based on covariation information is typically not enough to establish singular causation relations, as a singular co-occurrence of events consistent with known regularities may still just be coincidental. Information about causal mechanism variables seems to be relevant in this case. We have recently extended our generalized power PC model of singular causation judgments to provide a formal answer to the question of why mechanism information is helpful in this case (Stephan and Waldmann, 2022).

Under the causal Bayes net framework, causal mechanisms are modeled as intermediate nodes within causal chains or networks (see for example, Danks, 2005; Woodward, 2011) (see also Stephan et al., 2021). The original version of our generalized model was applied to the basic common-effect causal model shown in Figure 5.1a with two causes converging on an effect. In Stephan and Waldmann (2022) we applied the model to more complex causal structures that include intermediate mechanism nodes. One such structure containing mechanism nodes is shown in Figure 5.1b. This model can be thought of as an augmented version of the basic common-effect model in which the mechanisms underlying the direct causal arrows connecting C and A with E have been explicitly represented. In this augmented causal model, assuming that the causal Markov assumption holds (or assuming probabilistic modularity as proposed in Woodward, 2003), the original strength parameters w_c and w_a can now be re-represented as the products of single link strengths of the two paths: $w_c = w_{cmc} \cdot w_{mce}$ and $w_a = w_{ama} \cdot w_{mae}$ (see, for example, Waldmann et al., 2008). Similarly, the probability that c is the singular cause of e corresponds to the probability c caused m_c times the probability that m_c caused e: $P(c \rightarrow e|c,m_c,e) = P(c \rightarrow m_c|c,m_c,e) \cdot P(m_c \rightarrow e|c,m_c,e)$. The two equations allow us to see under which conditions the observation that a target cause's mechanism is active ($M_C = 1$ or m_c) increases a reasoner's confidence that the target cause c is the singular cause of the target effect e. Since the strength w_{mce} of the link connecting M_C to E will be higher than the strength w_c of the overall (unelaborated) causal path from C to E for $w_c < 1.0$, the probability that m_c caused e will on average be higher than the probability that c caused e in situations in which M_C is unobserved: $P(m_c \rightarrow e|m_c,e) > P(c \rightarrow e|c,e)$. Observing m_c will then lead to an increase in the probability that c is the singular cause of e if we can be certain that m_c was caused by c. One situation in which we can be certain that c caused m_c is when C is a necessary cause of its mechanism variable M_C. $P(c \rightarrow m_c|c,m_c)$ is 1.0 in this case and, as a result, $P(c \rightarrow e|c,m_c,e)$ reduces to $P(m_c \rightarrow e|c,m_c,e)$.

Learning about the absence instead of the presence of mechanism variables may also help in assessing whether c caused e. For example, if C can cause E only via M_C, and M_C is discovered to be absent in a singular case, c can be ruled out as the singular cause of e. Conditionalizing on situations in which $M_C = 0$, w_c takes on a value of 0 and, as result, $P(c \rightarrow e|c, \neg m_c, e)$ also equals 0. By contrast, if we discover in a situation that the alternative cause's mechanism variable M_A is absent, then we can be certain that c is the singular cause of e. In this case $w_a = 0$ and Equation 2 reduces to

$$P(c \rightarrow e \mid c, \neg m_A, e) = \frac{w_c}{w_c} = 1.0.$$

The previous analysis showed that causal mechanism information helps to assess singular causation relations because it allows us to insert more specific values for the causal strength parameters. In Stephan and Waldmann (2022) we showed that causal mechanism information also helps to specify the temporal relations between the potential causes of a target effect. This is necessary when the causes can alternatively produce their effect via different possible mechanism paths. For example, in the shooting scenario one might consider the different ways via which being hit by a bullet can cause people to die. The bullet might either kill somebody by hurting their heart or their aorta. These different possible mechanism paths are not only associated with different causal strengths, but also with different causal latencies. Bullets hurting the heart not only kill more reliably than bullets destroying the aorta, they also kill quicker.

A causal structure in which the causes C and A generate their common effect E via different possible mechanism paths is shown in Figure 5.1c. The gamma distributions attached to the final causal links connecting the different mechanism nodes to the effect illustrate that the links are assumed to differ in their causal latencies. In particular, C and A each have one fast and one slow causal path. For C the fast causal path is the one via M_{C1} and for A the fast causal path is the one via M_{A1}. These different latency distributions assigned to the different mechanism paths imply that the α value will change depending on which mechanism components of the target and the alternative cause are observed to be active on a singular occasion. For example, if both potential causes activate the mechanism components that have the same causal latency (e.g., $M_{C1} = 1$ and $M_{A1} = 1$), then α would be 0.5. By contrast, in a situation in which C activates M_{C1} and A activates its slower mechanism variable M_{A2}, then α would take on a small value. In the reverse case, α would take on a high value.

An illustration of the scenario we used in the first experiment in Stephan and Waldmann (2022) is shown in Figure 5.5. Subjects learned about a kingdom in which one castle was located in the Southwest and another one in the Southeast, and in which the King's palace was located in the North.

The scenario was about the medical emergency system of the kingdom. Subjects learned that the only healer in the kingdom was living in the King's palace, and that the castles, to call the healer in case of a medical emergency, had to send out carrier pigeons.

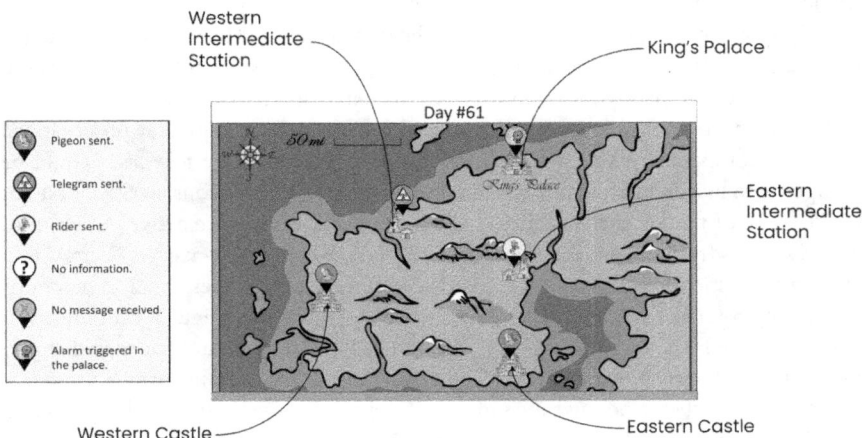

Figure 5.5 Illustration of the scenario used in Experiment 1 in Stephan and Waldmann (2022).

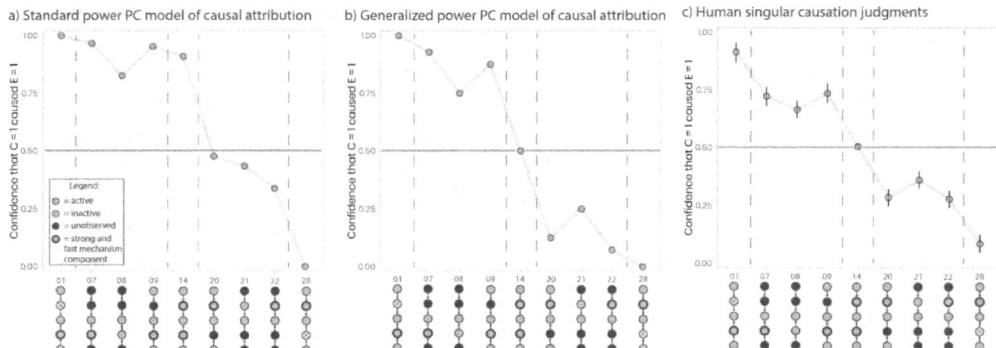

Figure 5.6 Model predictions and results (means and 95% CIs) of a subset of test cases used in Experiment 1 in Stephan and Waldmann (2022). Note. Asterisks in the neuron diagrams refer to the target cause.

Subjects learned that the pigeons could not fly the whole distance to the palace, which is why each castle had installed intermediate stations. To establish different possible mechanism paths, two possibilities were introduced of how incoming emergency signals could be forwarded to the palace at these intermediate stations. One possibility was telegraph towers and the other was pony riders stationed next to the telegraph towers (see Figure 5.5). The pony riders were described as back-ups ensuring that emergency signals could be forwarded if a telegraph tower was blacked out. The routes the pony riders had to take on their way to the palace were described as dangerous and it was pointed out that pony riders might get lost on their way to the palace. We hypothesized that subjects would assume that telegraph towers have a higher causal strength as well as a shorter causal latency than pony riders. Subjects were informed that they would observe what happened on different days and that the different events would be illustrated using different event icons (see Figure 5.5).

Subjects were informed that, for each day, they would be asked to indicate how strongly they believed that the observed alarm in the King's palace had been caused by the Western [Eastern] castle on that day. A demo video can be found at https://osf.io/ycv8u/.

Subjects were then asked to evaluate twenty-eight different singular observations that were compatible with the instructed causal structure. These test cases could be grouped into five different categories. For example, one category consists of all cases in which none of the alternative cause's mechanism components are active. A subset of nine test cases from the five different categories is shown on the x-axes in Figure 5.6 in the form of simplified neuron diagrams. The bottom nodes of these neuron diagrams marked by asterisks represent the target cause to which the singular causation test queries referred. The last four test cases (cases 20, 21, 22, and 28 in the original study) mirror the first four shown test cases. The middle case (case 14 in the original study) is a "symmetric" test case because the same event types are instantiated for the target and the alternative cause. The graphs in Figure 5.6 show the predictions made by the standard model (a) and the generalized model (b). For the first four test cases both models make similar qualitative predictions, but the predictions differ for the remaining test cases. For the symmetrical test case, for example, the standard model predicts that subjects should be confident that the target cause was the singular cause of the effect. In this test case the target cause activates its strong and fast mechanism path. As we have seen, the standard model predicts high values for $P(c \rightarrow e|c,e)$ whenever the causal strength of the target cause is high. The generalized model, by contrast, predicts that reasoners should be uncertain in this case because the alternative cause also activates its strong and fast mechanism path, and thus has a fifty percent probability of successfully preempting the target cause. A further notable difference between the models is the contrast between the predictions for the first and the last four test cases. Since the last four test case mirror the first ones, the generalized model predicts that singular causation judgments for the last four cases should mirror those for the first four cases. For example, the difference between the test cases 09 and 20 is that target and alternative cause have switched. The generalized model predicts that $P(c \rightarrow e|c,e)$ for test case 20 corresponds to $1 - P(c \rightarrow e|c,e)$ for test case 09. The standard model does not make this prediction. As the standard model solely focusing on causal strength and neglects temporal information, it predicts an advantage of the target cause in all these cases.

The mean singular causation judgments for the nine test cases are shown in Figure 5.5c. We have found that their ratings (including those given for the remaining test cases) were predicted best by the generalized model. By contrast, the standard model as well as further alternative models that we included in our analyses failed to account for subjects' singular causation ratings. In sum, the results of this experiment demonstrate that people use and integrate mechanism information in an elaborate way when answering singular causation queries. The study shows that reasoners seem to understand that mechanism information helps with assessing singular causation relations because it allows us to insert more specific values for the strength and temporal parameters that are relevant for determining whether a target cause actually produced a target effect.

In Stephan and Waldmann (2022) we not only provided a formal account of why mechanism information is helpful for assessing singular causation relations, but also used our model to identify situations in which mechanism information is less useful. One factor diminishing the value of mechanism information is whether a mechanism path can also be activated by alternative causes. Observing the presence of a mechanism variable is more helpful for singular causation judgments when the target cause is the only cause that can activate this mechanism variable. A second factor diminishing the utility of mechanism information concerns the way in which the overall strength of the target cause (w_c) with respect to the target effect is distributed across the different components of its mechanism. We have used our model to show that, given constant levels of $w_c = w_{cmc} \cdot w_{mce}$ (see Figure 5.1b), the observation that the mechanism variable is active in a singular cause ($M_C = 1$) should lead to a stronger increase in the probability that c caused e when w_{mce} is the stronger component of the product $w_c = w_{cmc} \cdot w_{mce}$ than when it is the weaker component. We conducted two studies testing whether lay people understand the factors that reduce the utility of mechanism information. The studies showed that a subset of reasoners have a tentative understanding of the relevance of these factors. However, we also found that many people generally rely on the heuristic that mechanism information is always helpful.

Summary, open questions, and directions for future research

The generalized power PC model of singular causation judgments makes explicit how different types of information can be combined to determine how strongly a reasoner should believe that an observed effect event was actually caused by a potential target cause. Causal strength information is important for the assessment of singular causation relations because causes that reliably produce their effects are more likely to be successful than causes that only rarely generate an effect. Covariational information also allows us to learn about the prevalence and strength of alternative causes. For example, if an effect is known to occur only very rarely in the absence of the target cause, this means that alternative causes are sparse or weak. If alternative causes are sparse, then we should be more confident that an observed co-occurrence of a target cause and a potential effect was actually causal rather than coincidental, even if the target cause is generally relatively weak. A well-known example for this situation is the relation between smoking and lung cancer. Although smoking is a rather weak cause of lung cancer even in chain smokers, the probability that a singular instance of lung cancer in a heavy chain smoker was caused by that person's smoking is relatively high. The reason for this divergence is that lung cancer is extremely rare in people who are not smokers. The generalized power PC model of singular causation judgments provides a formal account of these facts.

Knowledge about the general strengths of causes is not sufficient to determine singular causation relations (see also Woodward, in this volume). Philosophical examples of redundant causation show that even deterministic general causes can fail to cause the effect in a specific situation if they are preempted by competing alternative causes. Philosophical process theories of causality attempt to solve the problem of causal preemption by referring to the transfer of energy or the exchange of conserved quantities between cause and effect (e.g., Dowe, 1992, 2007) (see also Wolff, 2007; Wolff, Barbey, and Hausknecht, 2010; Wolff and Thorstad, 2017). Counterfactual accounts of singular causation (e.g., Halpern and Hitchcock, 2015; Halpern and Pearl, 2005) aim to solve the problem of causal preemption by defining causality as causal dependence of the effect on the cause by counterfactually holding constant suitable causal factors (see also Hitchcock, 2009).

Our model implements a different solution to the problem of preemption. People often will rely on temporal information to determine the preemptive relation between potential causes of an effect. We have identified two types of temporal information that help with determining causal preemption: onset times and causal latencies. Our model makes explicit how these factors can be integrated and combined with causal strength knowledge to assess whether a cause was preempted by a potential alternative cause. Our experiments support the assumptions of the model.

In research on causal reasoning, causal mechanism and covariation-based theories have for a long time been regarded as competing alternative accounts of causal inference. But in fact, both frameworks are compatible with each other, as has been shown, for example, by Danks (2005). Both types of theories traditionally have been applied to explain different tasks of causal inference, though. Covariation theories have mostly been used to explain how people infer general causation relationships (e.g.,

Cheng, 1997; Gopnik et al., 2004; Griffiths and Tenenbaum, 2005; Novick and Cheng, 2004), while mechanism theories have focused on explaining singular causation judgments (e.g., Ahn et al., 1995). According to the causal Bayes net framework, mechanisms can be understood as a sequence of mediating variables within causal networks, and knowledge about them can be acquired based on covariational information. We have shown that mechanism knowledge can constrain inferences and thereby help with determining the singular cause of an effect. What had been missing in the literature is a formal explanation of why mechanism information can be useful to assess singular causation, and when its contribution is limited. In Stephan and Waldmann (2022) we used the generalized power PC model of singular causation judgments to provide a formal analysis along with empirical evidence demonstrating the value of the model.

Despite the success of the generalized model there are still important open empirical and theoretical questions. So far, we have only tested relatively simple scenarios. For example, in all experiments in Stephan, Mayrhofer, and Waldmann (2020) and Stephan and Waldmann (2022), we limited the causal model to two potential causes of a single effect. In everyday life reasoners will only very rarely be in a situation in which the number of potential causes is so small. It would therefore be interesting to assess in future studies how well participants perform in more complex situations. We suspect that subjects' performance will decrease rather quickly with increasing complexity.

Another interesting question is how singular causation judgments are generated in situations in which there are unknown background causes of an effect. Although we studied such a scenario in Stephan and Waldmann (2018), in all experiments in which we specifically tested the role of temporal relations (Stephan, Mayrhofer, and Waldmann, 2020), the status of all relevant causes as present or absent was explicitly mentioned. However, in the real world it is common that effects are not only determined by observed but also by unobserved causes that need to be considered in the judgments. In such situations it appears to be at first sight impossible to conclude confidently that the target cause actually produced the target effect because the possibility of preemption by an unobservable cause cannot be ruled out. However, people can nevertheless make rational inferences given suitable background assumptions. In situations with unobserved background causes, the individual parameter values for b_a and w_a cannot be estimated. However, as has been shown by Cheng (1997), the influence of unobserved background causes can be estimated by the probability of the effect in the absence of the target cause: $P(e|\neg c) = b_a \cdot w_a$ if the background causes are assumed to be generative, independent, and not interacting with the target cause. The more difficult problem is to judge potential preemptive relations between the target and the unobserved alternative causes. How can the value of our model's α parameter be specified in this kind of situation? One possibility is that reasoners in such cases simply rely on certain default values for α. For example, setting α to 0.5 would mean that we remain uncertain about the preemptive relation between the potential causes. As a conservative solution, α could be set to 1.0, which would reflect the assumption that the target cause is always preempted by an alternative cause whenever at least one of the alternative causes is simultaneously present and sufficient for the effect (which is estimated by $P(e|\neg c)$). In this case, the resulting value for $P(c \to e|c,e)$ can be thought of as a measure of the lower boundary of a range within which the true probability of c having caused e lies.

Alternatively, reasoners may have in some cases more specific intuitions about preemptive relations (Stephan, Mayrhofer, and Waldmann, 2020). In contexts with unobserved background causes, temporal information can be extracted from the observable background rate of the effect. The background rate can be modeled using exponential functions (cf. Bramley et al., 2018). In situations in which the target cause and the unobserved background causes are all present, the distribution of the effect rate is a mixture in which the gamma distribution that represents the causal latency of the target cause is superimposed on the exponential distribution of the unobserved background causes.

When the unobserved background cause is absent, then only the gamma distribution of the target cause can be observed. Thus, if the rate in which the effect occurs in the presence of the target cause is much higher than in its absence, this is an indicator that the target cause has a very short causal latency. A short causal latency makes it less likely than a long latency that the target cause is preempted by a background cause (see Lagnado and Speekenbrink, 2010, for supporting evidence). One interesting future study thus would be to test if reasoners report higher degrees of confidence that c caused e if they have learned that the presence of the target cause leads to a steep increase in the effect's rate than if they have observed that the effect rate only mildly increases in the presence of the target cause.

Another limitation of the present studies is that we have only tested static test situations, that is, situations in which subjects receive information about the status of events in a specific case rather than having observed the unfolding of events. While we are frequently asked to make judgments about events in the past, we also often find ourselves in situations in which we witness events developing in front of our eyes. In such cases, we will directly experience the relevant temporal relations, which may either be consistent or inconsistent with our expectations. For example, if we have learned in the past that a cause typically generates the effect very quickly, but then observe a long delay between the events, it seems reasonable to be cautious to infer that the two events were causally linked.

Our studies so far focused on binary events in both the model and the scenarios we tested. Research on forensic epidemiology (see Freeman and Zeegers, 2016, for an overview) has often studied cases that involve continuous variables. In this literature various quantitative measures of culpability have been suggested. For example, one could ask whether a plaintiff's disease has actually resulted from a particular quantitative amount of toxic exposure. It would be interesting to use these models as an inspiration for an extension of the generalized model to also capture intuitions about singular causation involving continuous variables.

Finally, there are further cues to singular causation that have been proposed that still need to be integrated into our model. For example, one additional cue suggested by Cartwright (2015; 2017) is information about the presence of "required support factors," by which she means enabling conditions that are necessary for a cause to produce the effect. Another cue currently not considered by our model is knowledge about the absence of preventive or disabling factors. These concepts can be easily integrated within our framework. Enabling factors can, for example, be represented as additional factors that interact with the target cause (Novick and Cheng, 2004). Disablers can either be explicitly represented as inhibitory causes or can be implicitly encoded as affecting causal strength (Stephan et al., 2021). Yet another useful cue is information about the occurrence of known side effects of a causal process because such side effects may provide diagnostic evidence that an unobserved cause – or one of the mechanism variables – have indeed been present on a singular occasion. For example, the high levels of the element iridium at the KT boundary are considered indirect evidence that the extinction of the dinosaurs was caused by the impact of a massive asteroid[2] (see Woodward, 1990). High levels of iridium are not a causally relevant part of the causal chain via which asteroid impacts lead to the eradication of earthly species. They are, however, a strong indicator that a massive impact had occurred 65 million years ago.

Despite the considerable progress in formalizing singular causation in the past years, more needs to be done to develop an account that also addresses more complex cases. It seems important to transition in future research from laboratory studies to analyses of real-world cases, for example in law or medicine, to obtain a better impression of the strengths and shortcomings of the generalized model and to develop it further.

Notes

1 Another relevant cue is information about *spatial* relations between the causal events. For example, in the preemption scenario about Suzy and Billy, we may learn that only Suzy's rock actually came into spatial contact with the bottle. In many cases, however, only temporal but not spatial relations between causes and effects can be observed (e.g., *smoking → cancer*).
2 We thank James Woodward for this illustrative example.

References

Ahn, W., C.W. Kalish, D.L. Medin, and S.A. Gelman (1995). "The role of covariation versus mechanism information in causal attribution." *Cognition*, 54(3): 299–352.
Beebee, H., C. Hitchcock, and P. Menzies (2009). *The Oxford Handbook of Causation*. Oxford: Oxford University Press.
Bird, A. (2005). "Abductive knowledge and Holmesian inference." In T.S. Gendler and J. Hawthorne (eds.), *Oxford Studies in Epistemology* (1–31). Oxford: Oxford University Press.
Bird, A. (2007). "Inference to the only explanation." *Philosophy and Phenomenological Research*, 74(2): 424–32.
Bird, A. (2010). "Eliminative abduction: examples from medicine." *Studies in History and Philosophy of Science Part A*, 41(4): 345–52.
Bramley, N.R., T. Gerstenberg, R. Mayrhofer, and D.A. Lagnado (2018). "Time in causal structure learning." *Journal of Experimental Psychology: Learning, Memory, and Cognition*, 44(12): 1880—910.

Buehner, M.J., P.W. Cheng, and D. Clifford (2003). "From covariation to causation: a test of the assumption of causal power." *Journal of Experimental Psychology: Learning, Memory, and Cognition*, 29(6): 1119–140.
Cartwright, N. (2015). "Single case causes: What is evidence and why." In J. Reiss (ed.), *Philosophy of Science in Practice*. Dordrecht: Springer.
Cartwright, N. (2017). "How to learn about causes in the single case." *CHESS Working Paper no 2017–2004*. https://www.dur.ac.uk/resources/chess/CHESSK4UWP_2017_04_Cartwright.pdf.
Cheng, P.W. (1997). "From covariation to causation: A causal power theory." *Psychological Review*, 104(2): 367–405.
Cheng, P.W. and M.J. Buehner (2012). "Causal learning." In K.J. Holyoak (ed.), *The Oxford Handbook of Thinking and Reasoning* (210–33). New York: Oxford University Press.
Cheng, P.W. and L.R. Novick (1991). "Causes versus enabling conditions." *Cognition*, 40(1–2): 83–120.
Cheng, P.W. and L.R. Novick (2005). "Constraints and nonconstraints in causal learning: Reply to White (2005) and to Luhmann and Ahn (2005)." *Psychological Review*, 112(3): 694–706.
Craver, C.F. and L. Darden (2013). *In Search of Mechanisms: Discoveries Across the Life Sciences*. Chicago: The University of Chicago Press.
Danks, D. (2005). "The supposed competition between theories of human causal inference." *Philosophical Psychology*, 18(2): 259–72.
Danks, D. (2017). Singular causation. In M.R. Waldmann (ed.), *The Oxford Handbook of Causal Reasoning* (201–15). New York: Oxford University Press.
Dowe, P. (1992). "Wesley salmon's process theory of causality and the conserved quantity theory." *Philosophy of Science*, 59(2): 195–216.
Dowe, P. (2007). *Physical Causation*. Cambridge: Cambridge University Press.
Freeman, M. and M.P. Zeegers (2016). *Forensic Epidemiology: Principles and Practice*. New York: Academic Press.
Glymour, C. (2001). *The Mind's Arrows: Bayes Nets and Graphical Causal Models in Psychology*. Cambridge, MA: MIT Press.
Glymour, C. (2003). "Learning, Prediction and Causal Bayes Nets." *Trends in Cognitive Sciences*, 7(1): 43–8.
Gopnik, A., C. Glymour, D.M. Sobel, L.E. Schulz, T. Kushnir, and D. Danks (2004). "A theory of causal learning in children: Causal maps and bayes nets." *Psychological Review*, 111(1): 3–32.
Griffiths, T.L. and J.B. Tenenbaum (2005). Structure and strength in causal induction. *Cognitive Psychology*, 51(4): 334–84.
Halpern, J.Y. and C. Hitchcock (2015). "Graded causation and defaults." *The British Journal for the Philosophy of Science*, 66(2): 413–57.
Halpern, J.Y. and J. Pearl (2005). "Causes and explanations: A structural-model approach. Part I: Causes." *The British Journal for the Philosophy of Science*, 56(4): 843–87.
Hitchcock, C. (2007). "Prevention, preemption, and the principle of sufficient reason." *The Philosophical Review*, 116(4): 495–532.
Hitchcock, C. (2009). "Causal modelling." In H. Beebee, C. Hitchcock, and P. Menzies (eds.), *The Oxford Handbook of Causation* (299–314). New York: Oxford University Press.
Hume, D. (1748/1975). *An Enquiry Concerning Human Understanding*. Oxford: Oxford University Press.
Johnson, S.G. and W. Ahn (2017). "Causal mechanisms." In M.R. Waldmann (ed.), *The Oxford Handbook of Causal Reasoning* (127–46). New York: Oxford University Press.

Johnson, S.G. and F.C. Keil (2018). "Statistical and mechanistic information in evaluating causal claims." In T.T. Rogers, M. Rau, X. Zhu, and C.W. Kalish (eds.), *Proceedings of the 40th Annual Conference of the Cognitive Science Society* (618–23). Austin, TX: Cognitive Science Society.

Kahneman, D. and D.T. Miller (1986). "Norm theory: Comparing reality to its alternatives." *Psychological Review, 93*(2): 136–53.

Kominsky, J.F., J. Phillips, T. Gerstenberg, D. Lagnado, and J. Knobe (2015). "Causal superseding." *Cognition, 137*: 196–209.

Lagnado, D.A. and M. Speekenbrink (2010). "The influence of delays in real-time causal learning." *The Open Psychology Journal, 3*(1): 184–95.

Liljeholm, M. and P.W. Cheng (2007). "When is a cause the 'same'? Coherent generalization across contexts." *Psychological Science, 18*(11): 1014–21.

Meder, B., R. Mayrhofer, and M.R. Waldmann (2014). "Structure induction in diagnostic causal reasoning." *Psychological Review, 121*(3): 277–301.

Novick, L.R. and P.W. Cheng (2004). "Assessing interactive causal influence." *Psychological Review, 111*(2), 455–85.

Paul, L.A. and E.J. Hall (2013). *Causation: A User's Guide*. New York: Oxford University Press.

Pearl, J. (1988). *Probabilistic Reasoning in Intelligent Systems: Networks of Plausible Inference*. San Francisco, CA: Morgan Kaufmann.

Pearl, J. (2000). *Causality: Models, Reasoning and Inference*. Cambridge: Cambridge University Press.

Rehder, B. (2014). "Independence and dependence in human causal reasoning." *Cognitive Psychology, 72*: 54–107.

Samland, J. and M.R. Waldmann (2016). "How prescriptive norms influence causal inferences." *Cognition, 156*: 164–76.

Samland, J., M. Josephs, M.R. Waldmann, and H. Rakoczy. (2016). "The role of prescriptive norms and knowledge in children's and adults' causal selection." *Journal of Experimental Psychology: General, 145*(2): 125.

Shortle, J.F., J.M. Thompson, D. Gross, and C.M. Harris (2018). *Fundamentals of Queueing Theory*. New Jersey: John Wiley & Sons.

Sloman, S. (2005). *Causal Models: How People Think About the World and its Alternatives*. New York: Oxford University Press.

Stephan, S. and M.R. Waldmann (2018). "Preemption in singular causation judgments: A computational model." *Topics in Cognitive Science, 10*(1): 242–57.

Stephan, S. and M.R. Waldmann (2022). "The role of mechanism knowledge in singular causation judgments." *Cognition*, 2018, 104924.

Stephan, S., R. Mayrhofer, and M.R. Waldmann (2020). "Time and singular causation—a computational model." *Cognitive Science, 44*(7): e12871.

Stephan, S., K. Tentori, S. Pighin, and M.R. Waldmann (2021). "Interpolating causal mechanisms: The paradox of knowing more." *Journal of Experimental Psychology: General*.

Waldmann, M.R. (2000). "Competition among causes but not effects in predictive and diagnostic learning." *Journal of Experimental Psychology: Learning, Memory, and Cognition, 26*(1): 53–76.

Waldmann, M.R. (ed.). (2017). *The Oxford Handbook of Causal Reasoning*. New York: Oxford University Press.

Waldmann, M.R. and Y. Hagmayer (2013). "Causal reasoning." In D. Reisberg (ed.), *Oxford Handbook of Cognitive Ppsychology* (733–52). New York: Oxford University Press.

Waldmann, M.R., P.W. Cheng, Y. Hagmayer, and A.P. Blaisdell (2008). "Causal learning in rats and humans: a minimal rational model." In N. Chater and M. Oaksford (eds.), *Prospects for Bayesian Cognitive Science* (453–84). Oxford: Oxford University Press.

Wolff, P. (2007). "Representing causation." *Journal of Experimental Psychology: General, 136*(1): 82–111.

Wolff, P., A.K. Barbey, and M. Hausknecht (2010). "For want of a nail: How absences cause events." *Journal of Experimental Psychology: General, 139*(2): 191–221.

Wolff, P. and R. Thorstad (2017). "Force dynamics." In M.R. Waldmann (ed.), *The Oxford Handbook of Causal Reasoning* (147–68). New York: Oxford University Press.

Woodward, J. (1990). "Supervenience and singular causal statements." *Royal Institute of Philosophy Supplement, 27*: 211–46.

Woodward, J. (2003). *Making Things Happen: A Theory of Causal Explanation*. Oxford: Oxford University Press.

Woodward, J. (2011). "Mechanisms revisited." *Synthese, 183*(3): 409–27.

6

Cause, "Cause," and Norm[1]

John Schwenkler and Eric Sievers

1 Introduction

In an important passage in her seminal paper "Causality and Determination," G.E.M. Anscombe calls attention to the variety of words that are used to express causal concepts:

> The word "cause" itself is highly general. [...] I mean: the word "cause" can be *added* to a language in which are already represented many causal concepts. A small selection: *scrape, push, wet, carry, eat, burn, knock over, keep off, squash, make* (e.g., noises, paper boats), *hurt.*
>
> Anscombe 1981, p. 137

The italicized words are quite diverse, but these "special causal verbs" (ibid.) are unified conceptually in that they all describe kinds of causation: that is, ways of *making* things happen, of *bringing about* events or changes of state in oneself or other things, of *creating* things or *destroying* them—most generally, of *acting on* things in such a way that in virtue of this activity, those things end up different than they otherwise would be.

Special causal verbs like those in Anscombe's list make up a great part of our ordinary ways of describing causation. Indeed, among the hundred most commonly used verbs according to the Corpus of Contemporary American English (COCA) (see

Table 6.1 The 100 most commonly used English verbs according to the Corpus of Contemporary American English. Those in **boldface** can be used to express causal concepts. From http://www.wordfrequency.info, retrieved June 14, 2019.[2]

---

be, have, do, say, go, can, **get**, would, **make**, know, will, think, **take**, see, **come**, could, want, look, use, find, **give**, tell, work, may, should, call, try, ask, need, feel, become, **leave**, **put**, mean, **keep**, **let**, **begin**, seem, **help**, talk, **turn**, **start**, might, **show**, hear, **play**, **run**, **move**, like, live, believe, **hold**, **bring**, happen, must, **write**, **provide**, **sit**, **stand**, lose, **pay**, meet, include, **continue**, **set**, learn, **change**, **lead**, understand, watch, follow, **stop**, **create**, speak, read, **allow**, **add**, **spend**, **grow**, **open**, **walk**, win, offer, remember, love, consider, appear, **buy**, wait, **serve**, die, **send**, expect, **build**, stay, fall, **cut**, reach, **kill**, remain

Table 6.1), about forty can be used in ways that express causal concepts in the broad sense indicated above. If, for example, someone says that

(1) Tony *had* the cup of coffee that Beth *got* for him to drink, *using* to sweeten it some of the sugar that Keith had *put* in the cupboard.

—then she says a great deal about what in philosophy we might want to call Tony's, Beth's, and Keith's having *caused* various things to be the case, or to happen. Yet the sentence in (1) does this *without* using a "highly general" word like "cause" or any of its variants. Indeed, the verb "cause" is not itself very commonly used: it shows up at #135 on COCA's verb frequency list, behind all the special causal verbs identified in Table 1 as well as several more. When people talk about causing, it is usually these special causal verbs that they use.[3]

Further evidence suggests that when the verb "cause" *is* used in ordinary speech and writing, this is very often in a way that expresses some "special" variety of causal relation rather than the general relation that is usually the interest of metaphysicians and philosophers of science. For example, Sytsma et al. (2019) present evidence from corpus analysis supporting the hypothesis that the most frequent use of "cause" is to assign *responsibility* to a person for something *bad* that happened—a pattern of use that is different from the one they observed for other causal verbs like "create," "generate," "induce," "lead to," "make," and "produce." In addition, Wolff (2003) presents experimental evidence finding that people prefer to use periphrastic causal verbs like "cause," "enable," and "prevent" over lexical causatives like "break," "pop," "melt," and "burn" when the agent and patient are separated by the operation of an intermediate entity, and vice versa: for example, the statement

(2) The girl caused the vase to break.

is preferred over

(3) The girl broke the vase.

when the vase in question breaks after being hit by a ball that the girl bounces off her foot, whereas (3) is preferred to (2) when the girl throws the ball directly at the vase.[4]

Facts like these, about the ordinary usage of "cause" and other causal verbs, bear directly on experimental work that uses verbal reports to study the psychology of causal thinking. Consider, for example, the well-known *pen vignette* presented in Knobe and Fraser (2008):

The receptionist in the philosophy department keeps her desk stocked with pens. The administrative assistants are allowed to take the pens, but faculty members are supposed to buy their own.

The administrative assistants typically do take the pens. Unfortunately, so do the faculty members. The receptionist has repeatedly emailed them reminders that only administrative assistants are allowed to take the pens.

On Monday morning, one of the administrative assistants encounters Professor Smith walking past the receptionist's desk. Both take pens. Later that day, the receptionist needs to take an important message ... but she has a problem. There are no pens left on her desk.

Having presented this vignette, Knobe and Fraser found that participants agreed much more with the statement that *Professor Smith* caused the receptionist's problem than the statement that *the administrative assistant* did so—a finding they take to support the hypothesis that "moral judgments ... play a direct role in the process by which causal judgments are generated" (Knobe and Fraser 2008, p. 443). In light of the above, however, we should be concerned that it is only one *kind* of causal judgment—namely, the kind made with a statement of the form

(C1) *X* caused *Y*

—where *X* is an intentional agent and *Y* is an outcome with negative valence—that this experiment investigates directly. (Knobe and Fraser's other (2008) experiment has the same structure: it concerns a pair of siblings who log in at the same time to a computer, which then crashes, and participants then consider who *caused* the computer to crash.) A review of the literature shows that this focus is hardly exceptional in recent experimental work on causal thinking. Consider, for example, the following list of sentences that were used as test statements or test questions in a selection of highly cited studies:

"Lauren caused the system to crash." (Livengood, Sytsma and Rose, 2017)

"The attending doctor's decision caused the patient's recovery." (Hitchcock and Knobe, 2009)

"Did Sam cause the bottle to fall off the wall?" (Walsh and Sloman, 2011)

"Turnbull caused Poole's death." (Alicke, Rose, and Bloom, 2011)

"Billy caused the motion detector to go off." (Kominsky and Phillips, 2019)

Despite the many differences between these sentences, they all have the use of the word "cause" in common as a way to link an agent with an outcome that can be construed as the result of what they did. This limitation has not stopped philosophers from using the results of experiments like these to support conclusions about *causal judgments* or the ordinary *concept of causation*, and not merely the ordinary use *of the word "cause"*: for example, alongside Knobe and Fraser's (2008, p. 443) conclusion that "moral judgments ... play a direct role in the process by which causal judgments are generated," Hitchcock and Knobe (2009, p. 604) conclude from their findings that the "concept of actual causation enables us to pick out those factors that are particularly suitable as targets of intervention," while Livengood, Sytsma and Rose (2017, p. 292) take their findings to support the hypothesis that "folk causal attributions are inherently normative and are closely related to responsibility judgments." By contrast, the evidence surveyed above suggests that investigations that concern only what we may call *"cause"-judgments*, or judgments that are expressed with the ordinary use of the English word "cause," may be revealing only of a partial and possibly unrepresentative range of causal thought and talk.

To address this lacuna, the present chapter presents a series of experiments that elicit causal judgments using statements of a different form than (C1) above. In particular, our interest is in exploring the extent to which the previously observed effects of normative considerations on causal judgments of the form (C1) extend as well to those of the form

(C2) *X V*-ed *Y*

—where "*V*" is a "special causal verb" like those in Anscombe's list. Our principal finding is that in many cases the effects do not extend in this way, and moreover that the cases where we *do* find the same pattern are those where the causal verb used has a negative valence of its own. We draw two main conclusions from this finding. First, it supports directly our contention that the almost exclusive focus on statements in the form of (C1) in the experimental study of causal judgments has led to findings that are *unrepresentative* of the full range of ordinary causal thinking and provides a proof of concept as to how those judgments can be studied in their full variety. Second, as we discuss in more detail below, the results of our experiments provide significant indirect support for the contention that the effect of moral considerations on causal judgments in the form of (C1) reflect the fact that judgments in this form are most often used to assign *responsibility* for an event, and not just to describe the causal structure of what happened. (For similar views, see Livengood, Sytsma, and Rose 2017; Samland and Waldmann 2016; Sytsma, Livengood, and Rose 2012; Sytsma et al., 2019; Sytsma forthcoming.) It is not causal judgments in general that result from a process in which prior moral judgments play a role, but perhaps only those judgments that express a determination of moral responsibility.

2 Experiments

The principal aim of our experiments was to explore whether the above-discussed influence of norms on agreement with statements of the form

(C1) *X* caused *Y*

would also appear in connection with statements of the form

(C2) *X V*-ed *Y*

—where "*V*" is a causal verb other than the generic "cause." To explore this, we began with a well-known case from the prior literature, then replicated and extended our findings using some cases of our own.

Experiment 1: The pilfering professor

Above we referenced Knobe and Fraser's (2008) *pen case*, which is one of the earliest demonstrations of the influence of norms on causal judgment. As we noted there, Knobe and Fraser's finding, confirmed in replications and extensions of the case (Hitchcock and Knobe, 2009; Systma, Livengood, and Rose, 2012), was that agreement with the statement that

(4) [Professor Smith/The administrative assistant] caused the problem.

is affected by whether or not the person described was *allowed* to take the receptionist's pens. Specifically, participants are more inclined to agree that someone caused the receptionist's problem if that person *violated a norm* by taking one of her pens.

It is arguable, however, that agreement with a judgment like (4) is less a way of describing what a person *did* or *brought about* than of *blaming* them for a bad outcome, or saying that they were *responsible for* this consequence of their disallowed action. As one of our experimental participants wrote to us following the conclusion of an experiment that used this case:

An administrative assistant took a pen and a professor took a pen. [...] I think the Professor Smith did help cause the problem since he wasn't supposed to take a pen (and apparently didn't return the one he used). But it also is at the fault of the Admin Assistant since they didn't return the pen they used.

Our participant gets something importantly right: if the professor and the administrative assistant both take pens from the receptionist's desk, then under *that* description what they do seems to be the same. Because of this, the statement that one or the other of them "caused the problem" seems in a way to reach beyond this description of the causal structure of the scenario, to a further judgment that applies a concept of blameworthiness or moral responsibility.

We should also notice, however, that the phrase "took a pen" *itself* describes a way of causing something to happen. The linguist Beth Levin identifies this use of "took" as belonging to the subclass of "Verbs of Possessional Deprivation" that she calls "*steal* verbs": as with verbs like *abduct, capture, confiscate, liberate, pilfer, snatch,* and so on, to say that someone *took* something is to "describe the removal of something from someone's possession" (Levin 1993, §10.5, pp. 128–9). It makes sense, then, to investigate whether the application of this causal description is likewise sensitive to whether the action it describes was a violation of a moral or statistical norm—i.e., whether the influence of norms on agreement with (4) extends as well to agreement with the simple statement that

(5) [Professor Smith/The administrative assistant] took a pen.

If it does not, then this will be our first piece of evidence that the effect of norms on causal judgments may be limited in the way we have hypothesized.

To do this, we began by replacing Knobe and Fraser's original vignette with the following:

> The receptionist in the philosophy department tries to keep her desk stocked with pens. [Administrative assistants/Faculty members] are allowed to use these pens, but [faculty members/administrative assistants] in the department are not allowed to use them. They are expected to buy their own.
>
> On Monday morning, Professor Smith needs a pen for grading exams, and decides to go to the receptionist's office to look for one. At the same time, an administrative assistant also decides to go to the receptionist's office to look for a pen. Later that day, the receptionist needs to sign a document ... but she has a problem. There are no pens left on her desk, and while she is trying to find one she misses an important call.

Here, the *permissible* version of the scenario is the one in which Professor Smith, whose action is described in both of the test statements presented below, was allowed to take the receptionist's pens, while the *impermissible* version of the scenario is the one in which he was not allowed to do this. Following the vignette each participant evaluated two comprehension statements and then indicated their agreement with the following test statements on a standard seven-point Likert scale:

Caused   Professor Smith caused the problem.

Took   Professor Smith took a pen from the receptionist's desk.

All statements were presented on a single page, with the comprehension statements coming first followed by the two test statements, which occurred in a randomized order. We predicted that, while we would replicate Knobe and Fraser's finding of a significant effect of the permissibility of Professor Smith's action on agreement with **Caused**, this effect would *not* be observed in connection with ratings of **Took**, even though this statement also involves a causal concept.

Three points should be emphasized about the structure of this very simple experiment. The first is that, unlike Knobe and Fraser's original, the text of our pen vignette does not say explicitly that either Professor Smith or the administrative assistant took one of the receptionist's pens from her desk, but only that each of them *went to look* for one in her office. The purpose of this was to ensure that judgments of who *took* the pen, no less than judgments of who *caused* the problem, required participants to make an inference beyond the explicitly stated facts of the case. Our interest was in determining whether this causal inference would be affected in each case by the normative status of the agent's decision.

Our second point is concessive: it is clear that there are important differences between the structure of the causal process described in **Caused** and the structure of the causal process described in **Took**, including (i) that it is only in **Caused** that the agent is related explicitly to an independent event or state of affairs (here, the "problem" faced by the secretary) that might be viewed as the outcome of what they did, and (ii) that **Took**, unlike **Caused**, does not describe an outcome that results from the *joint* behavior of the two agents in the scenario. Together these points mean that, to the extent that the norm effect is supposed to arise just as a result of the role of normative considerations in making certain counterfactuals more salient than others (as in the account of Hitchcock and Knobe, 2009), it might therefore be expected not to extend to **Took**. However, we thought it important to treat this as an open question, since as we explain just below there was at least some prima facie reason to think that evaluations of **Took** might have been influenced by normative considerations as well. We will revisit this matter in more detail in introducing our third and fourth experiments, which were designed to address both of these concerns.

Finally, and related to our second point, it is important to the structure of this experiment that the event described in **Took**—Professor Smith's taking a pen from the receptionist's desk—*is itself* either a violation of a norm, or not a violation of a norm, depending on the version of the vignette in question. This is what made it prima facie possible that our participants' agreement with **Took** would have been subject to normative influence: for while there is *a* sense in which the professor will have done the same thing whether or not he was allowed to do what he did, it is possible that the tendency to describe him as *taking* a pen will be affected by whether doing so was a violation of a norm. As we shall see, however, there was in fact no such effect.

One hundred and twenty-six people (71 percent male, average age=31.6 years) participated in this experiment, of whom fifty-five were excluded for failing a comprehension check. This experiment, like all the other experiments in this study, was administered on Qualtrics, and all participants were recruited from Amazon's Mechanical Turk platform. A 2x2 mixed ANOVA with Statement (**Caused**, **Took**) as a within-subjects factor and Condition (Permissible, Impermissible) as a between-subjects factor revealed a significant main effect of Statement, $F(1,68)=30.66$, $p<.001$, a significant within-subjects interaction between Statement and Norm, $F(1,68)=9.19$, $p=.003$, and a main between-subjects effect of Condition, $F(1,68)=10.772$, $p=.002$. Subsequent analyses revealed a significant effect of condition on ratings of **Caused**, $F(1,68)=14.21$, $p=<.001$, $d=.90$, as participants agreed more that Professor Smith had caused the problem in the *impermissible* condition, where he was not allowed to take the pen ($M=5.32$, $SD=1.51$), than in the *permissible* condition, where he was allowed to take it ($M=3.70$, $SD=2.08$). However, there was no such effect of whether the professor's behavior was permissible or impermissible on ratings of **Took**, $F(1,68)=.31$, $p=.58$, $d=.13$, as participants agreed equally that Professor Smith had taken a pen whether he was allowed to take one ($M=5.97$, $SD=1.12$) or not ($M=5.82$, $SD=1.14$). These findings are illustrated in Figure 6.1.

This experiment replicated the previously observed effect of normative considerations on agreement with **Caused** statements for our modified version of the Pen case. People agreed more that Professor Smith had *caused the problem* when he was not allowed to take pens from the receptionist's desk than when he was allowed to take them. However, we found that this effect of normative considerations on causal judgments was limited: it did not extend to ratings of **Took**, a statement that describes a causal process using a "special causal verb" in the form of (C2). Our subsequent experiments sought to extend this pattern in connection with a number of different ways of expressing causal concepts.

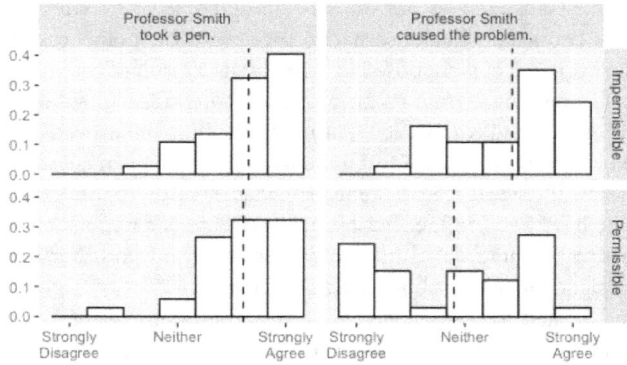

Figure 6.1 Results of Experiment 1. Bars indicate the proportion of participants who chose each response option in the corresponding condition, and dashed lines indicate mean response.

Experiment 2: Mrs. Smith's missing keys

Our second experiment sought to replicate the findings from Experiment 1 using a novel vignette and a different pair of causal verbs. Of particular interest was the potential influence of norms on periphrastic causative constructions with the following form:

(C3) *X* made *Y* *V*

—where *X* and *Y* are agents, and *V* describes an action that *Y* performs due to *X*'s influence. Part of what makes the construction in (C3) interesting is that, as noted above (see Table 6.1), 'make' occurs much more frequently than "cause" in everyday speech and writing.[5]

Three hundred and fourteen individuals (49 percent male, average age=37 years) participated in this experiment. Ninety-eight were excluded for failing a comprehension check. Participants began by reading one of two versions of the following vignette:

> On Tuesday evening, Mr. Smith borrowed his wife's car for a trip to the grocery store. The next day, Mrs. Smith couldn't find her keys when it was time to go to work. After ten minutes of looking, she found them in the dresser drawer –
>
> *Permissible variant:* even though she had always told Mr. Smith not to leave things there.
>
> *Impermissible variant:* just where Mr. Smith had told her he was going to leave them.
>
> Mrs. Smith ended up late to an important appointment.

After reading the vignette, participants rated three comprehension statements and then rated their agreement with one of the following test statements on a standard seven-point Likert scale:

Cause   Mr. Smith caused Mrs. Smith to be late to her appointment.

Made   Mr. Smith made Mrs. Smith late to her appointment.

Put   Mr. Smith put the keys in the dresser drawer.

In contrast with our first experiment, Experiment 2 used an exclusively between-subjects design: the three test questions were randomized so that each participant only saw one of them. Otherwise, the three points that we emphasized in connection with Experiment 1 remain relevant here: while **Caused** and **Made** both relate Mr. Smith's action counterfactually to his wife's eventual lateness, the description of his action supplied by **Put** does not, and moreover this last description does not concern an outcome that results *jointly* from the behavior of two agents. However, the statement in **Put** does concern an action that either is (in the permissible variant) or is not (in the impermissible variant) a violation of a norm, under the description in question. Finally, as with our first experiment, neither version of our vignette says explicitly where Mr. Smith put the keys, which means that participants were required to make an inference from the information supplied to them in order to evaluate the description of his action in **Put**.

In line with prior work, we hypothesized that participants would agree more strongly with **Caused** when they read the *impermissible* version of the vignette, in which the keys were found where Mr. Smith was not supposed to put them, than when they read the *permissible* version, where the keys were found where he said. We also predicted that, similar to Experiment 1, agreement with **Put** would be unaffected by the difference between the two vignettes. Finally, we expected the pattern of agreement

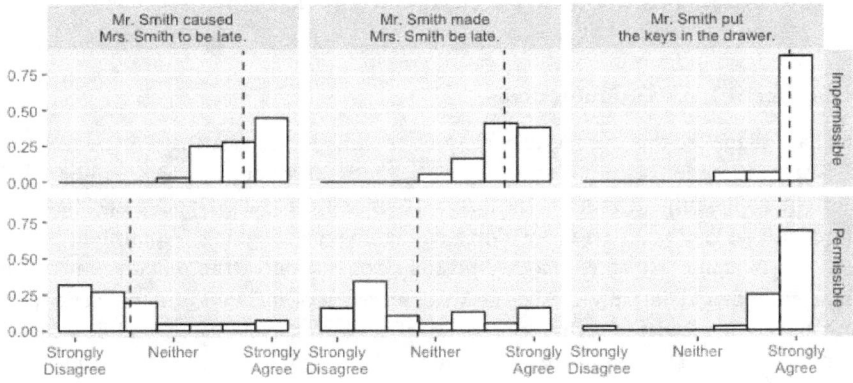

Figure 6.2 Results of Experiment 2. Bars indicate the proportion of participants who chose each response option in the corresponding condition, and dashed lines indicate mean response.

with **Made** to parallel the agreement with **Caused** rather than **Put**, since to say that Mr. Smith *made his wife late* is thereby to blame him, or hold him responsible, for this outcome of what he did. This prediction reflects the intuition that, as with **Caused**, the most natural reading of **Made** in this context is as a statement that assigns responsibility for a bad outcome.

Once again, the results of this experiment were in line with our predictions. A 2x3 ANOVA revealed main effects of Condition (Permissible, Impermissible), $F(1,210)=141.09$, $p<.001$, and Statement (**Caused, Made, Put**), $F(2,210)=55.06$, $p<.001$, as well as a significant interaction between Statement and Condition, $F(2,210)=23.62$, $p<.001$. Subsequent analyses showed that the effect of Condition was significant only on ratings of **Caused**, $F(1,76)=10.85$, $p<.001$, $d=2.43$, and **Made**, $F(1,73)=50.21$, $p<.001$, $d=1.65$, and not on ratings of **Put**, $F(1,61)=.99$, $p=.323$, $d=.24$. That is, participants agreed more that Mr. Smith had *caused* Mrs. Smith to be late when the keys were found in an impermissible location ($M=6.14$, $SD=.90$) rather than a permissible one ($M=2.64$, $SD=1.83$), and likewise they agreed more that Mr. Smith had *made* Mrs. Smith be late when the keys were found in an impermissible location ($M=6.11$, $SD=.88$) rather than a permissible one ($M=3.44$, $SD=2.11$), but they agreed equally that Mr. Smith had *put* the keys in the dresser drawer whether doing so was permissible ($M=6.68$, $SD=.54$) or impermissible ($M=6.81$, $SD=.54$). These results are illustrated in Figure 6.3.

These findings indicate that agreement with sentences of the form "X made Y V" can be influenced by normative considerations in the same way as agreement with those of the form "X caused Y." However, we also found that judgments of whether Mr. Smith *put* something somewhere were not influenced by normative considerations in this way. Moreover, unlike Experiment 1 the participants in this experiment saw only one of the three test questions, and so the difference between the pattern of ratings for **Caused** and **Made** compared to **Put** cannot have been due to their making implicit comparisons between them—that is, it is not as if participants could have been treating **Caused** as the "true" causal judgment, so that the norm effect was swallowed up by it. Indeed, we observed the same effect of norm on ratings of **Made**, but not on ratings of **Put**, even as each participant was presented with only one of these statements.

Experiment 3: Alex's double dose

We have suggested that our participants' greater willingness to say that Professor Smith *caused* the receptionist's problem, and that Mr. Smith *caused* or *made* Mrs. Smith (to be) late to her appointment, is due to the fact that these uses of "caused" and "made" have the function of *blaming* a person for doing something, or assigning responsibility for a negative outcome. However, another possible explanation of the difference between these findings and the pattern of results we observed in connection with the verbs "take" and "put" is that the latter verbs are both *lexical* causatives, while "cause" and (as we used it in Experiment 2) "make" both appear in *periphrastic* causal constructions. Our third experiment addressed this possibility by exploring the potential effects of normative considerations on agreement with statements containing a lexical causative that *is* used frequently to express blame or assign responsibility, namely the verb *kill*.

One hundred and thirty-eight participants (71 percent male, average age=33 years) participated in this experiment. Thirty-four were excluded for failing a comprehension check. Each participant began by reading the following vignette, which draws on some elements of a similar vignette presented in Phillips and Kominsky (2016):

> Alex and Benni are conducting a science experiment on a mouse.
>
> [Alex/Benni] is supposed to inject the mouse with a solution containing 10 milliliters of a poisonous chemical compound called AX 300. AX 300 is poisonous to mice in 10 milliliter doses, though it is lethal only in doses of 20 milliliters or more.
>
> Meanwhile, [Benni/Alex] is supposed to inject the mouse with a solution containing 10 milliliters of VT 4000, a chemical compound that will counter the effects of AX 300.
>
> But [Benni/Alex] secretly decides to load her syringe with a 10 milliliter dose of AX 300, instead. The double dose proves to be lethal, and the mouse dies immediately.

Following the vignette participants indicated their agreement with each of three test statements regarding Alex's actions, presented in random order, on a standard seven-point Likert scale:

Caused   Alex caused the mouse to die.

Killed   Alex killed the mouse.

Injected   Alex injected the mouse with AX 300.

Here, the *impermissible* condition is that in which Alex, who is described in all three statements, is the one who violates a norm by loading her syringe with AX 300 rather than the antidote, while the *permissible* condition is that in which Alex is supposed to inject the mouse with AX 300 and it is Benni who violates the norm instead. We predicted that, since in this context saying that Alex *killed* the mouse is a way of blaming Alex or attributing responsibility to her for the mouse's death, participants would agree more with both **Killed** and **Caused** when Alex's actions were impermissible than when Alex does what she is supposed to do. Further, we predicted that we would not observe this pattern for agreement with **Injected**, since this description of what happened is not so normatively laden.

As with our first and second experiments, the description of Alex's action in **Injected** differed from the description in **Caused** in that it does not relate her action explicitly to a further outcome that depends counterfactually on it, nor does it describe something that was a joint effect of her action and Benni's. However, the description given in **Killed** was arguably different in this regard, given that "kill" plausibly contains the sense "cause to die" (though for skepticism concerning this analysis, see Fodor, 1970 and Wierzbicka, 1975). Moreover, as with the statements **Took** (in Experiment 1) and

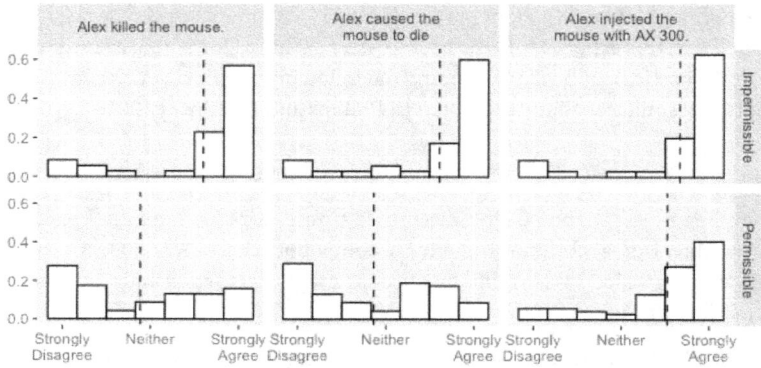

Figure 6.3 Results of Experiment 3. Bars indicate the proportion of participants who chose each response option in the corresponding condition, and dashed lines indicate mean response.

Put (in Experiment 2), the judgment that Alex *injected* the mouse with poison is itself a description of her as doing something that either did or did not violate a norm. Finally, as with our first two experiments, the vignette used in Experiment 3 does not say explicitly whether Alex had injected the mouse with AX 300, killed the mouse, or caused it to die, and so participants needed to make an inference from the information supplied in order to evaluate each of the three statements.

The results of Experiment 3 confirmed all three of our predictions. A 2x3 ANOVA revealed main effects of Condition, $F(1,102)=19.84$, $p<.001$, and Statement, $F(2,204)=36.24$, $p<.001$, as well as a significant interaction between Statement and Condition, $F(2,204)=13.72$, $p<.001$. Subsequent analyses showed Condition had a highly significant effect on ratings of **Caused**, $F(1,102)=26.4$, $p<.001$, $d=1.06$, and **Killed**, $F(1,102)=22.15$, $p<.001$, $d=.98$, while there was no significant effect of Condition on ratings of **Injected**, $F(1,102)=1.313$, $p=.254$, $d=.24$. That is, participants agreed more that Alex had *caused* the mouse to die when she acted impermissibly ($M=5.83, SD=1.95$) than when she acted permissibly ($M=3.58, SD=2.19$) in loading her syringe with AX 300, and likewise they agreed more that Alex had *killed* the mouse when she was not supposed to inject the mouse with AX 300 ($M=5.80, SD=2.00$) than when she was supposed to do this ($M=3.65, SD=2.29$), but they agreed about equally that Alex had *injected* the mouse with poison whether doing so was permissible ($M=6.00, SD=1.86$) or impermissible ($M=5.56, SD=1.81$). These results are illustrated in Figure 6.3.

These findings challenge the possible interpretation of our previous findings as resting just on the difference between lexical and periphrastic causative constructions and provide further support for our contention that the tendency to identify a norm-violating agent as the one who *caused* something bad to happen or *made* someone do an undesired thing reflects the tendency to blame that person for what they did, or hold them morally responsible for it. Whether Alex violated a norm in loading her syringe with AX 300 had a significant effect on participants' willingness to say that she *killed* the mouse and she *caused* it to die, but it did not have such an effect on their judgment of whether she *injected the mouse* with AX 300—since this description of what Alex did applied equally whether or not she violated a norm in doing it.

Experiment 4: The shape playground

One barrier to using vignettes as stimuli in eliciting judgments of actual causation is that so much of our ordinary language uses causal verbs simply in the description of what happens. As we have noted, the vignettes that we used in Experiments 1–3 all get around this difficulty by avoiding any explicit description of the causal processes we were interested in having participants form judgments about: thus our version of the pen vignette differs from Knobe and Fraser's (2008) original in that nowhere in our vignette does it say that Professor Smith took a pen, and the vignettes used in Experiments 2 and 3 also left implicit what Mr. Smith had done with the keys and Alex had done to the mouse.

However, another way of inviting participants to draw inferences about causal processes from stimuli that do not represent those processes explicitly is by using animations, rather than text-based stimuli, as experimental prompts. A large body of research has shown that participants readily infer (or even perceive: cf. Anscombe, 1981, pp. 136–8; Siegel, 2009; Helton, 2018) causal interactions and agential behavior on the basis of 2D stimuli consisting in nothing more than the movements of simple shapes (for reviews, see Scholl and Tremoulet, 2000; Danks, 2009). Paradigms that employ such materials provide a way of exploring causal judgments that avoids the potential pitfall described just above, since in them the causal structure of the scenario under consideration is not *described* to participants at all, and they must instead *infer* its causal structure on the basis of what they see.[6]

Our final experiment attempted to extend and replicate our earlier findings in a way that builds on this research, by displaying a simple animation and inviting participants to make causal judgments about it. Three hundred and nineteen participants (61 percent male, average age=34 years), of whom one hundred and fifty-six were excluded for failing a comprehension check, watched one of two thirty-second animations that depicted the motion of several geometric shapes. These animations are illustrated in Figure 6.4, and can be viewed in full at http://www.schwenkler.org/cause-norm.html. At the beginning of each animation (Figure 6.4, Slide 1) a circle and a square were located next to a rectangular box, above which was a rectangular shape containing outlined images of a square and a circle. Each time one of the outlined images changed from red to green, the corresponding shape rose up and landed on the box—according to the pattern "circle, square, circle, square, . . ." (Figure 6.4, Slides 2–3 and 6). Each time a shape jumped on the box, a triangle that was on a different box rose into the air as the box rose up underneath it (Figure 6.4, Slides 4 and 7). Finally, after three rounds of taking turns jumping on the platform, the circle and the square both jumped on the platform at once, and the triangle rose higher into the air than usual and then fell to the ground, shattering into pieces.

These events proceeded according to one of two conditions. In the *impermissible condition*, as illustrated in Slides 9–12 of Figure 6.4, before the circle and the square jumped simultaneously onto the box the signal above it illuminated only the circular

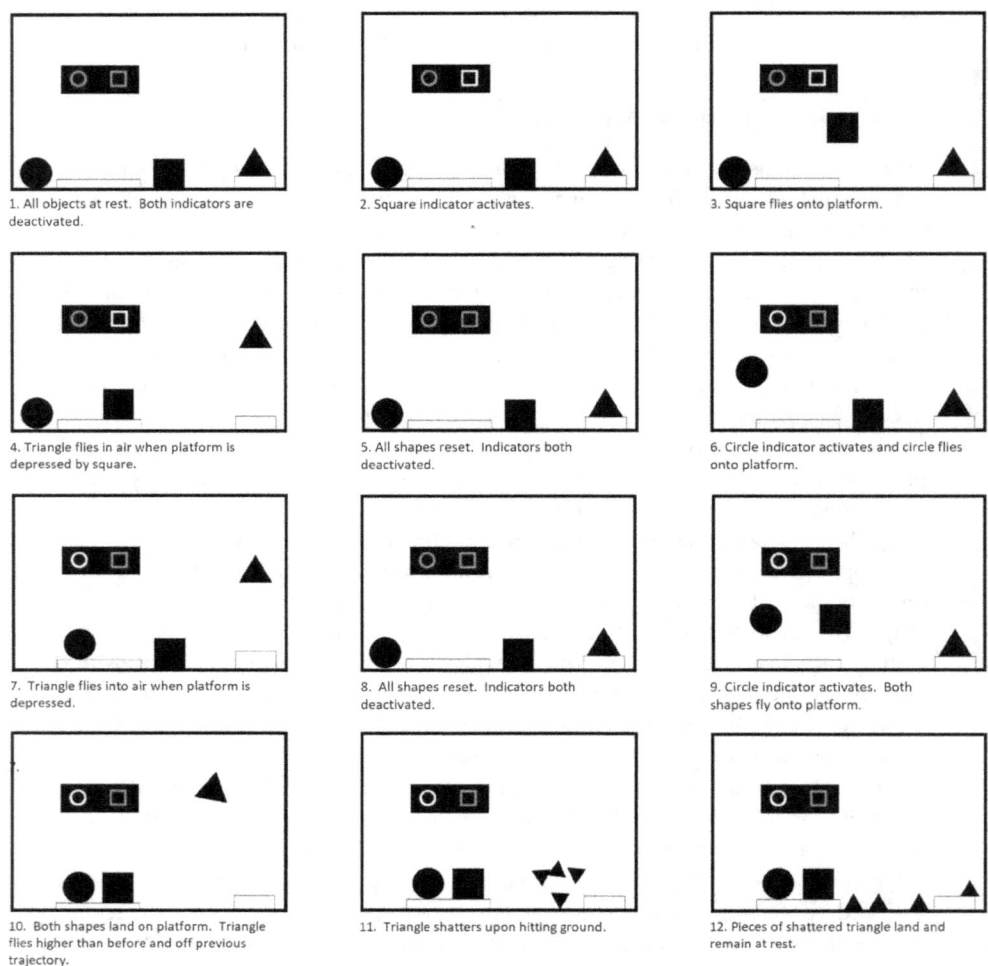

Figure 6.4 Illustration of the animation used in Experiment 4. The pattern in slides 2–8 was repeated three times before the final event shown in slides 9–12 began. Shown here is the impermissible condition, in which only the circle was "supposed" to jump onto the platform at the end, as indicated by the fact that only its indicator light activates. By contrast, in the permissible condition the indicator light for both shapes activated at the point shown in slide 9, and remained so until the end of the animation. (Note that the original materials used red and green indicators, respectively, instead of grey and white.)

shape, indicating that the square had jumped out of turn. By contrast, in the *permissible condition* the signal illuminated both shapes at once, indicating that both of them were allowed to jump.[7] Following a comprehension question designed to ensure that they had picked up on the rule that the jumping shapes were supposed to follow, each participant responded to the following three test statements, presented in random order, by choosing which of the phrases "square," "circle," or "circle and the square" best completed each one:

Broke	At the end, the _____ broke the triangle.	
Bounced	At the end, the _____ bounced the triangle into the air.	
Caused	At the end, the _____ caused the triangle to break.	

We predicted that, in line with the findings of our earlier experiments, participants would tend to choose "square" to complete both **Caused** and **Broke** more frequently in the permissible condition than the impermissible condition, and that we would not observe this pattern in connection with **Bounced**. (Recall that it is the square that jumps "out of turn" in the impermissible condition, but follows the direction of the signal in the permissible one.) Our analyses also confirmed these predictions, as planned comparisons found a significant effect of Condition on the percentage of participants who chose "square" to complete **Caused** ($t=6.42$, $p<.001$) and **Broke** ($t=5.47$, $p<.001$), but not on the percentage of participants who chose "square" to complete **Bounced** ($t=1.48$, $p=.140$). That is, participants judged consistently that *both* shapes had bounced and broken the triangle, and caused the triangle to break, in the permissible condition, when both shapes obeyed the signal in jumping together onto the platform. By contrast, in the impermissible condition, in which the square's final jump was out of turn, a similar proportion of participants judged that both shapes had *bounced* the triangle into the air, while significantly larger proportions judged that the square had *broken* the triangle and *caused* it to break. The full results of this experiment are presented in Table 6.2 and illustrated in Figure 6.5.

The structure of this experiment differed in an important way from the structure of our first three, and this difference helps to address the concessive point that we raised in our discussion of Experiment 1. As with those experiments, the description of either shape as having *bounced* the triangle into the air required participants to make an inference that went beyond what was immediately depicted in the experiment, and concerned an action that either was or was not a violation of a norm, under the description given. However, unlike the description of Professor Smith as having *taken* a pen, of Mr. Smith as having *put* the keys in the dresser drawer, and of Alex as having *injected* the mouse with AX 300, the description supplied in **Bounced** is easily understood as describing an event (the triangle's going into the air) that can be construed as depending counterfactually on the activity of two separate agents (the

Table 6.2 Results of Experiment 4. Percentages indicate the proportion of participants who chose each response option.

Statement	Condition	"circle"	"square"	"circle and the square"
Broke	Impermissible	2.78%	31.94%	65.28%
	Permissible	1.10%	1.10%	97.80%
Bounced	Impermissible	5.56%	15.28%	79.17%
	Permissible	0%	7.69%	92.31%
Caused	Impermissible	4.17%	38.89%	56.94%
	Permissible	0%	1.10%	98.90%

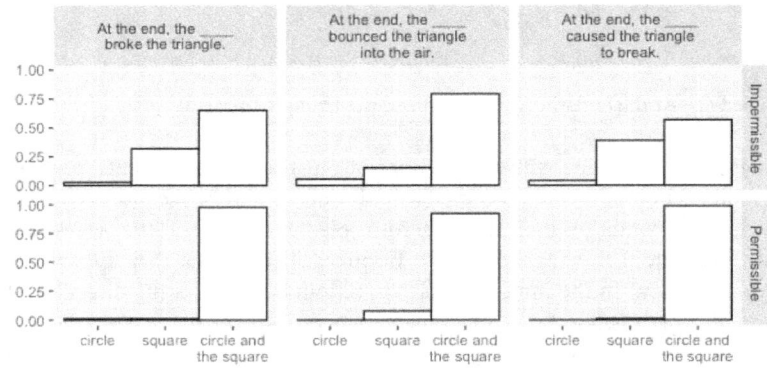

Figure 6.5 Results of Experiment 4. Bars indicate the proportion of participants who chose each response option in the corresponding condition.

circle and the square). Because of this, the lack of a significant effect of norm on ratings of this statement was especially revealing: it suggests that our earlier findings were not just due to the distinctive causal structure of the events described in **Take** (in Experiment 1), **Put** (in Experiment 2) and **Injected** (in Experiment 3), since the event described in **Bounced** had just the causal structure described in those judgments that have been found in the past, and in the other experiments in the present study, to be affected by moral norms. Because of this, we take the insensitivity of these statements to normative considerations as evidence that participants were treating them as doing a quite different thing from the judgments expressed in our several **Caused** statements and in **Made**, **Killed**, and **Broke**: rather than expressing a judgment of moral responsibility, their role was to describe the causal structure of the scenario that participants had just been shown.

These findings replicate and extend the results of our first three experiments, while also illustrating the value of causal perception paradigms for the philosophical study of causal judgments. When the square's final jump was permissible, response patterns were similar across **Caused**, **Broke**, and **Bounced**, as participants tended to identify both the square and the circle as having done the thing in question. By contrast, in the norm-violating condition participants selected "square" at similar rates for **Caused** and **Broke** but were less likely to do so for **Bounced**. Indeed, participants selected "square" at similar rates to complete **Bounced** regardless of whether a norm was violated. This contrasts with their judgments of which of the shapes *broke* the triangle and *caused* the triangle to break.

3. Discussion

What is the structure of ordinary causal thinking? Following Knobe (2010), we may distinguish accounts of human causal cognition that depict it as broadly *scientific* in character from those that depict it as *moralized* through and through. According to accounts of the first kind, human beings aim to make sense of the world in roughly the same way that, at least in the ideal, scientists reach conclusions about their domains of expertise: they draw on "observation, experimentation, [and] the construction of explanatory theories" (Knobe, 2010, p. 315) in filling out their understanding of how the world works. Knobe finds this account to be undermined by evidence showing the influence of moral norms on causal judgments: the process of causal cognition, he argues, is "suffused through and through with moral considerations" (ibid., p. 317) in a way that reveals that this process does not even *aim* at developing the kind of objective, purely evidence-based model of causal structure that these accounts imagine.

The evidence that we have presented in this chapter gives reason to think that this very strong conclusion is overstated. The extensive influence of normative considerations on what we have called *"cause"-judgments*, or judgments that are ordinarily expressed with the use of the English verb "cause," is not an influence on *causal judgment in general*—i.e., on the much broader family of judgments that are expressed with the use of special causal verbs like "take," "put," "inject," "bounce," and so on. Many of these latter judgments, we have shown, are totally unaffected by whether the action they describe was a violation of a moral norm—and to the extent that they are so affected, it seems to be because they involve causal concepts, such as the one expressed by the use of "kill" in our third experiment and "break" in our fourth one, that possess their own moral valence.

How should we understand these findings, and what is the model of causal cognition that they support? We contend that these findings can be explained by reflecting on two quite different causal tasks that were faced by the participants in our four experiments. One of these tasks was to *describe* the causal structure of a scenario, to identify *what happened* in a way that brings it under various specific causal concepts expressed by words like those in Anscombe's list. Doing this requires collecting, from observation and also from inference, various facts relating to what happened, and putting these facts together in order to generate a description of what took place. And our chief finding was these descriptions tend to be unaffected by the normative valence of the events they concern—so that, for example, the question whether Professor Smith *took a pen* doesn't seem depend at all on whether doing so was a violation of a moral norm.

Along with this descriptive task, the other task our participants faced was that of forming a conclusion about how the facts of the case they considered related to a further question, namely that of which of the parties in the scenario was *responsible* for a negative outcome of it. Across all of our experiments we found that it is when causal concepts are used in this latter way—to say, for instance, whether or not it was Professor Smith who *caused the problem* that the secretary eventually faced, or whether Mr. Smith *made his wife late* by doing what he undeniably did, viz., putting her keys in the dresser drawer, or whether Alex *killed the mouse* when she injected it with a poisonous substance—that the judgments they figure in are subject to normative influence. It is when words like "cause," "make," and "kill" are used to express what we may call *responsibility concepts*, or concepts of who is responsible and therefore blameworthy for a certain negative outcome, that the use of these words is affected by moral considerations.

The difference between the two tasks that were faced by our participants can be analogized to the difference between two tasks facing judges and jurors in a court of law: on the one hand, that of establishing what are the facts that are relevant to determining the responsibility of a given party for a certain outcome; and on the other, that of reaching this further determination of guilt or innocence.[8] H.L.A. Hart and Tony Honoré appeal to this distinction in their visionary work *Causation in the Law*, where they outline what they call an "apparent paradox" that turns on how we understand the relationship between causation and responsibility:

> Much modern thought on causation in the law rests on the contention that the statement that someone has caused harm either means no more than that the harm would not have happened without ("but for") his action or where (as in normal legal usage and in all ordinary speech) it apparently means more than this, it is a disguised way of asserting the "normative" judgment that he is responsible, i.e., that it is proper or just to blame or punish him or make him pay. On this view to say that a person caused harm is not really, though ostensibly it is, to give a *ground* or *reason* for holding him responsible in the first [that is, "but-for"] sense; for we are only in a position to say that he has caused harm when we have decided that he is responsible.
>
> Hart and Honoré, 1959, p. 66

Hart and Honoré's two senses of "cause" correspond to the two kinds of causal judgment that were elicited from participants in our experiments: their concept of "but for" causation, or what in the Restatements (see fn. 8 above) is called "philosophic" or "factual" causation, is the concept involved in what above we called *describing* the causal structure of a scenario, while their "normative" causal concept is, as they suggest, the one involved in identifying the party that was morally responsible for an outcome—i.e., the concept that in the Restatements is described as that of "substantial cause" or "harm within the scope of liability." Our argument here has turned on the simple observation that many of our ordinary causal judgments fall into the first of these categories, and that these descriptions are largely presupposed by "cause"-judgments that express a determination of moral responsibility. The evidence we have presented here strongly suggests that ordinary causal judgment is influenced by normative considerations in the way proposed by Knobe only to the extent that it expresses a conclusion of this latter sort.

While these parallel notions of causation are conceptually distinct, people don't always keep them separate in practice. It is for this reason that contemporary law establishes procedural safeguards to prevent jurors from conflating these two lines of inquiry. Such safeguards aim to ensure that complex legal judgments mirror the way in which our common-sense causal reasoning unfolds. For example, the relevant portions of Rule 701 of the Federal Rules of Evidence limit witness testimony to statements which are "rationally based on the witness's perception" and "helpful to clearly understanding the witness's testimony or to determining a fact in issue" (Fed. R. Evid. 701). In other words, a witness cannot be asked to form a conclusion, but can only assist the court in establishing facts relevant to the case. For this reason, judges and jury are often referred to as the "fact finder" during this stage of a trial. Forming a conclusion is the duty of the jury at the end of the trial, *after* the facts "in issue" have been established.

Judgments of moral or legal responsibility, including those implying the "normative" or "substantial" concept of causation that the ordinary use of "cause" most often expresses, are *conclusions* in the sense just defined, and we cannot form conclusions until we get our facts straight. In this way, causal action-descriptions are structurally prior, and conceptually quite different, from causal conclusions. Hart and Honoré note this difference when they point out the distinction between simple causal action statements such as "He pushed it" and "He broke it" with what they call "the most obvious and fundamental case of all for the attribution of responsibility: the case in which we can simply say 'He did it'" (1959, p. 73). Our data, however, strongly suggest that it is not necessarily anything inherent in the content of verbs like "push," "break," and "do" that accounts for this distinction. As our fourth experiment reveals, the claim that so-and-so *broke* such-and-such can, in the right context, function to express a judgment of moral responsibility that is affected by normative considerations in just the same way as "So-and-so did it" or "So-and-so caused such-and-such to break." Our second and third experiments showed that something similar can happen with the ordinary use of "make" and "kill": our participants' use of these words was equivalent to their use of "cause," and gave them a way of saying something quite different than what they said using verbs like "put" and "inject." It is a task for further research to explore the factors that influence whether the use of various verbs is liable to be treated as doing one or the other of these things—whether describing facts about the causal relationships between various entities, events, and states of affairs, or conveying normatively valenced conclusions that assign responsibility for what happened.

Notes

1   David Rose was significantly involved in this project at an early stage, and we thank him for his valuable contributions. For discussion of this material, we thank Samantha Berthelette, Randy Clarke, Josh Knobe, Justin Sytsma, several members of the FSU Philosophical Psychology Group, and an audience at the 2020 meeting of the SSPP. We also thank Kevin Reuter for detailed comments on an earlier version of the chapter. Funds to compensate experimental participants were provided by FSU's Small Grants Program and by a Developing Scholar Award to JS. JS acknowledges the support of an Academic Cross-Training Fellowship from the John F. Templeton Foundation.
2   There is no canonical list of which English verbs are causal, nor any uncontroversial criterion for determining which verbs are. (For an attempt at providing both of these things, see Schwenkler (in prep.).) As such, the decision of which verbs to highlight in Table 1 reflect our own considered judgments. To touch on a few of the controversial or borderline cases: we judge that *have* is used causally in a sentence like "Beth had a milkshake" (i.e., she consumed it), *get* is used causally in "Jim got the keys out of the drawer" (i.e., he removed them), *sit* is used causally in "Annie sat the doll in the chair" (i.e., she made it to sit there), and *stand* is used causally in "Al stood the books on the

shelf" (i.e., he made them to stand there). However, since the list in Table 6.1 is merely illustrative, nothing in our argument hinges on whether we are correct in every case, nor on deciding what exactly "correctness" in this context would be.

3   Notice that this point holds even if many of the words in our list, like "have," "get," "sit," and "stand," aren't used causally very often (when they are used). It's enough that some of them, like "put," "build," "cut," and "kill," seem to have *only* a causal use: for the frequency data reveal that we use *each* of these words more often than we use "cause," thus talking about causation using each of these special causal verbs more often than we talk about it using "cause."

4   For similar findings, see Bar-Asher Siegal, Bassel, and Hagmayer (forthcoming, in prep.)

5   We should note that "make" is used most often as a lexical causative, in sentences like "We made a mistake" and "Sally made dinner." However, corpus data from iWeb (http://www.english-corpora.org/iweb/, retrieved July 17, 2019) show that the construction "made $X\ V$" is still used over three times more frequently than "caused X to V" (32,962 occurrences vs. 9,272).

6   For other recent work that uses this approach, see Wolff (2003, 2007) and Wolff and Thorstad (2016).

7   We thank Samantha Berthelette for giving us the idea to convey the normative structure of the scenario in this way.

8   Indeed, it is precisely in order to separate these two causal notions that The Restatements (Second) of Torts draws a distinction between what it calls "philosophic cause" and "substantial cause" (Restatement, Third, of Torts: § 431 cmt. a). The former term implies an extended counterfactual causal concept in which background conditions and events play causal roles in bringing about an event, while the latter term uses cause "in the popular sense, in which there always lurks the idea of responsibility" (ibid.). And the most recent treatment of causation in The Restatements (Third) of Torts preserves this traditional distinction with updated language by distinguishing "factual cause" from "harm within the scope of liability (which has historically been called 'proximate cause')" (Restatement, Third, Torts: Liability for Physical and Emotional Harm § 6 cmt. b at 67–8). In this case, the latter is used to distinguish the causal agents which the court may hold liable from those which are too attenuated to fall "within the scope of liability." In other words, what has traditionally been called proximate cause is a concept used to assign responsibility.

References

Alicke, M.D. (1992). "Culpable causation." *Journal of Personality and Social Psychology* 63(3): 368.

Alicke, M.D., D. Rose, and D. Bloom (2011). "Causation, norm violation, and culpable control." *The Journal of Philosophy* 108(12): 670–96.

American Law Institute (1965). "Restatement of the Law Second, Torts." St. Paul: American Law Institute Publishers.

American Law Institute (2010). "Restatement of the Law Third, Torts, Liability for Physical and Emotional Harm." St. Paul: American Law Institute Publishers.

Anscombe, G.E.M. (1981). "Causality and determination." *Collected Philosophical Papers, Vol. II: Metaphysics and the Philosophy of Mind* (133–47). Minneapolis: University of Minnesota Press.

Bar-Asher Siegal, E., N. Bassel, and Y. Hagmayer (forthcoming). "Causal selection—the linguistic take. *Experiments in Linguistic Meaning 1*.

Bar-Asher Siegal, E., N. Bassel, and Y. Hagmayer (in prep.). "The role of agency in causal selection."

Danks, D. (2009). "The psychology of causal perception and reasoning." In H. Beebee, C. Hitchcock, and P. Menzies (eds.), *The Oxford Handbook of Causation* (447–70). New York: Oxford University Press.

Danks, D., D. Rose, and E. Machery (2014). "Demoralizing causation." *Philosophical Studies 171*(2): 251–77.

Fodor, J. (1970). "Three reasons for not deriving 'kill' from 'cause to die.'" *Linguistic Inquiry 1*(4): 429–38.

Godfrey-Smith, P. (2009). "Causal pluralism." In H. Beebee, C. Hitchcock, and P. Menzies (eds.), *The Oxford Handbook of Causation* (326–37). Oxford: Oxford University Press.

Hall, N. (2004). "Two concepts of causation." In J. Collins, N. Hall, and L.A. Paul (eds.), *Causation and Counterfactuals* (225–76). Cambridge, MA: The MIT Press.

Hart, H.L.A. and T. Honoré (1959). *Causation in the Law*. Oxford: Oxford University Press.

Helton, G. (2018). "Visually perceiving the intentions of others." *Philosophical Quarterly 68*(271): 243–64.

Hitchcock, C. and J. Knobe (2009). "Cause and norm." *The Journal of Philosophy 106*(11): 587–612.

Kominsky, J.F. and J. Phillips (2019). "Immoral Professors and Malfunctioning Tools: Counterfactual Relevance Accounts Explain the Effect of Norm Violations on Causal Selection." *Cognitive Science 43*: e12792. doi:10.1111/cogs.12792

Knobe, J. (2010). "Person as scientist, person as moralist." *Behavioral and Brain Sciences 33*(4): 315–29. doi:10.1017/S0140525X10000907. https://www.cambridge.org/core/services/aop-cambridge-core/content/view/DC2DACD3A2997FB9E895A8C642A8F708/S0140525X10000907a.pdf/person-as-scientist-person-as-moralist.pdf

Knobe, J. and B. Fraser (2008). "Causal judgment and moral judgment: Two experiments." In W. Sinnott-Armstrong (ed.), *Moral Psychology, Vol. 2. The Cognitive Science of Morality: Intuition and Diversity* (441–7). Cambridge, MA: MIT Press.

Knobe, J., S. Prasada, and G.E. Newman (2013). "Dual character concepts and the normative dimension of conceptual representation." *Cognition 127*(2): 242–57.

Levin, B. (1993). *English Verb Classes and Alternations: A Preliminary Investigation*. Chicago: University of Chicago Press.

Livengood, J.M., J. Sytsma, and D. Rose (2017). "Following the FAD: Folk Attributions and Theories of Actual Causation." *Review of Philosophy and Psychology 8*(2): 273–94.

Phillips, J.S. and J.F. Kominsky (2016). "Causation and norms of proper functioning: Counterfactuals are (still) relevant." https://doi.org/10.31234/osf.io/dwajn

Samland, J., and M.R. Waldmann (2016). "How prescriptive norms influence causal inferences." *Cognition 156*: 165–76.

Scholl, B.J. and P.D. Tremoulet (2000). "Perceptual causality and animacy." *Trends in Cognitive Science 4*(8): 299–309.

Schwenkler, J. (in prep.). "The varieties of causation."

Siegel, S. (2009). "The visual experience of causation." *Philosophical Quarterly 59*(236): 519–40.

Sytsma, J. (forthcoming). "The responsibility account." In P. Willemsen and A. Wiegmann (eds.), *Advances in Experimental Philosophy of Causation*. London: Bloomsbury Academic.

Sytsma, J., J. Livengood, and D. Rose (2012). "Two types of typicality: Rethinking the role of statistical typicality in ordinary causal attributions." *Studies in History and Philosophy of Science Part C: Studies in History and Philosophy of Biological and Biomedical Sciences* 43(4): 814–20.

Sytsma, J., R. Bluhm, P. Willemsen, and K. Reuter (2019). "Causal attributions and corpus analysis." In E. Fischer and M. Curtis (ed.), *Methodological Advances in Experimental Philosophy*. London: Bloomsbury Academic.

Walsh, C.R. and S.A. Sloman (2011). "The meaning of cause and prevent: The role of causal mechanism." *Mind & Language* 26(1): 21–52.

Wierzbicka, A. (1975). "Why 'kill' does not mean 'cause to die': The semantics of action sentences." *Foundations of Language* 13(4): 491–528.

Wolff, P. (2003). "Direct causation in the linguistic encoding and individuation of causal events." *Cognition* 88: 1–48.

Wolff, P. (2007). "Representing causation." *Journal of Experimental Psychology: General* 136(1): 82–111.

Wolff, P. and R. Thorstad (2016). "Force dynamics." In M. Waldmann (ed.), *The Oxford Handbook of Causal Reasoning* (147–67). New York: Oxford University Press.

7

The Responsibility Account

Justin Sytsma

In this chapter, I lay out and defend one type of explanation of recent findings that norms impact people's causal judgments—the *responsibility account* (e.g., Sytsma et al., 2012; Livengood et al., 2017; Sytsma et al., 2019; Livengood and Sytsma, 2020; Sytsma and Livengood, 2021; Sytsma, forthcoming-a). To do so I will critically contrast this view with three other prominent types of explanation that have been put forward in the literature—the *pragmatic account* (e.g., Samland and Waldmann, 2016; Samland et al., 2016), the *bias account* (e.g., Alicke 1992, 2000; Alicke et al., 2011; Rose 2017), and *counterfactual accounts* (e.g., Hitchcock and Knobe, 2009; Halpern and Hitchcock, 2015; Kominsky et al., 2015; Icard et al., 2017; Kominsky and Phillips, 2019). The contrast is not straightforward, however, because while each of these views purports to explain the same basic findings, they arguably diverge in how they construe the broader phenomenon to be explained, and this is tied to the type of explanation offered.

To draw this out, consider the pen case first presented by Knobe and Fraser (2008), which has been widely offered as an illustrative example of the phenomenon in the subsequent literature. Participants were given the following vignette:

> The receptionist in the philosophy department keeps her desk stocked with pens. The administrative assistants are allowed to take the pens, but faculty members are supposed to buy their own.
>
> The administrative assistants typically do take the pens. Unfortunately, so do the faculty members. The receptionist has repeatedly e-mailed them reminders that only administrative assistants are allowed to take the pens.
>
> On Monday morning, one of the administrative assistants encounters Professor Smith walking past the receptionist's desk. Both take pens. Later that day, the receptionist needs to take an important message ... but she has a problem. There are no pens left on her desk.

In this scenario, two agents perform symmetric actions (both Professor Smith and the administrative assistant take pens) that jointly lead to a problem. The key difference is that one agent violates a norm (Professor Smith is not allowed to take pens) while the other does not (administrative assistants are allowed to take pens). After reading this vignette, participants were then asked to rate their agreement with two statements using a scale ranging from –3 ("not at all") to 3 ("fully"):

Professor Smith caused the problem.
The administrative assistant caused the problem.

Knobe and Fraser found that overall participants agreed far more strongly with the first claim (M=2.2) than with the second (M=–1.2). Call this the *norm effect*.

Each of the accounts in the literature purports to explain the norm effect, but what exactly is the scope of this effect? Focusing on the pen case, we can offer a minimal characterization of the basic phenomenon. First, Knobe and Fraser report the results of an empirical study that limited the "conversation" between experimenter and participant in notable ways, including that the participant's contribution to the conversation was restricted to rating the two statements. Minimally, the norm effect can be construed as being specific to such contexts, reflecting pragmatic factors owing to the experimental setup. Second, the statements that participants rated used the lemma "cause," having the form "X caused Y." Minimally, the norm effect can be construed as being specific to attributions employing this lemma. Third, in the pen case vignette the norm that Professor Smith violates is an explicit departmental rule: she takes a pen even though she was not allowed to do so. Minimally, the norm effect can be construed as being specific to norm violations of this type.[1]

The main types of explanation offered in the literature differ along one or more of these three dimensions, and so differ in how broad they ultimately take the norm effect to be. In this chapter, I detail these differences through the lens of my preferred explanation—the responsibility account. I begin by characterizing the phenomenon at issue, noting disagreements about the scope of the norm effect, focusing on how restricted the context for the effect is taken to be (Section 1), the scope of the judgments at issues (Section 2), and the range of norms involved (Section 3). In doing so, I'll lay out the primary alternative explanations of the norm effect that have been offered and very briefly summarize some of the recent evidence suggesting in favor of the responsibility account. In Section 4, I then add to this, reporting the results of two new, preregistered studies using a method not previously employed in these debates.

1 Context

Most of the explanations of the impact of norms on causal judgments that have been offered in the literature take this to be a general phenomenon that is revealed by the empirical studies, not an artifact created by the context of the studies themselves. The pragmatic account put forward by Samland and Waldmann challenges this assumption. Samland and Waldmann (2016) claim that the term "cause" can be understood in two different ways, one corresponding with what they refer to as *causality* and the other with *accountability*. While they offer a rather circular definition of "causality" that would require a good bit of unpacking—i.e., "causality in the narrow sense refers to contingent dependency relations between causes and effects that are generated by causal mechanisms" (p. 165)—the key distinction here is that it is taken to be purely descriptive, while accountability is taken to be sensitive to normative considerations. Samland and Waldmann then argue that in studies showing the norm effect, "pragmatic contextual features steer subjects toward an accountability understanding of the causal test question" (p. 165).

The most straightforward interpretation of Samland and Waldmann's view is that the dominant attributional use of the lemma "cause" expresses a purely descriptive concept (causality), but that in contexts like that found in Knobe and Fraser's study using the pen case, pragmatic factors lead participants to instead interpret the queries as asking for a judgment that is sensitive to normative considerations (accountability). Samland and Waldmann write that "the ambiguity of queries about the cause in scenarios demonstrating norm effects is grounded in the presupposition relation between accountability and causation," which is such that "agents are only held accountable for outcomes they have caused" (p. 165). They then note that in the pen case "the causal relations are trivial," such that "it is unlikely that subjects will think that they are supposed to solely judge this causal relation" (p. 165). What this suggests is not so much that Samland and Waldmann hold that the term "caused" is polysemous, but that in rather specific contexts they expect people to infer that the experimenters were actually interested in another concept altogether—one that presupposes relevant descriptive relations, but where information about norm violations is also relevant. The upshot is that according to the pragmatic account, studies showing the impact of norms on causal judgments miss their intended mark: they don't actually tell us anything about ordinary causal judgments.

Our responsibility account is in some ways similar to Samland and Waldmann's pragmatic account. Both views explain the norm effect in terms of participants taking the test statements to express a normative concept. While the pragmatic account holds that this is due to participants taking the statements to be intending to ask about something other than who caused the outcome, however, the responsibility account denies this. We contend that participants do in fact take the statements to be asking about who caused the outcome, but believe that the dominant use of "caused" in such statements expresses a normative concept. Specifically, we hold that the concept of causation expressed by the dominant attributional use of the lemma "cause," at least in English, is sensitive to both descriptive and normative considerations, being akin to concepts like responsibility and accountability. In this way, the responsibility account takes the norm effect to be notably broader than the pragmatic account does with regard to context: we hold that this is a general phenomenon, not one that is specific to the experimental contexts.

The responsibility account predicts that people's judgments about causal attributions (statements like "X caused Y") will generally be quite similar to their judgments about normative attributions such as responsibility attributions (statements like "X is responsible for Y"). There is also evidence for this claim both from corpus studies and experimental studies. First, Sytsma et al. (2019) present evidence suggesting that the dominant attributional use of "caused" as found in the Corpus of Contemporary American English is sensitive to normative information, being similar to the attributional use of "responsible" in this regard. Unlike other terms that plausibly express descriptive "causality" (such as "created," "induced," "led to"), "caused" and "responsible" tend to be disproportionately used in the context of negatively valenced outcomes, and a distributional semantic analysis shows that they are remarkably close together in semantic space. Such findings for ordinary English usage suggest against the norm effect being merely a pragmatic effect.

Second, a spate of papers have found a close correspondence between judgments about causal attributions and responsibility attributions, including a number of recent papers testing the norm effect that have shown that it occurs for both types of attribution and found no statistically significant difference between judgments about each. This includes recent studies testing variations on the pen case discussed above (Sytsma, 2021), the e-mail case tested below (Sytsma, 2021, ms-b; Sytsma and Schwenkler, ms), the machine case (see Hitchcock and Knobe 2009; Sytsma, forthcoming), and the motion detector case (see Kominsky et al., 2015; Sytsma, 2021). Further, not only have responses for causal attributions and responsibility attributions been found to be statistically indistinguishable when presenting the attributions between-subjects (Sytsma and Livengood, 2021; Sytsma, 2021, forthcoming, ms-a), but also when presenting them within-subjects, either on alternating pages (Schwenkler and Sytsma, ms) or together on the same page (Sytsma, forthcoming, ms-b). If the norm effect is due to pragmatic factors leading participants to interpret the causal queries as intending to elicit a normative judgment rather than the dominant descriptive use, then the effect should be notably diminished when participants are also given a normative attribution: pragmatic considerations should now promote interpreting the two attributions as intending to elicit different judgments. However, that is not what we find, suggesting that the norm effect is a general effect.

2 Causal judgments

The second point of disagreement that requires clarification concerns the scope of the "causal judgments" to be explained. As noted above, key examples of the norm effect in the literature have employed questions using the lemma "cause," prominently including the statements tested by Knobe and Fraser (2008), which were of the form "X caused Y."[2] A central question, then, is whether the main accounts of the norm effect in the literature are principally aiming to explain the impact of norms on causal attributions or hold that this is part of a broader phenomenon that calls for explanation.

Danks et al. (2014, p. 255) interpret a number of authors involved in the debate as making a broad claim, and perhaps as being committed to what they term the *Ubiquity Thesis*: "Normative considerations (broadly construed) influence causal cognition (broadly construed) and are perhaps even constitutive of various cognitive processes involved in aspects of causal cognition." Here, "causal cognition (broadly construed)" is taken to include both causal learning and causal reasoning, with causal perception and causal inference being counted as part of the former. What ties all of these processes together—what appending the adjective "causal" is meant to signify—and to what extent each of these processes warrant that adjective are complicated issues that Danks et al. do not engage with. Nonetheless, they contend that (at least some subset of) researchers in the debate are committed to the Ubiquity Thesis, and they present evidence that the norm effect isn't found for certain "causal" inferences.

Textual support for researchers being committed to the Ubiquity Thesis is minimal, however, with Danks et al. offering just a few quotes that concern "causal judgments" or "causal intuitions." These phrases could themselves be interpreted either broadly or narrowly, depending on how one understands the intent of "causal." More narrowly, "causal" can be understood first and foremost as reflecting the ordinary use of the lemma "cause." In fact, while Sytsma et al. (2012) are cited as an example of the broad claim, we only ever meant to be making a narrow claim: we focus on "the use of causal language" (p. 814)—on how likely people are to "say that an agent ... caused an outcome" (p. 815). And this is made clearer still in subsequent work where we explicitly state that we are concerned with causal attributions (e.g., Livengood et al., 2017; Sytsma et al., 2019; Livengood and Sytsma, 2020).

While focusing on the narrower claim about the ordinary use of the lemma "cause" might be taken to limit the interest of the norm effect, as Danks et al. in fact suggest, there are good reasons for this narrow focus. First, the primary aim of the responsibility account is to explain the effect shown in studies like those described above for the pen case, and such studies have overwhelmingly tested causal attributions. Second, we take it to be standard in philosophical discussions to assume that the ordinary concept of causation is *at least* expressed by the dominant attributional use of the lemma "cause." For example, Paul and Hall (2003, p. 2) focus on "our folk-theoretical notion of 'cause'," while Skow (2019) writes that "the most fundamental causal locution is 'X caused Y to Z by Ving'" (p. 18), although he notes that the "by Ving" is grammatically optional (p. 138). As such, if our account of the norm effect is correct—if we are correct that the ordinary concept of causation expressed by the dominant attributional use of "cause" is a normative concept—then this has notable implications for the philosophical discussions. Further, it would raise concerns about the sense in which "causal cognition (broadly construed)" is best considered *causal* if much of what is included diverges from the ordinary use of the root term.

It is unclear whether any of the participants in the present debate are committed to the Ubiquity Thesis, but this is itself problematic: it is unclear whether the Ubiquity Thesis applies because authors have often been unclear on what they take the scope of the norm effect to be. Further, even if the accounts at issue fall short of the broad claim given by the Ubiquity Thesis, there are nonetheless differences in how broad different researchers take the norm effect to be, and this corresponds with substantive differences in the types of explanations that have been offered.

The responsibility account is a narrow account in this regard, focusing on causal attributions and offering a linguistic/conceptual explanation of the phenomenon. Our account does not rule out that a similar effect might be found for other judgments, but neither does it make any specific predictions about them: it allows (of course) that the dominant use of some terms is descriptive, while the dominant use of others is normative. That said, we do expect that the range of terms typically used in a normative way might be surprising to many philosophers. This is in accord with the underlying motivation for our responsibility account, as laid out in Sytsma (2021): human cognition is generally quite attuned to recognizing applicable norms, detecting and responding to violations, and navigating factors that might exacerbate or mitigate those violations.

In contrast, the pragmatic, bias, and counterfactual accounts are broad accounts with regard to the judgments at issue for the norm effect. First, as seen above, the pragmatic account holds that the studies on the norm effect induce participants to interpret the queries as intending to ask a normative rather than a descriptive question. We would expect the same pragmatic pressures to hold for other terms that plausibly express causality (as Samland and Waldmann understand it). Second, the bias and counterfactual accounts both hold that the ordinary concept of causation is normative but that an underlying mechanism leads it to be applied in a normative way, producing the norm effect. While they differ with regard to the underlying mechanism that they posit, in each case the mechanism would be expected to reveal itself across a wider range of judgments than just those involving "cause."

The bias account contends that the norm effect comes about because the differential desire to blame (or praise) one of the agents leads people to exaggerate that agent's contribution to bringing about the outcome, pulling their causal judgments concerning that agent toward their blame (or praise) judgments. In other words, Alicke and colleagues hold that the desire to blame (or praise) biases the application of the descriptive concept of causation, generating judgments that are sensitive to normative considerations. As Rose (2017, p. 1327) puts it, the norm effect reflects "an *error*, rooted in a motivational bias to blame those who engage in harmful or offensive actions." Counterfactual accounts point to a different cognitive mechanism to explain the norm effect. Focusing on the account put forward by Hitchcock and Knobe (2009), they hold that norms impact those counterfactuals which people find relevant, and hence which counterfactuals they are most likely to consider. They then contend that the process by which people arrive at causal judgments works through the counterfactuals that they consider and, hence, that norms impact causal judgments only indirectly.

While the recent debate has in large part centered on judgments about statements using the lemma "cause," the explanations offered by the pragmatic, bias, and counterfactual accounts are not specific to such judgments: the mechanisms underpinning these explanations should reveal themselves in a larger class of judgments, presumably including judgments about other phrases that might be taken to express a descriptive causality relation (e.g., "created," "induced," "led to," "linked to," "because of"), and perhaps also counterfactual constructions (e.g., "if Professor Smith had not taken a pen, the problem would not have occurred"), statements involving lexical causatives (e.g., "Billy *deleted* the e-mails"), or causal inferences. There is currently a paucity of evidence suggesting that the norm effect consistently occurs across the range of judgments these views might predict, however, and some evidence that it does not. This includes the corpus evidence noted above (Sytsma et al., 2019), mixed results for "because" statements (see Footnote 2), evidence in this volume concerning causatives (Schwenkler and Sievers, 2022), and studies on causal inference (Danks et al., 2014).

The bias and counterfactual accounts should be expected to make predictions about a broader range of judgments because they explain the norm effect in terms of an underlying mechanism that isn't specific to judgments involving the lemma "cause." Theses mechanisms generate a number of further predictions that have not been borne out by the present data. First, like the pragmatic account, the bias and counterfactual accounts have difficulty explaining the close correspondence between judgments about causal attributions and judgments about responsibility attributions noted in the previous section (Sytsma, 2021). While the bias account would predict *some* correspondence between these judgments, to explain the extremely close correspondence found across a range of studies would require positing an implausibly strong bias. The basic worry for counterfactual accounts is a bit different: these accounts would seem to hold that there are two different mechanisms at play—the sensitivity of causal judgments to normative considerations being explained *indirectly* via the counterfactuals we consider while the sensitivity of responsibility judgments to normative considerations is explained *directly* in terms of responsibility being a normative concept—but it is implausible that two different mechanisms would produce statistically indistinguishable effects across a range of cases.

Second, the general mechanism posited by the bias account rests on people's "desire to praise or denigrate those whose actions we applaud or deride" (Alicke et al., 2011, p. 670). Such desires should be aroused not just by features of agents that are relevant to appropriately assessing their responsibility for an outcome, however, but also by "peripheral features of the event such as the actor's or victim's race or character" (p. 674). While information pertinent to assessing an agent's general character does have an impact on causal attributions, recent studies indicate that this effect is not driven by the desire to denigrate, but by an inference to the agent's knowledge and desires in performing the action, such that when the agent's knowledge and desires are made clear, peripheral features of the agent no longer show an effect (Sytsma, ms-c).

Third, the general mechanism posited by counterfactual accounts hinges on the overall normality of the actions described (as discussed further in the next section), but a pair of recent papers find that causal attributions sometimes diverge from what would be predicted on the basis of norms alone. First, Sytsma and Livengood (2021) argue that sometimes acting in accord with the relevant norms renders the actor responsible for a negative outcome that results. We suggest that the switch version of the trolley problem is one such case: while popular sentiment holds that the agent ought to flip the switch, saving five innocents at the expense of one, it also seems that in doing so the agent shares in the responsibility for the one person's death since that person was in no danger prior to the agent's intervention. What we find is that causal judgments for this case are similar to both people's normative judgments and their responsibility judgments, with ratings for each being higher when the agent flips the switch than when the agent refrains. This is in line with the responsibility account, but runs counter to counterfactual accounts, which would expect an *inverse* relationship between normative judgments and causal judgments. Second, according to counterfactual accounts, the valence of the outcome should not matter for causal judgments—just the normality of the actions. However, Schwenkler and Sytsma (ms) have found that the norm effect is also reversed when the norm-conforming agent knowingly acts to bring about a good outcome, while the norm-violating agent acts for malicious reasons.

3 Norms

The third point of disagreement that requires clarification concerns the scope of the norms at issue for the norm effect. The prototypical examples from the literature, such as the pen case, involve agents violating explicit rules, such as when Professor Smith takes a pen in violation of department policy. This is an example of a *proscriptive norm*: a norm specifying what ought not to be done. The compliment of proscriptive norms are *prescriptive norms*: norms that specify what ought to be done. Together these can be referred to as *injunctive norms*.[3]

Injunctive norms are in line with standard discussions of normativity in philosophy and psychology, which have generally focused on our ability to recognize and enforce *oughts*. For instance, Darwall (2001) opens his *Routledge Encyclopedia of Philosophy* entry on "Normativity" by stating the issue in just this way, writing that "normative judgments concern oughts: what one ought to do, desire, believe, infer, conclude, think, feel and so on." The implicit or explicit rules corresponding with such oughts are then standardly referred to as "norms." As Kelly and Setman (2020) summarize in their *Stanford Encyclopedia of Philosophy* entry on "The Psychology of Normative Cognition":

> Norms are the social rules that mark out what is appropriate, allowed, required, or forbidden in different situations for various community members. These rules are informal in the sense that although they are sometimes represented in formal laws, such as the rule governing which side of the road to drive on, they need not be explicitly codified to effectively influence behavior.

One thing to note here is that the norms at issue are not restricted to those oughts that we are likely to classify as distinctively moral. Although debate rages concerning how to classify norms (see O'Neill, 2017), including how to distinguish between moral and non-moral norms, the key point for present purposes is that while normativity covers moral norms, it is not exhausted by them. And similarly for injunctive norms.

The pragmatic, bias, and responsibility accounts all operate on this standard understanding of norms where they're tied to oughts. As suggested by Danks et al.'s focus on "normative considerations (broadly construed)" in their statement of the Ubiquity Thesis discussed above, however, some participants in the debate have embraced a more expansive notion of norms. Specifically, counterfactual accounts operate on a broad conception of normality. To illustrate, Hitchcock and Knobe (2009) distinguish between two meanings for the term "norm." The first corresponds with injunctive norms: these are "norms that actually tell us what ought to happen under certain circumstances" and include "purely moral norms, where violating the norm would be intrinsically wrong" in addition to more general norms including legal norms and "norms arising from policies adopted by social institutions," as well as norms of proper functioning that "apply to artifacts and biological organisms (and their components)" (pp. 597–8). Hitchcock and Knobe's second meaning for "norm" diverges from the sense laid out above, however, instead concerning what is typical or atypical. They refer to these as *statistical norms* and write that "these norms simply capture information about the relative frequencies of certain events" (p. 597).

As such, statistical norms are descriptive, while injunctive norms are normative (in the standard sense).

Counterfactual accounts like that given by Hitchcock and Knobe hold that the type of norm doesn't matter—that causal judgments are sensitive to both violations of injunctive norms and violations of statistical norms. In contrast, when I say that according to our responsibility account the dominant use of causal attributions employs a *normative* concept, this is specific to injunctive norms: we hold that causal attributions are *directly* sensitive to injunctive norms. That said, our account predicts that statistical norms will sometimes also impact causal attributions, although we hold that they do so indirectly, with statistical norms sometimes impacting our judgments about injunctive norms (Sytsma et al., 2012; Livengood et al., 2017).

We expect that the impact of statistical norms on causal attributions will work somewhat differently for attributions involving agents and attributions involving non-agents (see Sytsma, 2021). Focusing on agents, we have presented a body of evidence indicating that violations of statistical norms do not impact causal attributions in the same way that violations of injunctive norms do for scenarios like the Pen Case (Sytsma et al., 2012; Livengood et al., 2017; Sytsma, 2021). Instead, we've shown a striking pattern of findings that run counter to the predictions of counterfactual accounts but were predicted on the basis of our responsibility account. First, we found that causal attributions are insensitive to one type of statistical norm—*population-level statistical norms*, which concern what is typical or atypical for members of a relevant population to which the agent belongs. Second, we found that causal attributions are sensitive to another type of statistical norm—*agent-level statistical norms*, which concern what is typical or atypical for the agent herself—but only when the norm-violating agent knows about the likely outcome of her action; and, in such cases we found that the "norm effect" runs in the opposite direction to that observed for violations of injunctive norms, with causal ratings being higher when the agent acts typically than when she acts atypically.

Our predictions about these effects were based on thinking about responsibility judgments. Reflecting on the responsibility attributions that we would make, we expected that violations of population-level statistical norms would have little to no impact on causal attributions for scenarios like the pen case. We reasoned that excuses like "everyone was doing it" aren't generally taken to be good excuses and, as such, would not mitigate an agent's responsibility for a bad outcome. By contrast, for agent-level statistical norms we expected that causal ratings would be higher when the action is typical of the agent *and* when she knows that she is doing something she shouldn't and that a bad outcome might result. We reasoned that when the agent can be expected to know that a bad outcome might result from her behavior, people will be more likely to see her as being responsible for the outcome when she typically acts in this reckless way. Here it would just seem to be a matter of time before the agent brings about the outcome, blocking consideration of potential mitigating factors. While these predictions were based on the responsibility judgments that we would make, I've recently shown that the same complex pattern of effects found for causal attributions is also found for responsibility attributions in a broader sample (Sytsma, 2021). In fact, as noted above, ratings for the two types of attributions were not statistically significantly distinguishable.

Table 7.1 Summary of the scope of the norm effect for each view along the dimensions of context, judgments, and norms.

	Context	Judgments	Norms
Pragmatic	Narrow	Broad	Narrow
Responsibility	Broad	Narrow	Narrow
Bias	Broad	Broad	Narrow
Counterfactual	Broad	Broad	Broad

Summing up, while each of the main accounts on offer in the recent literature propose to explain the norm effect, they diverge with regard to how broad they expect this phenomenon to be, and do so along at least three dimensions—diverging with regard to the contexts that will elicit the effect, the judgments involved in the effect, and the norms that will give rise to it. These differences are summarized in Table 7.1. However, as sketched above, these assumptions about the extent of the norm effect are not all equally supported by the present data, and the details of the accounts shaping their treatment of the scope of the effect give rise to a number of further predictions that have not been borne out by subsequent studies. Perhaps most notably, while the close correspondence between judgments about causal attributions and responsibility attributions found in recent studies is directly predicted by our responsibility account, it is tough to convincingly reconcile with the competing accounts in the literature. To conclude this chapter, I expand on these findings, presenting the results of two new studies that further demonstrate that people tend to treat causal attributions and normative attributions as going together.

4 Rank ordering compound statements

In this section I extend the previous findings showing a close correspondence between judgments about causal attributions and responsibility attributions, presenting the results of two preregistered studies (osf.io/fpwq3/) using a novel design: rather than asking participants about separate attributions, I asked them to rank order compound statements involving both a causal attribution and a normative attribution—either responsibility (Study 1a) or blame (Study 1b).

4.1 Method

Each participant read the following vignette in which two agents perform actions that are symmetric, outside of one violating an injunctive norm (Billy) while the other does not (Suzy), and in so doing jointly bringing about a bad outcome:

> Billy and Suzy work for a company that has a central computer.
>
> To make sure that one person is always available to answer incoming phone calls, the company issued the following official policy: Billy is the only one permitted to

log into the central computer in the afternoons, whereas Suzy is the only one permitted to log into the central computer in the mornings. Billy is never permitted to log into the central computer in the morning.

Unfortunately, a problem has recently developed with the computer system: if two people log into the computer in the morning, some important work e-mails will be immediately deleted.

This morning, Billy and Suzy both log into the central computer at the same time. Immediately, some important work e-mails are deleted.[4]

After reading the vignette, participants were given two rank-ordering questions in random order, one about Billy and one about Suzy, followed by a comprehension check ("How many people need to log into the central computer in the morning for the e-mails to be deleted?" with options of 0, 1, 2, 3, and 4 or more). All questions were presented on the same page.

The rank-ordering questions each included four compound statements involving a causal attribution and a normative attribution, with the order of the two attributions being varied in the statements. To illustrate, the first ordering of the question about Billy in Study 1a read as follows (letters are added for convenience and were not presented to participants):

Please rank the following four claims about Billy in order of how much you agree with them, with (1) being the claim you most strongly agree with and (4) being the claim you most strongly disagree with:

[A] Billy did **not** cause the e-mails to be deleted *and* Billy is **not** responsible for the e-mails being deleted.
[B] Billy did **not** cause the e-mails to be deleted *but* Billy is responsible for the e-mails being deleted.
[C] Billy caused the e-mails to be deleted *but* Billy is **not** responsible for the e-mails being deleted.
[D] Billy caused the e-mails to be deleted *and* Billy is responsible for the e-mails being deleted.

In the second ordering, the normative attributions preceded the causal attributions. For example, the second ordering for [D] would now read: "Billy is responsible for the e-mails being deleted *and* Billy caused the e-mails to be deleted." The questions about Suzy were identical, except for "Suzy" replacing each instance of "Billy." Similarly, the questions in Study 1b were identical to those in Study 1a, except for "to blame" replacing each instance of "responsible." For each question, the order of the four options was randomized.

Participants for each study were recruited through advertising for a free personality test on Google with the ads being displayed in North America.[5] Prior to the test questions, participants answered basic demographic questions. After the test questions they took a ten-item Big Five personality inventory. Participants were restricted to native English speakers, sixteen years of age or older, who indicated that they had not previously taken the survey, and who completed the three test questions. Results were collected from 200 participants who met the restrictions and passed the comprehension check (100 per study and 50 per condition).[6] These participants were 73.0 percent women (three non-binary) with an average age of 46.7 years and ranging in age from sixteen to eighty.

4.2 Predictions

The responsibility account predicts that there will still be a pronounced norm effect for the causal attributions in these studies, despite participants now being able to clearly register their normative judgments. As such, I predict that for the norm-violating agent, Billy, participants will tend to rank one of the two statements affirming causation ([C], [D]) in first place and to rank one of the two statements denying causation ([A], [B]) in last place; and I predict that the opposite pattern will be found for the norm-conforming agent, Suzy. In addition, the responsibility account predicts that participants will treat the causal attributions and the normative attributions similarly, showing a stronger preference/dispreference for the "and" statements compared to the "but" statements. More specifically, I predict that for Billy, participants will tend to show the strongest preference for [D] and the strongest dispreference for [A], while for Suzy they will tend to show the strongest preference for [A] and the strongest dispreference for [D].

The pragmatic account makes contrasting predictions. According to this view, when asking about compound attributions we would expect pragmatic considerations to lead participants to read "caused" and "responsible"/"blame" in contrasting senses since this would make the claims more informative, whereas reading them in the same sense would render them redundant. As such, advocates of the pragmatic account should expect the norm effect for causal attributions to largely disappear, with participants interpreting "caused" in the (supposedly) dominant descriptive sense. While Samland and Waldmann (2016, p. 165) claim that "the causal relations are trivial" for cases like this, as noted above, it is in fact unclear whether we would expect people to hold that *both* agents caused the outcome or that *neither* agent caused the outcome on a purely descriptive reading. If the former, then their pragmatic account would predict that people will show the strongest preference for [D] for Billy and the strongest preference for [C] for Suzy, judging that while both caused the outcome, Billy but not Suzy is responsible for (to blame for) the outcome. If the latter, then they would predict that people will show the strongest preference for [B] for Billy and the strongest preference for [A] for Suzy, judging that while neither caused the outcome, Billy but not Suzy is responsible for (to blame for) the outcome.

4.3 Results

Rank orderings are shown in Figure 7.1. To analyze the results, I used the **pmr** package in R (Lee and Yu, 2013). I began by comparing the marginal frequencies between Studies 1a and 1b for each of the two rank-ordering questions. That is, for each of the two agents, I compared the number of participants ranking each statement ([A]–[D])

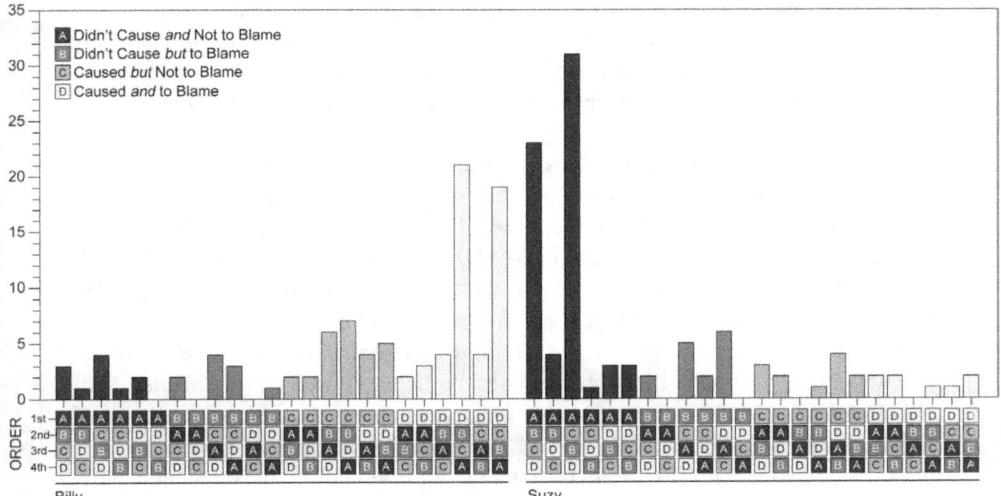

Figure 7.1 Histograms for each rank ordering for the questions in Studies 1a (top) and 1b (bottom).

in each position (1st–4th) between the two studies. The marginal frequencies were not significantly different for either Billy ($\chi^2=19.58$, $df=15$, $p=.19$) or Suzy ($\chi^2=14.17$, $df=15$, $p=.51$). In other words, the results were comparable whether combining causal attributions with responsibility attributions or with blame attributions. As such, I will collapse the two studies in the subsequent analysis. The same procedure was used to check for order effects, comparing marginal frequencies for each agent between the condition where the causal attribution was given first in each compound statement and the condition where it was given second. A significant order effect was found for the rankings for both Billy ($\chi^2=44.76$, $df=15$, $p<.001$) and Suzy ($\chi^2=25.79$, $df=15$, $p=.040$). As such, differences between the two orderings will be noted below. In brief, what we find is that the ordering impacted the relative preference for statements [**B**] and [**C**], but not [**A**] and [**D**].

To test whether the norm effect previously found for variations on the e-mail case using Likert items replicates for the rank ordering questions, I began by comparing the marginal frequencies between the rank orderings for the two agents. There was a significant difference ($\chi^2=368.02$ $df=15$, $p<.001$). More importantly, a significant majority of participants ranked one of the two items stating that the norm-violating agent, Billy, caused the outcome ([**C**], [**D**]) in first place (82.5%; $\chi^2=83.20$, $df=1$, $p<.001$) and a significant majority ranked one of the two items denying that Billy caused the outcome ([**A**], [**B**]) in last place (72%; $\chi^2=37.84$, $df=1$, $p<.001$). And the opposite was found for the norm-conforming agent, Suzy: a significant majority of participants ranked one of the two items denying that Suzy caused the outcome in first place (77.5%; $\chi^2=59.40$, $df=1$, $p<.001$) and a significant majority of participants ranked one of the two items affirming that Suzy caused the outcome in last place (78.5%; $\chi^2=63.84$, $df=1$, $p<.001$).[7] Thus, despite having options to register that Billy was responsible (to blame) for the outcome and that Suzy was not responsible (to blame) for the outcome, the norm effect was still in clear evidence, with participants preferring to say that Billy caused the outcome and participants preferring to say that Suzy did not cause the outcome. This runs strongly counter to what we would expect on the basis of the pragmatic account.

Looking more closely at the rankings for Billy, the mean ranks again suggest a clear preference for [D] and dispreference for [A], while [C] and [B] are similar: [A] 3.38, [B] 2.44, [C] 2.42, [D] 1.76.[8] This was confirmed by looking at the pairwise frequencies. A significant majority or participants ranked [D] *higher* than [A] (82%; χ^2=80.64, df=1, p<.001), *higher* than [B] (72%; χ^2=37.84, df=1, p<.001), and *higher* than [C] (70%; χ^2=31.20, df=1, p<.001). Similarly, a significant majority of participants ranked [A] *lower* than [B] (78%; χ^2=61.60, df=1, p<.001) and *lower* than [C] (77.5%; χ^2=59.40, df=1, p<.001). Finally, a very slight majority of participants ranked [C] *higher* than [B] (50.5%; χ^2=.005, df=1, p=.94). Further, a significant majority of participants ranked [D] first (62.5%; χ^2=12.00, df=1, p<.001) and a significant majority ranked [A] last (62%; χ^2=11.04, df=1, p<.001). Thus, the rankings for Billy confirm the prediction of the responsibility account.

The rankings for Billy also confirm the prediction of the pragmatic account, *on the assumption* that for a purely descriptive reading of "caused" participants will judge that *both* agents caused the outcome. As such, the pragmatic account would then make a different prediction from the responsibility account for Suzy (i.e., the pragmatic account would predict that participants will show the strongest preference for [C] and the strongest dispreference for [B]). If the pragmatic account instead predicted that participants would judge that *neither* agent caused the outcome, then the results for Billy run strongly counter to the prediction for this type of view: only a small minority ranked [B] first (9.5%; χ^2=129.6, df=1, p<.001) and only a small minority ranked [C] last (12.5%; χ^2=111, df=1, p<.001).

To further test for the preferred ordering for Billy, I used a weighted distance-based model with Spearman's footrule as the distance measure (Lee and Yu, 2012). The modal ranking given is [D] < [B] < [C] < [A], with parameter estimates of 0.46, 0.59, 0.13, and 0.55 (loglikelihood=532.17). The model was a good fit for the data as indicated by the sum of squares Pearson residuals (χ^2=91.34, df=24, p<.001). The same modal ranking was given for the Luce model and distance-based model, although the φ-component model reversed the order of [B] and [C].[9] As noted above, the relative order of preference for these two statements differed between the orderings: when the causal attribution was first in the statements, all four models showed a modal ranking of [D] < [C] < [B] < [A], with participants showing a relative preference for the "but" statement affirming the causal attribution ([C]) over the "but" statement denying the causal attribution ([B]); but when the normative attribution was first, all four models showed a modal ranking where these were reversed ([D] > [B] > [C] > [A]). Overall, the rankings suggest that participants did not have a strong preference between the "but" items, which is in keeping with the strong preference shown for affirming both attributions and the strong dispreference shown for denying both attributions.

Turning to the question about the norm-conforming agent, Suzy, we find a quite different pattern of results, with the mean ranks suggesting the opposite order of preference from that seen for Billy: [A] 1.58, [B] 2.62, [C] 2.39, [D] 3.42.[10] This was again confirmed by looking at the pairwise frequencies. A significant majority or participants ranked [A] *higher* than [B] (84%; χ^2=91.12, df=1, p<.001), *higher* than [C] (74%; χ^2=45.12, df=1, p<.001), and *higher* than [D] (84.5%; χ^2=93.84, df=1, p<.001). Similarly, a significant majority of participants ranked [D] *lower* than [B] (78%; χ^2=61.60, df=1, p<.001) and *lower* than [C] (79.5%; χ^2=68.44, df=1, p<.001). Finally, a slight majority of participants ranked [C] *higher* than [B] (55.5%; χ^2=2.20, df=1, p=.14, two-tailed). Further, a significant majority of participants ranked [A] first (67.5%; χ^2=23.80, df=1, p<.001) and a significant majority ranked [D] last (67%; χ^2=22.45, df=1, p<.001). Thus, the rankings for Suzy confirm the prediction of the responsibility account.

The rankings for Suzy also confirm the prediction of the pragmatic account, *on the assumption* that for a purely descriptive reading of "caused" participants will judge that *neither* agent caused the outcome. This assumption, however, would then generate the opposite prediction to the responsibility account for Billy, which runs counter to the findings detailed above. If the pragmatic account instead predicts that participants will judge that *both* agents caused the outcome, then the results for Suzy run strongly counter to the prediction of this type of view: only a small minority ranked [C] first (13%; χ^2=108.04, df=1, p<.001) and only a small minority ranked [B] last (17%; χ^2=85.80, df=1, p<.001). In other words, whichever prediction the pragmatic account makes about the supposedly "trivial" descriptive relations, the rankings for one of the two agents will run strongly counter to the prediction.

To further test for the preferred ordering for Suzy, I again used a weighted distance-based model with Spearman's footrule as the distance measure. The modal ranking given corresponds with the mean rank order—[A] > [C] > [B] > [D]—with parameter estimates of 0.58, 0.25, 0.51, and 0.63 (loglikelihood=504.30). The model was a good fit for the data as indicated by the sum of squares Pearson residuals (χ^2=91.34, df=24, p<.001). The same modal ranking was given for the Luce model, distance-based model, φ-component model. As with the question about Billy, however, the relative order of preference for [B] and [C] differed between the orderings: when the causal attribution was given first in the statements, all four models showed a modal ranking of [A] > [B] > [C] > [D]; but when the normative attribution was instead given first, all four models showed a modal ranking where these were reversed ([A] > [C] > [B] > [D]).

4.4 Discussion

As noted in the previous sections, a key piece of evidence in favor of the responsibility account, and against competing accounts, is the close correspondence between causal attributions and responsibility attributions. Some of these studies involve judgments solicited between-subjects, but some use a within-subjects design. While each is problematic for competing accounts, the latter is especially problematic for the pragmatic account. The close correspondence between causal attributions and responsibility attributions in the between-subjects studies *might* be explained in terms of pragmatic factors leading people to rate causal attributions similarly to how they would rate responsibility attributions, although the degree of correspondence is an issue for this type of view. When asking about the attributions together, however, we would expect the proposed pragmatic effect to be notably mitigated. If, for instance, the close correspondence in between-subjects studies is due to people interpreting the causal attribution as really asking about responsibility or accountability for pragmatic reasons, then we would expect participants to give divergent responses when asked about both attributions together: this should tend to promote interpreting the causal attribution as being intended in the dominant descriptive sense, according to Samland and Waldmann's reasoning.

This reasoning is even more clear for the present studies. In the studies reported in this section, participants did not simply rate a causal attribution and a normative attribution at the same time, but assessed joint statements combining both types of attributions. That is, assessing the statements required assessing both attributions together. If it is the case that the dominant sense of one is purely descriptive, while the other is partly normative, then pragmatic considerations should *if anything* reinforce reading each in the dominant sense since this would be maximally informative. However, despite this, we saw that participants showed a marked preference for affirming both for the norm-violating agent and denying both for the norm-conforming agent. This provides strong evidence against the pragmatic view. It appears that the norm effect is a general effect, not a pragmatic effect.

That the close correspondence between causal attributions and normative attributions remains despite pragmatic pressures that would seem to promote interpreting them as making different claims is equally strong evidence in favor of the responsibility account: the most straightforward explanation is that there is a notable commonalty in how people understand these attributions, with the dominant use of each being partly normative. In contrast, to explain these new findings advocates of the bias account would need to contend that the motivational bias it posits is so strong that even when directly comparing the two types of attributions people fail to keep them separate, with their desire to blame still infecting their causal judgments. Likewise, to explain these new findings advocates of counterfactual accounts would need to contend that the effect of norms on the counterfactuals that people consider is so strong that it overrides the pragmatic pressures to consider the difference between the two types of attributions, which would seem to emphasize the descriptive symmetry between the two agents' actions.

5 Conclusion

At this point, it is beyond dispute that the norm effect occurs for causal judgments: a wealth of findings shows that information about norms impacts people's causal judgments. But the extent of this phenomenon and, relatedly, how best to explain it has been heavily contested. Despite this, I believe that answers to these questions are becoming clear. We are not merely dealing with a pragmatic effect or an effect that otherwise owes to a general underlying mechanism that leads us to apply a purely descriptive concept in a way that appears normative; we are simply dealing with the judgments that result from the correct application of a normative concept akin to responsibility or accountability. In the face of the present evidence, this is the both the simplest and the most charitable explanation, requiring neither the posit of further mechanisms or general mistakes. The explanation of the norm effect is simply that we ordinarily use the lemma "cause" in a normative way.

Acknowledgments

I would like to thank Pascale Willemsen and an anonymous reviewer for helpful comments on a previous draft of this chapter and Jonathan Livengood for suggestions in the early stages of this project.

Notes

1   Further distinctions can be drawn, although I'll focus on these three. Most notably, focusing on the form "X caused Y," in the Pen Case the Xs are agents and the Y is a bad outcome. Work has varied both of these factors, however. With regard to X, the effect has also been found for non-agents (e.g., Hitchcock and Knobe, 2009; Sytsma, forthcoming) and for statements involving an agent's action or decision (e.g., Hitchcock and Knobe, 2009; Livengood et al., 2017). With regard to Y, while the effect has been reported for good outcomes (e.g., Hitchcock and Knobe, 2009; Kominsky et al., 2015), it has also been shown that it can be reversed with ratings being higher for the norm-conforming agent than the norm-violating agent (Schwenkler and Sytsma, ms).
2   There are a few exceptions to this general rule, however, such as the use of "made" in a study of children's judgments about the pen case by Samland et al. (2016) and the use of "because" in the fourth study by Kominsky et al. (2015). See Livengood and Machery (2007) and Livengood et al. (2017) for evidence that "X caused Y" and "Y because X" statements at least sometimes come apart, generating different judgments.
3   Note that the expression "prescriptive norm" is often used in the literature to refer to what I here term injunctive norms, including both prescriptive *and* proscriptive norms.
4   The vignette is based on the computer case presented by Knobe and Fraser (2008) and discussed in Sytsma et al. (2012), and is similar to the variations tested by Reuter et al. (2014), Kominsky et al. (2015), and Livengood et al. (2017), showing the expected norm effect with Likert-scale ratings of causal attributions. Further variations have been tested by Icard et al. (2017), Sytsma (2021), Sytsma and Livengood (2021), and Schwenkler and Sytsma (ms), among others.
5   One notable benefit of using a "push strategy" like this one (i.e., recruiting participants who were not directly looking to participate in research) is that participants are more likely to be "experimentally naïve" and less likely to be motivated to provide the responses that they think the experimenters are looking for (Haug, 2018). Samples collected using the recruitment strategy employed here have been previously compared against samples collected with other methods in replication studies. The present strategy has been consistently found to generate a diverse sample in terms of geography, socio-economic status, religiosity, political orientation, age, and education. Studies using this strategy have been previously reported in publications including,

e.g., Livengood et al. (2010), Feltz and Cokely (2011), Sytsma and Machery (2012), Murray et al. (2013), Machery et al. (2015), Kim et al. (2016), Livengood and Rose (2016), Sytsma and Reuter (2017), Sytsma and Ozdemir (2019), Reuter and Sytsma (2020), Fischer and Sytsma (2021), Fischer et al. (2021).

6   53/253 (20.9 percent) of participants failed the check question.

7   Similar results held for the first ordering (caused first), with a significant majority ranking [C] or [D] in first place for Billy (82%; χ^2=39.69, df=1, p<.001), a significant majority ranking [A] or [B] in last place for Billy (74%; χ^2=22.09, df=1, p<.001), a significant majority ranking [A] or [B] in first place for Suzy (74%; χ^2=22.09, df=1, p<.001), and a significant majority ranking [C] or [D] in last place for Suzy (77%; χ^2=28.09, df=1, p<.001). Similarly for the second ordering (caused second), with a significant majority ranking [C] or [D] in first place for Billy (83%; χ^2=42.25, df=1, p<.001), a significant majority ranking [A] or [B] in last place for Billy (70%; χ^2=15.21, df=1, p<.001), a significant majority ranking [A] or [B] in first place for Suzy (81%; χ^2=37.21, df=1, p<.001), and a significant majority ranking [C] or [D] in last place for Suzy (80%; χ^2=34.81, df=1, p<.001).

8   Mean ranks are similar for the first ordering ([A] 3.27, [B] 2.66, [C] 2.40, [D] 1.67) and the second ordering ([A] 3.48, [B] 2.23, [C] 2.44, [D] 1.85), although the relative order of [B] and [C] is shifted.

9   A pilot study (N=70) using the same design as Study 1a, but with the check question given on a second page with additional questions, showed this alternative ordering for Billy ([D] > [C] > [B] > [A]) for the mean ranks ([A] 3.56, [B] 2.60, [C] 2.34, [D] 1.50) and all four models. It showed the reverse ordering for Suzy ([A] > [B] > [C] > [D]) for the mean ranks ([A] 1.71, [B] 2.41, [C] 2.56, [D] 3.31) and all four models. Outside of the ordering of [B] and [C] the results were quite similar to those reported here; in fact, the marginal frequencies were not significantly different between the pilot and Study 1a for either Billy (χ^2=17.83, df=15, p=.27) or Suzy (χ^2=22.12, df=15, p=.10).

10 Mean ranks are similar for the first ordering ([A] 1.63, [B] 2.54, [C] 2.52, [D] 3.30) and the second ordering ([A] 1.51, [B] 2.69, [C] 2.26, [D] 3.54).

References

Alicke, M. (1992). "Culpable causation." *Journal of Personality and Social Psychology* 63: 368–78.

Alicke, M. (2000). "Culpable Control and the Psychology of Blame." *Psychological Bulletin* 126(4): 556–74.

Alicke, M., D. Rose, and D. Bloom (2011). "Causation, Norm Violation and Culpable Control." *Journal of Philosophy* 108: 670–96.

Danks, D., D. Rose, and E. Machery (2014). "Demoralizing Causation." *Philosophical Studies* 171: 251–77.

Darwall, S. (2001). "Normativity." In *The Routledge Encyclopedia of Philosophy*. Abingdon: Taylor and Francis. https://www.rep.routledge.com/articles/thematic/normativity/v-1

Fischer, E., P. Engelhardt, and J. Sytsma (2021). "Inappropriate stereotypical inferences? An adversarial collaboration in experimental ordinary language philosophy." *Synthese* 198(11): 10127–68.

Fischer, E. and J. Sytsma (2021). "Zombie Intuitions." *Cognition* 215: 104807.

Feltz, A. and E. Cokely (2011). "Individual differences in theory-of-mind judgments: Order effects and side effects." *Philosophical Psychology* 24(3): 343–55.

Halpern, J. and C. Hitchcock (2015). "Graded Causation and Defaults." *British Journal for the Philosophy of Science 66*: 413–57.

Haug, Matthew (2018). "Fast, Cheap, and Unethical? The Interplay of Morality and Methodology in Crowdsourced Survey Research." *Review of Philosophy and Psychology* 9(2): 363–79

Hitchcock, C. and J. Knobe (2009). "Cause and Norm." *The Journal of Philosophy 106*: 587–612.

Icard, T., J. Kominsky, and J. Knobe (2017). "Normality and Actual Causal Strength." *Cognition 161*: 80–93.

Kelly, D. and S. Setman (2020). "The Psychology of Normative Cognition." In E. Zalta (ed.), *The Stanford Encyclopedia of Philosophy* (Fall 2020 Edition). https://plato.stanford.edu/archives/fall2020/entries/psychology-normative-cognition/

Kim, H., N. Poth, K. Reuter, and J. Sytsma (2016). "Where is your pain? A Cross-cultural Comparison of the Concept of Pain in Americans and South Koreans." *Studia Philosophica Estonica* 9(1): 136–69.

Knobe, J. and B. Fraser (2008). "Causal judgments and moral judgment: Two experiments." In W. Sinnott-Armstrong (ed.), *Moral Psychology, Volume 2: The Cognitive Science of Morality* (441–7). Cambridge, MA: MIT Press.

Kominsky, J. and J. Phillips (2019). "Immoral Professors and Malfunctioning Tools: Counterfactual Relevance Accounts Explain the Effect of Norm Violations on Causal Selection." *Cognitive Science* 43(11): e12792.

Kominsky, J., J. Phillips, T. Gerstenberg, D. Lagnado, and J. Knobe (2015). "Causal superseding." *Cognition 137*: 196–209.

Lee, P. and P. Yu (2013). "An R package for analyzing and modeling ranking data." *BMC Medical Research Methodology 13*: 65.

Livengood, J. and E. Machery (2007). "The folk probably don't think what you think they think: Experiments on causation by absence." *Midwest Studies in Philosophy 31*: 107–27.

Livengood, J. and D. Rose (2016). "Experimental Philosophy and Causal Attribution." In J. Sytsma and W. Buckwalter (eds.), *A Companion to Experimental Philosophy* (434–49). Oxford: Wiley Blackwell.

Livengood, J. and J. Sytsma (2020). "Actual causation and compositionality." *Philosophy of Science* 87(1): 43–69.

Livengood, J., J. Sytsma, and D. Rose (2017). "Following the FAD: Folk attributions and theories of actual causation." *Review of Philosophy and Psychology* 8(2): 274–94.

Livengood, J., J. Sytsma, A. Feltz, R. Scheines, and E. Machery (2010). "Philosophical Temperament." *Philosophical Psychology* 23(3): 313–30.

Machery, E., J. Sytsma, and M. Deutsch (2015). "Speaker's Reference and Cross-cultural Semantics." In A. Bianchi (ed.), *On Reference* (62–76). Oxford: Oxford University Press.

Murray, D., J. Sytsma, and J. Livengood (2013). "God Knows (But does God Believe?)" *Philosophical Studies* 166: 83–107.

O'Neill, E. (2017). "Kinds of Norms." *Philosophy Compass* 12(5): e12416.

Paul, L. A. and N. Hall (2003). *Causation: A User's Guide*. Oxford: Oxford University Press.

Reuter, K. and J. Sytsma (2020). "Unfelt Pain." *Synthese 197*: 1777–801.

Reuter, K., L. Kirfel, R. van Riel, and L. Barlassina (2014). "The good, the bad, and the timely: how temporal order and moral judgment influence causal selection." *Frontiers in Psychology 5*: 1336.

Rose, D. (2017). "Folk Intuitions of Actual Causation: A Two-pronged Debunking Explanation." *Philosophical Studies* 174(5): 1323–61.

Samland, J. and M.R. Waldmann (2016). "How prescriptive norms influence causal inferences." *Cognition 156*: 164–76.

Samland, J., M. Josephs, M.R. Waldmann, and H. Rakoczy (2016). "The Role of Prescriptive Norms and Knowledge in Children's and Adults' Causal Selection." *Journal of Experimental Psychology: General 145*(2): 125–30.

Schwenkler, J. and E.T. Sievers (2022). "Cause, 'Cause', and Norm." To appear in P. Willemsen and A. Wiegmann (eds.), *Advances in Experimental Philosophy of Causation*, London: Bloomsbury Academic.

Schwenkler, J. and J. Sytsma (ms). "Reversing the Norm Effect on Causal Attributions." http://philsci-archive.pitt.edu/18220/

Skow, B. (2019). *Causation, Explanation, and the Metaphysics of Aspect*. Oxford: Oxford University Press.

Sytsma, J. (2021). "Causation, Responsibility, and Typicality." *Review of Philosophy and Psychology* 12: 699–719.

Sytsma, J. (forthcoming). "Crossed Wires: Blaming Artifacts for Bad Outcomes." *The Journal of Philosophy*.

Sytsma, J. (ms-a). "Structure and Norms: Investigating the Pattern of Effects for Causal Attributions." http://philsci-archive.pitt.edu/16626/

Sytsma, J. (ms-b). "Resituating the Influence of Relevant Alternative on Attributions." http://philsci-archive.pitt.edu/16957/

Sytsma, J. (ms-c). "The Character of Causation: Investigating the Impact of Character, Knowledge, and Desire on Causal Attributions." http://philsci-archive.pitt.edu/16739/

Sytsma, J. and J. Livengood (2021). "Causal Attributions and the Trolley Problem." *Philosophical Psychology* 34(8): 1167–91.

Sytsma, J. and E. Machery (2012). "On the Relevance of Folk Intuitions: A Reply to Talbot." *Consciousness and Cognition* 21: 654–60.

Sytsma, J. and E. Ozdemir (2019). "No Problem: Evidence that the Concept of Phenomenal Consciousness is Not Widespread." *Journal of Consciousness Studies* 26(9–10): 241–56.

Sytsma, J. and K. Reuter (2017). "Experimental Philosophy of Pain." *Journal of Indian Council of Philosophical Research* 34(3): 611–28.

Sytsma, J., J. Livengood, and D. Rose (2012). "Two types of typicality: Rethinking the role of statistical typicality in ordinary causal attributions." *Studies in History and Philosophy of Biological and Biomedical Sciences* 43: 814–20.

Sytsma, J., R. Bluhm, P. Willemsen, and K. Reuter (2019). "Causal Attributions and Corpus Analysis." In E. Fischer and M. Curtis (eds.), *Methodological Advances in Experimental Philosophy*, London: Bloomsbury Academic.

8

Causation in the Law and Experimental Philosophy[1]

Karolina Prochownik

1 Introduction

Experimental philosophers conduct empirical research on philosophical questions. Often, they are interested in intuitions and cognitive mechanisms that govern the application of philosophically relevant concepts of ordinary people and expert philosophers. The experimental philosophy research program has recently been extended to studying intuitions and psychological mechanisms underpinning the application of legally relevant concepts of laypeople and legal experts. The new field of "experimental jurisprudence" or "experimental philosophy of law" (below also "X-Phi of Law") has been focused on examining intuitions and psychological mechanisms underpinning lay and legal expert concepts such as intentionality, causation, reasonableness, consent, ownership, contracts (e.g., Kneer and Bourgeois-Gironde, 2017; Vilares et al., 2017; Macleod, 2019; Tobia, 2018; Sommers, 2020; Nancekivell et al., 2016; Wilkinson-Ryan, 2012). Besides, some researchers have been interested in whether folk and legal experts' intuitions overlap and whether they are consistent with the technical concepts of the law (e.g., Kneer and Bourgeois-Gironde, 2017; Prochownik et al., 2020).[2]

However, the theoretical justification of applying the experimental philosophy research methods to jurisprudence is still a matter of question.[3] One potential rationale is that legal theoreticians and practitioners sometimes argue in favor of particular legal concepts based on their assumed compatibility with their folk counterparts.[4] For instance, legal experts in criminal and tort law often appeal to the common sense of justice (Robinson and Darley, 1995, p. xv) or the ordinary meaning of causation (e.g., Macleod, 2019). Since legal professionals' judgments about folk concepts (such as justice or causation) are *empirical* (i.e., they concern facts about the actual content of the laypeople's concepts), it may be argued that their plausibility may be tested by rigorous *empirical* research on laypeople's intuitions (see also Macleod, 2019).[5] In this chapter, I take a moderate position that X-Phi of Law research is especially justified in these cases when legal theoreticians and practitioners (explicitly or implicitly) assume or aim at the congruence of particular legal concepts with their folk counterparts.[6]

In this respect, causation seems particularly susceptible to the X-Phi of Law research. Legal theoreticians and practitioners often believe that the legal concept of causation is or should be somewhat modeled on its folk counterpart. For instance, courts in the common law systems "have consistently stated that causation is simply a matter of common sense" (Herring, 2014, p. 86) and that "it is the plain man's notions of causation (and not the philosopher's or the scientist's) with which the law is concerned" (Hart and Honoré, 1985, p. 1). It is also quite common to support particular legal tests or theories of causation by appealing to their continuity with the folk understanding of causal relationships in the world. For instance, in the common law jurisprudence, Hart and Honoré argued that the folk causal notions, in which the legal terminology and thinking are rooted, relies on two contrasts: "between what is abnormal and what is normal in relation to any given thing or subject-matter, and between a free deliberate human action and all other conditions" (p. 33). They also criticized the "but for" test of causation in the law because it is not a core of ordinary causal thinking.[7]

A similar type of reasoning applies to legal theory in the continental law system. For instance, in an influential work of the Polish criminal law doctrine, Giezek (1994, p. 45, trans. K.P.) argued in favor of the so-called "theory of the condition corresponding to empirically proven regularity" (*teoria warunku odpowiadającego empirycznie potwierdzonej prawidłowości;* trans. K.P.) and against "but for" test of causation in terms of the congruence of the former and incongruence of the latter with the actual way people perceive and make causal judgments concerning relationships in the world:

> in contrast to the method of mental elimination ["but for test"], it ["theory of the condition corresponding to empirically proven regularity"] seems to be an accurate reflection of the actual process of establishing a causal link. The role of knowledge- and experience-generalizing regularities that occur between certain types of events is undoubtedly of primary importance in this process. ... They are—also from a purely psychological point of view—an indispensable element of perceiving and understanding the world.

Since such opinions of legal theoreticians and practitioners rely on certain empirical assumptions about how people make causal judgments (that are not empirically verified), we may speak of them in terms of *jurisprudential intuitions*. As long as jurisprudential intuitions about the ordinary concept of causation are used in the legal argumentation in favor or against certain legal theories or tests of causation, empirical testing of whether they are supported by ordinary intuitions may shed light on whether (and if so, which of them) are empirically sound.[8] In other words, since legal theoreticians and practitioners appeal to ordinary intuitions when arguing in favor or against certain legal theories of causation, it can be claimed that the empirical studies on such intuitions are an important source of insights, and perhaps even a tool of strengthening or weakening particular positions in this debate.[9] Moreover, sometimes the appeal to the ordinary concept of causation in the law is more implicit. For instance, legal codes frequently make use of causal terms (e.g., "cause," "results from," "outcome," "because of," "cause damages," "kills," "inflicts harm"),[10] but they do not provide their legal definitions. This suggests a common understanding of these notions by the code drafters and legislators—especially in criminal law where ordinary meaning interpretation is the default (e.g., see Wróbel and Zoll, 2012, p. 117, for the Polish criminal law doctrine).[11] What follows, the ordinary concept of causation and the extent to which it is congruent with the causal criteria in the legal theory and practice, seems a promising research direction in the X-Phi of law (see also Knobe and Shapiro, 2021).

Perhaps ironically, although beliefs that legal criteria of causation (should) somewhat reflect the folk notion of causation are pretty common in jurisprudence, legal systems adopt many tests and doctrines for assessing it. These different tests may sometimes lead to quite different conclusions about whether the causal link between the action or omission of an agent and the resulting outcome can be legally established. Such a variety in legal doctrines of causation may suggest the following: (a) that some theories of causation in the law are incongruent with the folk concept of causation (i.e., providing that there is one universally shared ordinary concept of causation, some jurisprudential intuitions on this matter may be unwarranted), (b) that different jurisprudential intuitions reflect different folk concepts of causation (i.e., providing there are several folk concepts of causation, different jurisprudential intuitions may be warranted), (c) that at least some legal theories of causation are based on technical rather than folk criteria (i.e., the assumption that these theories are modeled on the folk criteria is unwarranted). Putting aside potential implications of these possibilities for jurisprudence (I will come back to them in the final discussion), I will limit my further analysis to one group of theories of causation that is recurrent across the common law and continental law systems. I will call this group of legal theories "normative theories of causation" because they assume that norm violations are somewhat relevant for establishing causation in the law.[12]

Accordingly, I will proceed as follows: I will first delineate essential components of the normative theories of causation and provide examples from legal philosophy and criminal law theory from the common law and continental law traditions. Secondly, I will summarize empirical research indicating that normative theories of causation in the law are overall congruent with the folk criteria of causal ascription. I will argue that this research provides empirical support for these jurisprudential intuitions, which assume that norms are relevant for the ordinary concept of causation.[13] I will examine four different models explaining the connection between norms and causes in the X-Phi literature and how well they account for the basic components of the normative theories of causation in the law in terms of their recurrence across different legal systems and underlying psychological mechanisms (see Prochownik, 2021, pp. 9–10). Finally, I will discuss the challenges and limitations of the experimental research on causation for the law.

2 Causation in the law

Assessment of a causal link between an action and a harmful outcome is one of the first and essential components of the process of ascribing liability in criminal law.[14] The legal system must single out an agent's action from all the causal events preceding the harm as a legally relevant cause to hold the actor criminally liable for it. Thus, the fundamental problem of legal theory boils down to the question: which of the many causal conditions of a given event can be distinguished as its cause for the sake of attributing criminal responsibility? For instance, that Smith killed Jones may be causally conditioned by the fact that his boss fired him on the day before and that his mother gave birth to him thirty years ago, but these events will likely not be treated as legally relevant causes of the Jones's death. This issue is also known in philosophy as a causal selection problem (e.g., Hitchcock and Knobe, 2009).

Legal systems deal with the causal selection problem in different ways. Many solve it by introducing double criteria for assessing causation: (1) those that allow establishing causal connections between events in the world (factual or ontological criteria); (2) those that differentiate among these causal connections the legally relevant ones (normative or legal criteria). The most common test for factual causation in various legal systems is "but for test" (also known as *conditio sine qua non* or equivalence theory), which assumes that "an event X causes an event Y if, but for X, Y would not have occurred" (Fletcher, 1998, p. 62). Despite its popularity, the test is widely criticized as problematic and insufficient for assessing causation in the law (e.g., see Lagnado and Gerstenberg, 2017 for a review). In particular, sometimes, it is too inclusive (e.g., if Smith's mother did not give birth to him, he would not have killed Jones; hence her act of birth-giving would count as a cause of Jones's death), other times too exclusive (e.g., if Smith and Brown shot to Jones at the same time, and each of the bullets was enough to kill Jones, then neither of them would be a cause of his death). Due to these limitations, many legal systems introduce additional criteria to the "but for" causation.

In the common law jurisprudence, these additional criteria are known as legal or proximate cause. For instance, British legal theory of criminal law differentiates operating and substantial cause: an offender's action is a substantial cause of an outcome when it significantly contributes to its occurrence (Herring, 2014, p. 87), and its operative cause when it is not too distant from it (i.e., the causal chain initiated by the agent has not been broken by voluntary and deliberate action of a third party) (Herring, 2014, p. 88; Bohlander, 2009, p. 45). Similarly, American Model Penal Code specifies that the outcome must not be "too remote or accidental in its occurrence to have a [just] bearing on the person's liability or on the gravity of his offense" (MPC § 2.03[2]b and [3]b). For example, the mother giving birth to Smith seems too insignificant and remote to count as a cause of him killing Jones.

The continental legal theory also recognizes additional legal criteria. For instance, German criminal doctrine introduces an additional *normative criterion* either to the assessment of the causal link itself (e.g., *Adäquanztheorie* assumes that an event is a cause of an outcome only if the outcome is a normal consequence of this type of event), or, as a separate analysis of the relationship between the perpetrator and the outcome (e.g., the doctrine of *objektive Zurechnung* recognizes an additional stage of evaluating whether the actor violated a legal norm and whether this was connected to the outcome's occurrence) (Bohlander, 2009, p. 47). Thus, for instance, Smith's mother did not violate any legal norm by giving birth to him; therefore, the harm he caused cannot be normatively connected to her action.

2.1 Normative theories of causation in legal philosophy and legal doctrine

In this chapter, under the broad notion of normative theories of causation, I understand conceptions in legal philosophy and legal doctrines which assume that violations of norms (or normality broadly speaking) are somewhat relevant for ascribing causation in the law. For instance, the philosophical account of causation in the law by Hart and Honoré and the theory of objective attribution of outcome in the criminal law doctrine fall under this scope.[15] In this part of the chapter, I will examine some basic and recurrent components of these theories and some key differences.

Legal philosophy

Hart and Honoré place two contrasts at the root of the common concept of causation: (1) between normal and abnormal, (2) between voluntary and deliberate human actions and other events. Let us take a closer look at these contrasts and the relationship between them.

Regarding the first contrast, their argument goes that laypeople tend to choose an abnormal event as a cause of an outcome out of many conditions leading to it. This tendency to focus on the abnormal is supposedly related to the fact that laypeople seek explanations for those particular situations that are somehow out of the ordinary—accidents, catastrophes, other events that violate the typical and expected course of things (Hart and Honoré, 1985, p. 34). Notably, they understand causality as abnormality broadly in terms of "something which interferes with or intervenes in the course of events which would normally take place" (Hart and Honoré, 1985, p. 29). Such intervention may apply to many things (Hart and Honoré, 1985, p. 33), including "ordinary course of nature," "artefact of human habit, custom, or convention" (also "second 'nature,'" "man-made normal conditions," "man-made norms"; Hart and Honoré, 1985, p. 37–8), "normal functioning" (Hart and Honoré, 1985, p. 34), or "routine" (Hart and Honoré, 1985, pp. 38 and 41).

As an illustration, consider the following hypothetical case: a gardener omits to water flowers; as a result, the flowers die. Hart and Honoré observe that this gardener's omission "is not merely a breach of duty on his part, but also a deviation from a system or routine" (p. 38). Thus, there are two senses in which the gardener's omission may be considered "abnormal": (1) he violated his duty to water the flowers, (2) he deviated from his typical routine of watering them (Hart and Honoré, 1985, pp. 38 and 40). In other words, what is "normal" may refer to both moral or legal standards (e.g., if the gardener's obligation to water the flowers resulted from a promise or employment relationship) and statistical regularities (e.g., the gardener's typical watering of the flowers).

Suppose we accept this broad interpretation of what Hart and Honoré mean by "abnormal" and its essential role in the ordinary concept of causation. Then, it is not entirely clear what is the status of voluntary and deliberate human actions (their second contrast) in this concept. Since human actions may be perceived as interventions in the normal course of events, they may be singled out as *causes* already on this basis (in fact,

Hart and Honoré, 1985, pp. 41–2, seemed to have noticed that regarding not fully voluntary and voluntary actions).[16] Thus, it may seem puzzling why the legal philosophers distinguished the second contrast as essential to the folk concept of causation.

A potential solution to this puzzle brings the specification that "a voluntary human action ... has a special place in causal inquiries" (Hart and Honoré, 1985, p. 42). In particular, such actions deserve a special causal status (among other potentially "abnormal" events) because they often set the boundaries of ordinary causal investigations (Hart and Honoré, 1985, p. 42). Specifically, laypeople tend to end their search for a causal explanation when they can identify a voluntary and intentional human action in the causal chain leading to the outcome. As Hart and Honoré (1985) point out, "a deliberate human act is therefore most often a barrier and a goal in tracing back causes" (p. 44).

To sum up this part, Hart and Honoré endorse a set of jurisprudential intuitions regarding the ordinary concept of causation which they deem essential for the law. Namely, they claim that ordinary people solve causal selection problems by identifying deviations from the normal course of events, particularly those that result from voluntary and deliberate human actions.

Legal doctrine

Normative theories of causation in criminal law serve important practical goals: they provide criteria for assessing causation for the sake of ascribing liability for crimes in courts. Due to this function, these criteria may appear more specific and complex than the general ones identified by the legal philosophers. Primarily, criminal law doctrines focus on analyzing *legal norm* violations committed by human agents (and not any moral or statistical deviations) as a critical and additional step in analyzing the causal chain leading to crime. One instance of such theory, particularly influential in the continental law systems (e.g., German and Polish criminal law), is *Objektive Zurechnung* or *teoria obiektywnego przypisania skutku* ("objective attribution of outcome theory," trans. K.P.). In this part, I will reconstruct the key elements of this doctrine on the example of Polish criminal law.

According to the objective attribution of outcome theory, the test of factual causation (e.g., *sine qua non*) conducted at the very beginning of *causal* analysis in criminal cases is followed by a *normative* analysis of the agent's behavior as leading to the criminal outcome (e.g., Zoll et al., 2004, pp. 53–4). Namely, the objective attribution of outcome to the agent consists of two stages: (1) assessment of the unlawfulness of the offender's action in the light of the applicable legal norms, and (2) establishment of the normative connection between this unlawful action and the outcome (Bielski, 2012, p. 514).

The first stage determines whether the agent's behavior violated the rules of prudence in dealing with a legal good and brought about a higher than a socially acceptable threat to that legal good (Bielski, 2012, pp. 514–15; Góralski, 2009, p. 40). The occurrence of the legally prohibited outcome due to putting the legal good in danger must be objectively and *ex ante* predictable (Bielski, 2012, p. 518). By contrast, the second stage entails the *ex post* analysis of whether the norm-violating behavior was legally relevant to the occurrence of the prohibited outcome (Bielski, 2012, p. 520; Zoll et al., 2004, p. 54). This analysis consists of two elements: (a) assessment of a hypothetical causal relationship and (b) determining whether the aim of the legal norm violated by the agent was to protect the legal good against such outcome (Bielski, 2012, p. 520).

The first component (*a*) requires imagining a hypothetical course of events in which the legal norm had not been violated and determining whether the prohibited outcome would have occurred then (Bielski, 2012, p. 521). The outcome is attributed "had the offender behaved in line with the rules of conduct applying in the given circumstances, in the light of causal knowledge and experience, with a probability verging on certainty, the legally prohibited outcome would not have occurred" (Bielski, 2012, pp. 520-1, trans. K.P.). The second component of the analysis (*b*) boils down to assessing whether causing the certain outcome in a certain way by the perpetrator falls within the scope of protection of the violated legal norm (Bielski, 2012, p. 523). In other words, it is tested whether the aim of the legal norm in question was to protect the legal good from the danger that materialized in the legally prohibited outcome.

The objective ascription theory may be applied to both crimes of action and omission. While liability for criminal actions requires ascription of both causal and normative connection, liability for omissions requires determining only normative connection between the agent's omission and prohibited outcome (this includes imagining a hypothetical state of affairs in which a person who had a special legal duty to act would have acted as prescribed by the law).[17]

To sum up, according to the criminal law doctrine of objective outcome attribution, the key components of establishing the *normative* connection for crimes of actions and omissions is assessing whether an agent violated a legal norm (or a legally imposed duty) and whether the norm violation and the occurrence of the legally prohibited outcome were connected.

2.2 Previous and next steps

This part of the chapter has shown some common and recurrent features in thinking about causation in legal philosophy and legal doctrine, in the common law and continental law jurisprudence. A group of legal theories grants *norm violations* a special status in ascribing causation in the law, although they differ in the level of complexity. In the next part, I will assess these normative theories of causation in terms of their congruence with the ordinary causal intuitions characterized by current research in experimental philosophy and cognitive science. Before this step, I will summarize the main findings regarding the connection of norms and causes and their most prominent explanatory models in this literature.

3 Norms and causes: Different psychological models and their explanatory power for the causation in the law

In this part of the chapter, I argue that the normative theories of causation in legal philosophy and legal doctrine are *generally* congruent with the ordinary concept of causation, according to the state of the art in experimental philosophy and cognitive science. I examine four explanatory models in this literature regarding their *explanatory potential* for these theories.

3.1 Norms and causes in ordinary thought

There is a consensus in the X-Phi literature that the folk concept of causation is associated with norms. The impressive set of empirical findings supports this consensus (e.g., Alicke, Rose, and Bloom, 2011; Knobe and Fraser, 2008; Hitchcock and Knobe, 2009; Knobe, 2009; Kominsky et al, 2015; Phillips and Kominsky, 2016; Samland and Waldmann, 2016).[18] For instance, Knobe and Fraser (2008) presented lay participants with a hypothetical story of a receptionist who keeps pens on her desk. While administrative assistants are allowed to take the pens, professors are not. One day, though, both an administrative assistant and a professor take a pen from the desk. Later that day, no pens are left, and the receptionist cannot take an important message. After being presented with that story, participants were more likely to indicate that the professor *caused* the problem than the administrative assistant. These and other similar findings demonstrate that people tend to single out as causal the agent who violates a norm.

As such, these findings may provide *prima facie* evidence for the intuitive character of the normative theories of causation in the law. Consequently, jurisprudential intuitions of legal theoreticians and practitioners who believe that causal theories in the law (should) correspond to the ordinary causal intuitions and who adopt normative theories of causation seem generally supported by the empirical evidence so far.[19]

However, several competitive models offer different psychological explanations of these findings. Importantly, their explanatory power or how well they account for the essential components of the normative theories of causation in the law may vary. Therefore, in the next section, I examine the main psychological accounts and their implications for jurisprudence.

3.2 The "fantastic four": Different psychological accounts of the connection between norms and causes

There are four different models of the connection between causes and norms: *competence account, bias account, pragmatics account,* and *responsibility account*.[20]

According to the competence account (e.g., Hitchcock and Knobe, 2009; Knobe and Fraser, 2008), capacity for counterfactual thinking (e.g., Halpern and Pearl, 2005; Lagnado, Gerstenberg, and Zultan, 2013) is at the core of ordinary causal attributions. However, a "causal structure" of an event consists of many counterfactual possibilities which, if eliminated, would not lead to the event's occurrence (Hitchcock and Knobe, 2009). Laypeople solve this problem of causal selection by identifying the *abnormal* elements of the event as its actual causes. Namely, people counterfactually imagine what would have happened if the abnormal elements of the situation were replaced by a normal course of events or behavior that follows a norm. One of the key features of the competence account is the assumption that laypeople's appeals to norms manifest the competent application of the concept of causation.

There are two variants of this view in terms of the cognitive processes involved. Under one view, laypeople's ability for counterfactual thinking is affected by their representations of norms, determining what they choose as the actual event's causes (Hitchcock and Knobe, 2009). According to the second variant, the counterfactual thinking ability is inherently associated with norm representations. For instance, Knobe (2009, p. 242) argues that "the use of these [statistical and moral] considerations is simply built into the fundamental mechanisms that subserve people's counterfactual reasoning."

In either of the two variants, the competence model operates with a broad understanding of normality as consisting of prescriptive norms (e.g., moral or legal), statistical norms (e.g., frequency of events or statistical regularities in the world), and norms of proper functioning of objects and entities (Hitchcock and Knobe, 2009, pp. 597–8; see also Phillips and Kominsky, 2016). People tend to associate actual causes of events with deviations from normality because norms determine those situation's elements that are the most effective points of intervention (cf. Hitchcock and Knobe, 2009, p. 606). For instance, by intervening when a moral norm is violated, one may influence and stop repeating morally abnormal behavior in the future

A relevant research development by the proponents of the model concerns the phenomenon of *causal superseding*, which occurs when the causal connection between the primary agent's behavior and the outcome is subsequently undermined by a norm violation of the second agent (Kominsky et al., 2015, p. 196). For instance, the case of Carter vs. Towne, discussed by Hart and Honoré, considered the legal responsibility of a man who sold gunpowder to a boy who was injured by it. The court ruled that the causal link between the salesman's behavior and the injuries was broken by a subsequent behavior of the child's relatives who negligently hid the gunpowder in their house (Kominsky et al., 2015, p. 196; cf. Hart and Honoré, 1985, p. 154). The competence model offers the following explanation of this case: in a counterfactual scenario in which boy's relatives had not acted negligently, the salesman's behavior would have no longer been sufficient for the boy's injuries. Therefore, it is no longer perceived as their cause (cf. Kominsky et al., 2015, p. 198).

According to the *bias model*, "causal control"—the extent to which the agent has control over his action leading to a particular outcome—is one of the essential components of blame ascription. It is evaluated in terms of three factors: (1) uniqueness (whether the action is the sole or sufficient cause of the outcome), (2) proximity (whether there is a difference in time and space between the action and the outcome), and (3) effective control (whether the outcome would have occurred without this action) (Alicke, 2000, p. 561). Typically, laypeople take these factors into account when assessing the agent's causal control and, accordingly, the amount of blame he deserves (i.e., lower the degree of causal control, lesser the blame). Sometimes, however, spontaneous negative evaluations interfere and distort their assessments of causal control. Firstly, people may ascribe more causal control when they want to blame the agent for the negative event or outcome. Secondly, spontaneous evaluations may interfere directly with their attributions of blame (Alicke, 2000).

There are several significant similarities and differences between the bias and competence accounts. Both models acknowledge that moral evaluations affect folk ascriptions of causation, but for the bias model, this results in biased (not competent but erroneous) applications of this concept. Besides, the bias model assumes that various elements of a situation may trigger spontaneous evaluations (e.g., negative outcome, agent's intention, gender, or skin color), not only deviations from norms.[21] Finally, people consider norm violations vital because they may justify their judgments of blame or because they trigger spontaneous negative evaluations, not because they provide the most efficient intervention points (see Alicke, Rose, and Bloom, 2011, p. 692).

The *pragmatics model* (also "accountability hypothesis") assumes that the experimental findings on the connection between norms and causes can be better explained in terms of conversational pragmatics—that people often use causal language to express judgments of accountability (Samland and Waldmann, 2016). If so, then questions about causation in the previous studies could have been interpreted by participants as referring to the agent's accountability. Norm violations are relevant for ordinary judgments of accountability, but they may have no real impact on the folk concept of causation. In contrast to the competence account, the pragmatics model denies a deep and structural connection between thinking about causes and norms (Samland and Waldmann, 2016, p. 165). Besides, it predicts that people who interpret questions about causation in terms of accountability rely on a range of different factors besides norm violations (e.g., agent's intentionality). The impact of norms on causal judgments disappears if the interpretative openness of questions about causation is eliminated.

Finally, according to *the responsibility account*, norms are relevant for causal judgments because causal judgments express responsibility (e.g., Sytsma, Livengood, and Rose, 2012; Livengood, Sytsma, and Rose, 2017). Its key idea is that "causal attributions serve to indicate more than that an agent contributed to bringing about an outcome—they also give a normative evaluation of the action akin to saying that the agent is responsible or accountable for the outcome" (Sytsma, 2019, p. 5). From this perspective, *all* causal judgments are inherently normative.[22]

The responsibility and pragmatics accounts both assume that people express judgments of responsibility by making causal judgments. They also generate similar predictions. For instance, both predict that various factors which matter for responsibility (e.g., norm violations, intentionality) should be also relevant for causal ascriptions. However, according to the responsibility account, this is not an outcome of conversational pragmatics but of the fact that the folk concepts of causation and responsibility are closely related.[23]

3.3 Implications for causation in the law

Above, I indicated that the current state of X-Phi research supports the general compatibility of the folk understanding of causation and normative theories of causation in the law. In this part, I will compare the explanatory potential of the different psychological models of the connection between norms and causes for these legal theories. Namely, I will examine the extent to which these different models can account for the basic components of these theories in legal philosophy (theory of Hart and Honoré) and criminal law doctrine (objective attribution of outcome theory).

The *competence model* provides empirical support for the jurisprudential intuitions of Hart and Honoré concerning the folk concept of causation. According to the legal philosophers, ordinary people attribute causation by focusing on abnormal events and their contrast to what is conceived as broadly normal (natural or human-created order of things). Therefore, empirical findings showing that norms broadly speaking (i.e., prescriptive, statistical, and proper functioning norms) are involved in the ordinary judgments of causal selection support this essential component of this theory. However, legal-philosophical intuitions of Hart and Honoré regarding the special status of deliberate human actions among abnormal events is not supported by the findings of the competence model.[24]

The competence model can also account for the psychological basis of several principles of the objective attribution of outcome doctrine in criminal law. One of such principles is that for the attribution of the outcome to the agent, in addition to the factual causal connection, the normative connection between the unlawful agent's behavior (a legal norm violation) and the occurrence of the outcome must be established. Namely, the outcome ascription requires demonstrating that the agent's conduct was unlawful and "normatively connected" to the outcome. This is compatible with the competence model's finding that violations of prescriptive norms matter for assessing causal relationships. Another essential element of the normative connection analysis involves examining the "hypothetical causal link" (Bielski, 2012, p. 521): imagining a counterfactual scenario in which a perpetrator follows a legal norm that was actually violated and assessing whether the prohibited outcome would also result then. Hitchcock and Knobe (2009) and Kominsky and colleagues (2015) provided a counterfactual and hypothetical thinking model involving norms that may provide a psychological basis for this legal proceeding.

Finally, causal superseding (Kominsky et al., 2015) may shed light on another aspect of the doctrine of objective outcome attribution. In the Polish doctrine of criminal law: "The normative connection plays an important role in the event of the involvement of third parties in the causal course of events. An outcome cannot be attributed to an agent if, before its occurrence, another subject violating an important rule of conduct had joined in the causal course of events, and this way brought about a significant increase of the risk of the outcome occurrence" (Wróbel and Zoll, 2012, pp. 201–2; trans. K.P.). This component of the criminal law theory is in line with the ordinary causal thinking in the causal superseding scenarios.[25]

In sum, the competence model is generally compatible with and accounts well for several basic components of the objective outcome ascription doctrine (i.e., in terms of potential psychological mechanisms underlying its legal applications). Moreover, it may explain the popularity of this doctrine and its derivatives in different criminal law systems (e.g., Germany, Poland): such doctrines may spread because of their general congruence with people's causal intuitions.

However, some important incompatibilities also exist between the doctrine of the objective outcome ascription and the competence account. According to the legal doctrine, attribution of outcome to the agent requires establishing a factual causal connection in the first step and then a "purely" normative connection in the second step (i.e., these are two separate stages of the analysis). Whether this kind of legal distinction may be accounted for by the competence model depends on which version of this model is adopted. According to one version (e.g., Hitchcock and Knobe, 2009), purely descriptive causal judgments are in principle possible, even though norms are involved in causal selection. On the one hand, the general cognitive capacity for counterfactual thinking could account for the first step of the factual analysis of causation in the law (especially that the most widespread legal test for factual causation, *conditio sine qua non*, is based on counterfactual thinking).[26] On the other hand, the subsequent stage of "normative connection" analysis could reflect the psychological process of causal selection of the actual cause, which is affected by the representations of norms. According to the second version of the competence account (e.g., Knobe, 2009), causal judgments are *inherently* normative. From this perspective, the legal differentiation between factual and normative stages of outcome attribution would be purely technical and incongruent with the folk concept of causation.[27]

There is another *prima facie* incompatibility between the common notion of causation according to the competence account and the legal doctrine of objective outcome attribution. According to the competence model, the general representation of normality matters for the causal selection in ordinary thought (e.g., violations of legal and moral norms but also statistical regularities are equally good candidates for causes). In contrast, outcome attribution in criminal law depends solely on *legal* norm violations (i.e., the outcome cannot be attributed to the agent if he violated a social or statistical norm unless he also violated a legal norm). Nonetheless, the narrow understanding of "normative connection" in the law compared to the broad representation of normality according to the ordinary causal intuitions seems justified from the perspective of the particular goals of criminal law (e.g., holding people liable for the violations of criminal law specifically). To this limited extent, the competence model may still explain why legal norm violations are relevant for the legal doctrine of causation and provide potential psychological mechanisms that may be involved during the applications of this doctrine by lawyers.

Bias and *responsibility accounts*, just like the competence model, consider norm violations relevant for ordinary causal ascriptions (as well as for blame or responsibility attributions). In this respect, they also support general congruence between the common causal judgments and the essential criterion of the normative theories of causation in the law. However, different psychological mechanisms or processes account for the connection between causes and norms in ordinary thinking from these different perspectives. This, in turn, may lead to different implications (in terms of different explanatory potentials of these models) for the normative theories of causation in the law.

According to the *bias account*, people's spontaneous reactions to the negative features of the situation (e.g., outcome, action, or agent) may drive the urge to blame the agent and lead them to overestimate the causal control he had. Norm violations are relevant in this process because they may justify people's desire to blame the agent *post hoc* (e.g., "Smith is blameworthy because he violated the norm you 'shall not kill'"). Besides, norms themselves may drive the negative evaluations that bias causal assessment (e.g., since norm violations may trigger spontaneous negative reactions, norm violators are more likely to be perceived as causal). According to this model, norms are not special and play similar roles to many other situational factors (including features relevant for evaluating the situation, like the agent's intentionality, but also features irrelevant for it, such as gender or skin color of the agent).

The bias model may explain why normative theories of causation in the law treat norm violations as a criterion for establishing the causal connection (Hart and Honoré) or the normative connection (objective outcome ascription theory). Namely, the popularity of such legal theories could have been driven by the biases described above (e.g., norms' role in triggering spontaneous evaluations that bias causal judgments). However, I'd argue that the remaining assumptions of the bias model *cannot explain* and go against the basic principles of criminal law. In particular, the model assumes that people's assessments of intentionality and causation can affect each other. By contrast, these are two different stages of criminal responsibility attribution in the law (e.g., *mens rea* and *actus reus* in the common law systems). Besides, the bias model acknowledges the role of irrelevant factors, such as the agent's skin color or gender, in the ordinary attributions of causation and blame, which are not recognized by the law.

The proponents of the bias model could perhaps account for these basic criminal law principles as resulting from overriding biases that govern ordinary causal and blame ascriptions.[28] According to the model, people can make purely descriptive and unbiased judgments of causation (i.e., when spontaneous evaluations do not distort their causal assessment). Therefore, it could be argued that the criminal law system, as a result of many years of reflective and "cold" deliberations of legal scholars and practitioners, relies on the purely descriptive criteria of causal control (uniqueness, proximity, and effectiveness, according to the model).[29] However, adopting this position may undermine the normative theories of causation in the law as driven by the erroneous or "biased" application of the concept of causation (i.e., since privileging norms by these theories could result from the bias and, in that case, would violate the legal principle to rely on the descriptive causal criteria only). Therefore, adopting this response may lead to difficulties in explaining the normative theories of causation in the law.[30]

Finally, *responsibility* and *pragmatics models* assume that folk ascriptions of causation are sensitive to norms because norms are relevant for judgments of responsibility or accountability. Because people tend to express responsibility or accountability judgments by causal judgments, norms may affect their causal attributions. Another common ground between these models is situating norms among many factors that may affect causal decisions in this way (against the competence account, and consistently with the bias account, norms are granted no special status in ordinary causal ascriptions). Other factors, such as the agent's intentionality, should be equally relevant for the causal judgments that express responsibility judgments (since norm violations and intentionality are relevant for ascribing responsibility).

There are also relevant differences between these two accounts. For the pragmatics model, the impact of norms on causal judgments is a matter of conversational pragmatics. It occurs when questions about causation may be interpreted as questions about accountability. When the questions about causation are not interpretatively open, they are based on descriptive and counterfactual criteria, not normative ones. By contrast, for the responsibility account, the ordinary concept of causation is inherently normative by its very nature (the impact of norms on causation does not rely on the conversational context).

Although these two models are in principle congruent with the normative theories of causation in the law, their explanatory potential for the basic components of these theories seems relatively small. The responsibility account's central assumption is that there is psychological closeness and similarity between the concept of causation and responsibility. However, the view that causation indicates responsibility is incompatible with how the relationship between these two concepts is constructed in the criminal theory. Even when a court successfully establishes the causal (and normative) connection between the agent's unlawful action and the prohibited outcome, this does not mean that the agent is legally responsible for the crime. Although the outcome may be objectively ascribed to the defendant, he might not be held criminally responsible due to, for instance, being a minor or psychologically impaired, acting under the force of a third party, or acting in self-defense. Holding the agent legally responsible for the crime is an outcome of a complex, multi-stage process, in which attributing causation is only one step (typically initial, sometimes not even a necessary one[31]). Therefore, at least according to the criminal law doctrine, causation does not indicate responsibility.[32]

However, it should be noted that although the explanatory power of the responsibility model for the normative theories of causation in the law seems relatively small, this does not exclude the possibility that the model captures some essential features of the folk causal judgments. This possibility, which should be subject to further research, might suggest that the normative legal theories are based on technical, conceptual distinctions that are counterintuitive to the folk or do not exhaust all the different ways ordinary people make causal judgments.

The *pragmatics model* also provides *prima facie* evidence in favor of the general congruence between the normative legal theories and folk causal judgments. Yet, its explanatory potential for these legal theories seems rather small. In particular, the proponents of this model assume that the relationship between norms and causes is a matter of conversational pragmatics. As already noted above, the criminal law doctrine provides clear and precise criteria of the causal analyses in the law and separates them from legal accountability. Therefore, it is unlikely that it's the interpretative openness of the legal criteria that accounts for the role of norms in ascribing causation (or that norms are relevant for the legal theories due to the interpretative confusion of causation with accountability).

To conclude this part of the analysis, although all four psychological models support the general congruence between the ordinary concept and the normative theories of causation in the law, the competence model accounts for these theories' basic and recurrent components to the greatest extent. Namely, many factors that, according to the competence model, play a role in the folk causal cognition seem to also play a role in the legal philosophy and the criminal law doctrine of causation. Therefore, the competence model supports the jurisprudential intuitions regarding the connection between causes and norms in these theories and describes possible psychological mechanisms explaining these intuitions. What follows from this analysis for jurisprudence *so far*: legal theorists who assume that legal theories of causation are (or should be) congruent with the folk concept of causation and are the proponents of the normative theories of causation in the law, are to the greatest extent, supported by the competence model.

However, it should be noted that simply because a psychological model is compatible and supports certain ideas in legal philosophy and doctrine does not entail that the model correctly characterizes folk causal judgments. This is an empirical question that should be subject to more extensive empirical research in the future and cannot be answered in this chapter. For instance, further research may show that another psychological account better captures the essential components of the folk causal judgments than the competence account or any of the accounts described above.[33] Consequently, it may turn out that jurisprudential intuitions regarding the connection between norms and causes in ordinary thinking are not empirically supported or are supported to a lesser extent than follows from the current analysis. In particular, normative theories of causation could be partially or entirely a product of technical legal reasoning.[34] Therefore, in the final part of this chapter, I will examine the limitations of the current findings and some potential implications of future empirical research for causation in the law.

4 Challenges and limitations of the experimental philosophy research for the legal theories of causation

Above I examined the implications of X-Phi research on causes and norms in terms of their explanatory potential for normative theories of causation in the law. I suggested that this research may explain why these theories of causation are widespread in legal philosophy and doctrine across different legal systems. In this respect, this research may have similar potential to the cultural evolutionary approaches to the spread of other cultural ideas or beliefs (e.g., Sperber, 1996; Norenzayan, 2013; De Cruz and De Smedt, 2014). Namely, ordinary causal intuitions may underlie the cultural spread of particular legal theories and doctrines.[35]

However, there are multiple challenges ahead of the experimental research on the ordinary concept of causation and legal theory in the light of this research. One of the future research directions includes conducting systematic empirical studies on the folk concept of causation, including the question of whether there is a unified set of causal intuitions that govern people's causal inferences or whether causal intuitions vary across demographic and individual factors (e.g., culture, age, gender, personality).[36] The first part of the experimental research on causation may be associated with the so-called "positive program" of X-Phi, aiming to contribute to the traditional conceptual analysis by conducting empirical research on folk intuitions. The second part of this research may belong to the "negative program" of X-Phi that examines whether people's intuitions are reliable or susceptible to demographic and individual variation (e.g., Knobe and Nichols, 2017).

One possible outcome of such empirical inquiries is identifying a unified concept of causation (i.e., that people universally rely on a certain set of causal intuitions supported by specific psychological mechanisms). Alternatively, there may be several or even multiple folk concepts of causation (i.e., that people rely on different sets of causal intuitions supported by different psychological mechanisms). These potential research directions and findings may have different implications for the X-Phi of Law and legal philosophy and doctrine in general.

In this chapter, I only examined one type of legal theory of causation: theories that consider norms as relevant criteria for applying causation in the law. However, different legal theories of causation co-occur not only *across* legal systems but also *within* legal systems (in fact, a lot of discussion in jurisprudence is dedicated to these different theories and which is the most appropriate one for the law; e.g., see Moore, 2019, for a review). Therefore, future X-Phi of Law research should examine the scope of compatibility of different theories of causation in legal philosophy and doctrine with the folk causal intuitions.[37] X-Phi of Law may also face a challenge of explaining the variety of the legal theories of causation in the law.

Particular directions of the future X-Phi of Law research will largely depend on the prior empirical findings on the universality or variety in ordinary causal intuitions. For instance, if there is a unified folk concept of causation, then some legal theories of causation may be more congruent with ordinary causal intuitions than others. If, on the other hand, causal intuitions vary depending on demographic or individual factors, then perhaps this could account for different theories of causation in the law. In the latter case, it may also be more challenging to decide between these theories based solely on the congruence with ordinary intuitions (e.g., variety in everyday causal intuition may also support adopting purely technical doctrines of causation in the law).

Therefore, some critical challenges also await legal scholars in response to X-Phi research. As pointed out, legal scholars often indicate or assume that the legal concept of causation is modeled on its folk counterpart but do not provide empirical validation of such claims. X-Phi may provide the empirical data that enable the evaluation of such statements in jurisprudence. In particular, if the future X-Phi research supports the existence of the singular and universally shared folk concept of causation, then legal scholars may be able to identify those theories of causation in the law that are congruent with this concept. However, suppose the future X-Phi research reveals several or multiple ordinary concepts of causation (e.g., that people rely on a different set of causal intuitions depending on demographic or individual factors). In that case, the task of the legal theoreticians and practitioners may be much more difficult. There are at least two possible responses of legal scholars to the latter scenario.

On the one hand, legal scholars might argue that since common causal intuitions vary depending on demographic or individual factors, they are unable to provide insights into legal theories at all (such an argument could be reminiscent of the negative program of experimental philosophy against the use of intuitions in philosophy because of their *unreliable* character[38]). In other words, the variety within the ordinary concept of causation could provide an argument in favor of purely technical legal criteria for attributing causation for the sake of assessing legal responsibility. This would also be followed by the abandonment of the postulates in legal theory and practice that legal views of causation (should) reflect the folk causal concepts. Otherwise, courts' decisions regarding the interpretation and application of the ordinary causal evaluation criteria could be arbitrary. This, in turn, could have negative consequences for the social perception and overall security of the system of justice (e.g., different judges could refer to a different set of ordinary intuitions).

The second possible response of the lawyers is more nuanced and depends on the character of the future representative empirical findings. Suppose the differentiation of ordinary causal intuitions occurs at the level of whole populations (e.g., cultures or legal traditions) and not individuals within these populations. In that case, legal scholars may still aim to have theories of causation that reflect the causal intuitions shared in the population where the law applies. However, individual-level differences in respect to causal concepts within the same population (e.g., individual differences in the same culture or legal system) seem more problematic for the consistency between the legal and ordinary concepts of causation. For instance, if folk causal intuitions within one population differ significantly and unsystematically (such that we would not be able to distinguish any stable pattern of causal thinking in the group), this may undermine lawyers' reliance on the ordinary causal concepts. However, if the causal intuitions differ due to individual factors, but several systematic patterns of causal thinking can be distinguished, then lawyers may decide to incorporate *some* of the ordinary criteria of causal analyses into the legal doctrine. For instance, those causal theories which are congruent with a set of common causal intuitions *and* satisfy the particular aims and functions of the law to the greatest extent (e.g., a function of justice) may be preferred by the legal scholars over others.

Regardless of which of the above scenarios is confirmed by the future X-Phi research, the relationship between empirical findings and legal policy is not straightforward. As argued in this chapter, X-Phi of Law may provide insights relevant especially for these legal-theoretical discussions that use arguments from common intuitions in favor of or against specific legal theories of causation (e.g., Hart and Honoré, 1985; Giezek, 1994), but this is not to be confused with the policy claim that laws *should* be based on folk causal intuitions or that the legal criteria should strictly follow the folk criteria (see Tobia, in preparation). There are several reasons why legal philosophy and doctrine may occasionally depart from ordinary intuitions. For example, according to the criminal law doctrine examined above, to objectively attribute an outcome to the agent, factual causal link and normative connection need to be established in separate steps. Providing that the competence model is right about the relationship of causes and norms in ordinary thinking, the separation of two stages that are usually inseparable in folk thinking may seem artificial from the layman's perspective. Yet, it could be argued that criminal law has to be more precise than folk thinking to adequately fulfill the function of justice. Therefore, particular demands of clarity and transparency on the legal criteria might provide one law-specific reason for this partial departure from the way laypeople reason.

Even if we accept that there should be some general level of convergence between legal concepts and equivalent common concepts (e.g., Robinson and Darley, 1995), it remains a matter for discussion in jurisprudence *to what extent* legal concepts of causation should rely on the folk criteria of causal judgments, and to what extent they should involve technical criteria. On the one hand, because of the special functions that theories of causation play in holding people who violate legal norms accountable at courts, it may be justified to develop (at least partially) technical legal criteria that would better serve this purpose. On the other hand, one may argue that X-Phi research provides general insights about the ordinary concept of causation (e.g., criteria people typically base their causal judgments on) and the potential psychological mechanisms involved. These may be too general to provide a model for the causal analyses in the law (which, due to the law's special character and functions, need to be more specific).

In light of all the above challenges and limitations, the analysis presented here has modest overtones. It boils down to an indication that research on ordinary causal intuitions may provide potentially relevant insights for assessing diverse theories and doctrines of attributing causation in the law (primarily to the extent that these theories are based on certain assumptions about the content of ordinary intuition). More precisely, what follows from the current analysis is that the research on common causal intuitions *so far* demonstrates that jurisprudential intuitions of some prominent legal theoreticians about the folk concept of causation are actually *empirically supported* (i.e., ordinary people take norms into account when ascribing causation, which is reflected in the normative theories of causation). However, more fine-grained research remains to be done regarding explanatory models behind the connection of causes and norms, the existence of singular or many ordinary folk concepts of causation, and the potential implications of such findings for different legal theories of causation. While future empirical research should shed more light on what the folk concept of causation *is*, it is a separate question what law theorists and practitioners *should* do (if anything) in the face of these findings.

Acknowledgments

I would like to thank Felipe Oliveira de Sousa and an anonymous reviewer for very helpful comments and suggestions to the previous version of this chapter.

This work was supported by the DFG-CAPES research grant "Experimental Legal Philosophy: The Concept of Law Revisited" (project number 434400506).

Notes

1 This chapter is based on a chapter of the Ph.D. thesis "Conditions of Criminal Responsibility from the Perspective of Experimental Legal Philosophy" (2019), defended at the Faculty of Law of Jagiellonian University.
2 This line of research on particular legal concepts does not exhaust all ongoing research projects in X-Phi of Law. Other projects examine intuitions and psychological mechanisms underpinning concepts of general relevance for jurisprudence: the concept of law (Donelson and Hannikainen, 2020), the concept of rule (Struchiner, Hannikainen, and de Almeida, 2020), and legal interpretation (Tobia, 2020). See Tobia (forthcoming) and Prochownik (2021) for more comprehensive overviews of different research projects.
3 See Tobia (forthcoming) and Prochownik (2019) for more comprehensive justifications of this approach.

4   Another recent argument for the general compatibility between legal concepts and their ordinary counterpart concepts states that rule of law principles (e.g., publicity, clarity, fair notice, consistency) are better satisfied when the law is accessible to laypeople (see Tobia, in preparation; forthcoming).
5   However, this rationale does not seem to apply to all legal concepts equally. Legal systems are abundant with purely technical concepts with no equivalents in common thinking and language (e.g., mortgage). Besides, some ordinary concepts acquire secondary and technical meaning in the law (e.g., *mens rea* concept of the law often partially departs from the folk concept of intentionality) (see von der Pfordten, 2009, for a discussion of different legal concepts). In these cases, conducting empirical research on folk intuitions may seem less justified (e.g., what examining folk intuitions concerning mortgage would bring us, except for, perhaps, an idea if the folk understand the legal notion?). Or at least it may be limited to a specific group of subjects and questions, for instance, whether legal experts' concept of intentionality is in line with the technical legal concept of *mens rea* (Kneer and Bourgeois-Gironde, 2017) or whether the lawyers consistently apply the concept of a mortgage.
6   This claim should not be confused with a stronger normative position that the law *should* follow folk intuitions in these cases—law-specific reasons or goals may justify departure from folk notions. Instead, learning about the content of folk concepts and how they function in everyday people's thinking may *inform* normative debates about whether folk criteria should or should not be followed when making or interpreting the law (see also Tobia, in preparation, for a discussion).
7   For instance, they point out that: "The general utility in legal cases of the question 'Would this harm have happened without this event, act, or omission?' as a test of causal connection does not spring from the fact that a condition *sine qua non* is the fundamental element in the notion of causation or its sole factual component; for this is not the case" (Hart and Honoré, 1985, pp. 128–9).
8   Thus, this endeavor may be compared to a more general X-Phi research program that examines whether ordinary people share philosophical intuitions that support certain philosophical theories (e.g., Sytsma and Livengood, 2015, pp. 9–10; Stich and Tobia, 2016, pp. 5 and 9).
9   This proposal can be rephrased in the form of a conditional assertion: if legal theorists and practitioners assume that theories of causation in the law should be informed by the ordinary understanding and application of this concept—where the compatibility or incompatibility of these theories with the common causal understanding serves as an argument for or against the acceptance of these theories in the law—then they should consider empirical research on the understanding and application of causal notions by the ordinary people.
10 See, for instance, the Penal Code of Poland (1997) or the Model Penal Code (1962).
11 Therefore, I will focus on criminal law in this analysis.
12 This should not be confused with the theories of causation that are normative in the sense that they involve certain policy-driven criteria about what should count as a "cause" in the law (which may but do not have to rely on the notion of norm violation—for instance, proximate cause in the common law system; see, for example, Moore, 2019).
13 Note that this does not automatically imply that other jurisprudential intuitions regarding the folk concept of causation are unwarranted (e.g., there may be several folk concepts of causation that may be compatible with different legal theories of causation).

14 This is particularly so for "crimes of harmful consequences" (e.g., Fletcher, 1998, p. 61), which require a certain result to occur for the crime to be committed (e.g., there is no murder without a dead body).

15 In the chapter, I focus on these two normative theories of causation in the law, but there may be other examples. For instance, according to some formulations of proximate causation, abnormal events, under certain circumstances, break the causal chain between the actor and the outcome (e.g., Moore, 2019; Herring, 2014, p. 93). See Knobe and Shapiro (2021) for a discussion of proximate causation from the cognitive science perspective.

16 See Philippa Foot (1963) for similar criticism.

17 This is a consequence of the fact that omissions are not treated as causal by the Polish doctrine of criminal law. However, recent X-Phi research suggests that folk people perceive both actions and omissions as causal (Willemsen, 2018).

18 See Willemsen and Kirfel (2018) for a literature review.

19 Note that I argue in favor of the general-level congruence between ordinary people thinking and the legal theories in the sense that norms are relevant in solving the causal selection problem for both. However, particular variants of these legal theories may provide additional criteria for solving that problem. Thus, it is a matter of question whether these additional criteria fit or depart from the ordinary causal intuitions (I will come back to this issue in the ending discussion).

20 I will focus here on the discussion of the basic assumptions of these models. Due to the space limit, I will not review the empirical evidence for each of them.

21 Additionally, it seems that only violations of prescriptive norms (not *any* norms) may trigger spontaneous evaluations distorting causal control assessments for the bias model.

22 This is similar to the view that norms belong to the competent application of the concept of causation. However, descriptive causal judgments are in principle possible for some proponents of the competence model (e.g., Hitchcock and Knobe, 2009; Willemsen and Kirfel, 2018, pp. 5–6).

23 Note that the bias account also grants a role to factors relevant for responsibility (i.e., agent's intentionality) in causal judgments. Still, it is incompatible with the responsibility model in giving such a role to factors irrelevant for responsibility (e.g., agent's gender or skin color).

24 A second difference between Hart and Honoré and the competence model concerns the role granted to counterfactual thinking in folk causal cognition. While it does not seem very important for the legal-philosophical account, it is crucial for the competence model (Hitchcock and Knobe, 2009, p. 601, footnote 22). This difference may result because X-Phi aims to explain the psychological mechanisms involved in ordinary causal thinking and not only to describe its main components (as traditional philosophical accounts).

25 Kominsky and colleagues' model (2015) also postulates psychological mechanisms and factors involved in causal superseding: counterfactual thinking involving norm representations and analyzing the sufficiency of the agent's behavior to bring about the outcome. These psychological processes could be involved in the legal reasoning involving such cases.

26 According to the model by Hitchcock and Knobe (2009), "causal structure" consists of all possible counterfactual scenarios that would not lead to a certain outcome. Perhaps legal *sine qua non* test, which is based on a similar idea, could be rooted in this general counterfactual thinking capacity.

27 Note that this potential incongruence with the ordinary concept does not need to speak against the technical understanding of the "normative connection" and its separation from the factual causal analysis in the law. Adopting specific technical criteria, such as differentiating separate stages of causal and normative assessments, may be due to the criminal law's special functions. For instance, because the legal criteria are generally more specific and clearer than the folk criteria, they may better warrant equal treatment and just trial for all defendants. See Tobia (in preparation; forthcoming) for a discussion of descriptive and normative questions in jurisprudence.
28 See Güver and Kneer (forthcoming) for recent findings that favor the bias interpretation of laypeople's susceptibility to the norm effects on causal attributions.
29 Note that although the law is not biased, actual lawyers' judgments still may be (e.g., Kneer and Bourgeois-Gironde, 2017).
30 Perhaps one way of explaining these potential inconsistencies would be to claim that the legal theories of causation sometimes follow ordinary "unbiased" judgments, other times ordinary "biased" judgments (or that there are some inconsistencies in the legal concept of causation that result from the complexities of the ordinary causal judgments).
31 For example, in the case of omissions or attempted crimes.
32 However, it should be noted that according to some views in common-law jurisprudence, proximate causation judgments express judgments of responsibility (see Knobe and Shapiro, 2021, and Moore, 2009, for critical discussions). If empirically supported by future research, the responsibility account could therefore support such legal-philosophical intuitions as consistent with (some) ordinary causal intuitions.
33 See, for instance, Güver and Kneer (forthcoming).
34 Importantly, this would not necessarily imply that the legal community should reject these legal theories, but simply that their justification by the appeal to ordinary causal intuitions would no longer hold.
35 More generally, various folk intuitions may be involved in the cultural transmission of different legal theories and doctrines.
36 The hypothesis that there are many folk concepts of causation was expressed already by Hart and Honoré (1985, pp. 27–8), making it another jurisprudential intuition to be empirically verified.
37 For some recent contributions to this X-Phi of Law project in the common law system, see Macleod (2019) on the "but for" test in the law and Knobe and Shapiro (2021) on proximate causation.
38 See Machery (2017) for a review.

References

American Law Institute (1985). *Model penal code: official draft and explanatory notes: complete text of model penal code as adopted at the 1962 annual meeting of the American Law Institute at Washington, D.C., May 24, 1962*. Philadelphia, PA: The Institute.

Alicke, M.D. (2000). "Culpable control and the psychology of blame." *Psychological Bulletin* 126(4): 556–74.

Alicke, M. D., D. Rose, and D. Bloom (2011). "Causation, norm violation, and culpable control." *The Journal of Philosophy* 108(12), 670–96.

Bielski, M. (2012). "Kryteria obiektywnego przypisania skutku na tle współczesnej polskiej dogmatyki prawa karnego." In P. Kardas, T. Sroka, and W. Wróbel (eds.), *Państwo prawa i prawo karne. Księga Jubileuszowa Profesora Andrzeja Zolla*, Vol. 2 (503–28). Warszawa: Wolters Kluwer.

Bohlander, M. (2009). *Principles of German Criminal Law*. Oxford, Portland, OR: Hart Publishing.

De Cruz, H., and J. De Smedt (2014). *A natural history of natural theology: The cognitive science of theology and philosophy of religion*. Cambridge, MA: MIT Press.

Donelson, R., and I. Hannikainen (2020). "Fuller and the folk: the inner morality of law revisited." In T. Lombrozo, J. Knobe, and S. Nichols (eds.), *Oxford Studies in Experimental Philosophy*, Vol. 3 (6–28). Oxford: Oxford University Press.

Fletcher, G.P. (1998). *Basic Concepts of Criminal Law*. New York: Oxford University Press.

Foot, P. (1963). "Hart and Honoré: Causation in the law." *Philosophical Review* 72(4): 505–15.

Giezek, J. (1994). *Przyczynowość oraz przypisanie skutku w prawie karnym*. Wrocław: Wydawnictwo Uniwersytetu Wrocławskiego.

Góralski, P. (2009). "Związek przyczynowy w prawie karnym na tle orzecznictwa sądowego." *Prokuratura i prawo*, 1233–2577, 6: 26–45.

Güver, L., and M. Kneer (forthcoming). Causation and the silly norm effect. In K. Prochownik, and S. Magen (Eds.), *Advances in experimental philosophy of law*. Bloomsbury.

Halpern, J.Y. and J. Pearl (2005). "Causes and explanations: A structural-model approach. Part I: Causes." *The British Journal for the Philosophy of Science* 56(4): 843–87.

Hart, H.L.A. and T. Honoré (1985). *Causation in the Law* (2nd ed.). Oxford: Oxford University Press.

Herring, J. (2014). *Criminal Law: Text, Cases, and Materials* (6th ed.). Oxford: Oxford University Press.

Hitchcock, C. and J. Knobe (2009). "Cause and norm." *The Journal of Philosophy* 106(11), 587–612.

Kneer, M. and S. Bourgeois-Gironde (2017). "Mens rea ascription, expertise and outcome effects: Professional judges surveyed." *Cognition* 169: 139–46.

Knobe, J. (2009). "Folk judgments of causation." *Studies in History and Philosophy of Science Part A* 40(2): 238–42.

Knobe, J., and B. Fraser (2008). "Causal judgment and moral judgment: Two experiments." In W. Sinnott-Armstrong (ed.), *Moral Psychology*, Vol. 2 (441–88). Cambridge, MA: MIT Press.

Knobe, J., and S. Nichols (2017). "Experimental philosophy." In E. Zalta (ed.), *The Stanford Encyclopedia of Philosophy* (Winter 2017 ed.). Stanford, CA: Stanford University. Retrieved from: https://plato.stanford.edu/archives/win2017/entries/experimental-philosophy/

Knobe, J. and S.J. Shapiro (2021). "Proximate cause explained: An essay in experimental jurisprudence." *University of Chicago Law Review* 88: 165–236.

Kominsky, J.F., J. Phillips, T. Gerstenberg, D. Lagnado, and J. Knobe (2015). "Causal superseding." *Cognition* 137: 196–209.

Lagnado, D.A., T. Gerstenberg, and R.I. Zultan (2013). "Causal responsibility and counterfactuals." *Cognitive Science* 37(6): 1036–73.

Lagnado, D.A. and T. Gerstenberg (2017). "Causation in legal and moral reasoning." In MR. Waldmann (ed.), *The Oxford Handbook of Causal Reasoning* (565–601). Oxford: Oxford University Press.

Livengood, J., J. Sytsma, and D. Rose (2017). "Following the FAD: Folk attributions and theories of actual causation." *Review of Philosophy and Psychology* 8(2): 273–94.

Macleod, J. (2019). "Ordinary causation: A study in experimental statutory interpretation." *Indiana Law Journal* 94(3): 956–1029.

Machery, E. (2017). "Philosophy within its proper bounds." Oxford: Oxford University Press.

Moore, M.S. (2009). *Causation and Responsibility: An Essay in Law, Morals, and Metaphysics*. Oxford: Oxford University Press.

Moore, M.S. (2019). "Causation in the law." In E. Zalta (ed.), *The Stanford Encyclopedia of Philosophy* (Winter 2019 ed.), Stanford, CA: Stanford University. Retrieved from: https://plato.stanford.edu/archives/win2019/entries/causation-law/

Nancekivell, S., J. Millar, P. Summers, and O. Friedman (2016). "Ownership rights." In J. Sytsma and W. Buckwalter (eds.), *A Companion to Experimental Philosophy* (247–56). Oxford: Wiley-Blackwell.

Norenzayan, A. (2013). *Big Gods: How Religion Transformed Cooperation and Conflict*. Princeton: Princeton University Press.

Penal Code of Poland, Act of 6 June 1997, Journal of Laws, No. 88, Item 553 (1997). https://isap.sejm.gov.pl/isap.nsf/download.xsp/WDU19970880553/U/D19970553Lj.pdf (text in English retrieved from https://www.legislationline.org/download/id/7354/file/Poland_CC_1997_en.pdf).

Phillips, J.S. and J.F. Kominsky (2016). "Causation and norms of proper functioning: Counterfactuals are (still) relevant." In G. Gunzelmann, A. Howes, T. Tenbrink, and E.J. Davelaar (eds.), *Proceedings of the 39th Annual Conference of the Cognitive Science Society* (931–6). Austin, TX: Cognitive Science Society.

Prochownik, K. (2019). *Conditions of Criminal Responsibility from the Perspective of Experimental Legal Philosophy* (unpublished doctoral dissertation). Krakow: Jagiellonian University.

Prochownik, K. M. (2021). "The experimental philosophy of law: New ways, old questions, and how not to get lost." *Philosophy Compass* 16(12), e12791.

Prochownik, K., M. Krebs, A. Wiegmann, and J. Horvath (2020). "Not as bad as painted? Legal expertise, intentionality ascription, and outcome effects revisited." In S. Denison., M. Mack, Y. Xu, and B.C. Armstrong (eds.), *Proceedings of the 42nd Annual Conference of the Cognitive Science Society* (1930–6). Cognitive Science Society.

Robinson, P.H. and J.M. Darley (1995). *Justice, Liability, and Blame: Community Views and the Criminal Law*. Boulder, CO: Westview Press.

Samland, J., and M.R. Waldmann (2016). "How prescriptive norms influence causal inferences." *Cognition* 156: 164–76.

Sommers, R. (2020). "Commonsense consent." *Yale Law Journal* 129: 2232–605.

Sperber, D. (1996). *Explaining Culture*. Oxford: Blackwell Publishers.

Stich, S. and K. Tobia (2016). "Experimental philosophy and the philosophical tradition." In J. Sytsma and W. Buckwalter (eds.), *A Companion to Experimental Philosophy* (5–21). Oxford: Wiley-Blackwell.

Struchiner, N., I. Hannikainen, and G. Almeida (2020). "An Experimental Guide to Vehicles in the Park." *Judgment and Decision Making* 15(3).

Sytsma, J. (2019). *The Character of Causation: Investigating the Impact of Character, Knowledge, and Desire on Causal Attributions*. Retrieved from: http://philsci-archive.pitt.edu/16739/

Sytsma, J. and J. Livengood (2015). *The Theory and Practice of Experimental Philosophy*. Peterborough, Ontario: Broadview Press.

Sytsma, J., J. Livengood, and D. Rose (2012). "Two types of typicality: Rethinking the role of statistical typicality in ordinary causal attributions." *Studies in History and Philosophy of Science Part C: Studies in History and Philosophy of Biological and Biomedical Sciences* 43(4): 814–20.

Tobia, K.P. (2018). "How people judge what is reasonable." *Alabama Law Review* 70: 293–359.

Tobia, K.P. (2020, April 6). *Legal Concepts and Legal Expertise*. Manuscript in preparation. Retrieved from https://ssrn.com/abstract=3536564

Tobia, K.P. (forthcoming). "Experimental jurisprudence." 89. *University of Chicago Law Review*. Retrieved from: https://ssrn.com/abstract=3680107

Vilares, I., M.J. Wesley, W.Y. Ahn, R.J. Bonnie, M. Hoffman, O.D. Jones, ... and P.R. Montague, (2017). "Predicting the knowledge–recklessness distinction in the human brain." *Proceedings of the National Academy of Sciences* 114(12): 3222–7.

von der Pfordten, D. (2009). "About concepts in law." In J.C. Hage and D. von der Pfordten (eds.), *Concepts in Law* (17–34). Netherlands: Springer.

Willemsen, P. (2018). "Omissions and expectations: a new approach to the things we failed to do." *Synthese* 195(4): 1587–614.

Willemsen, P. and L. Kirfel (2018). "Recent empirical work on the relationship between causal judgements and norms." *Philosophy Compass* 14(1): e12562.

Wilkinson-Ryan, T. (2012). "Legal promise and psychological contract." *Wake Forest Law Review* 47: 843–73.

Wróbel, W. and A. Zoll (2012). *Polskie prawo karne. Część ogólna. Podręcznik*. Kraków: Wydawnictwo "Znak."

Zoll, A., G. Bogdan, Z. Ćwiąkalski, P. Kardas, P. Majewski, J. Raglewski, M. Szewczyk, and W. Wróbel (2004). "Kodeks karny: część ogólna: komentarz do art." 1–116. kodeksu karnego (2nd ed.). Kraków: Kantor Wydawniczy "Zakamycze."

9

Children and Adults Don't Think They Are Free: A Skeptical Look at Agent Causationism

Lukas S. Huber, Kevin Reuter, and Trix Cacchione

1 Introduction

Imagine you walk by a table. On the table is a plate of cookies. They look delicious, though not particularly healthy. You think it over and decide to take a cookie. You eat it, and it is indeed delicious. A researcher appears and wants to ask you some questions about free will and your decision to take a cookie. "You took a cookie," the researcher says. "But could you have done otherwise?"

Philosophers have noticed a crucial ambiguity in this type of question. The phrase "could you have done otherwise" can be understood in two different ways (Hobbes, 1839/1646; Nichols, 2004; Turner and Nahmias, 2006): according to an *unconditional reading*, the question asks whether you could have done otherwise if your beliefs and desires were exactly the same. In contrast, the *conditional reading* allows for changes to your original state of mind, and hence asks whether you would have done otherwise if you'd had some other beliefs and desires. The conditional reading is compatible with determinism, while the unconditional is not.

Consequently, if we are interested to know how people think about free will, it will not be sufficient to ask them whether they believe that they could have done otherwise. Importantly, we also need to find out whether people interpret the phrase "could have done otherwise" conditionally or unconditionally. Recently, a number of empirical studies (Nichols, 2006; Nichols and Knobe, 2007; Sarkissian et al., 2010) have been interpreted as demonstrating that (at least) many of us entertain an unconditional notion of free will. It would seem that many people believe that they could have chosen not to eat the cookie, even if everything (else) had been exactly the same.

One popular way to make sense of this is agent causationism. This is the view that people *believe* they can prevent causal chains from happening as well as start new causal chains. Our primary concern in this chapter is thus not whether agent causation exists, but only whether people think of themselves as agent causationists. Applied to the case at hand, we are interested in whether people think they can intervene in the causal process leading from their desire to actually taking the cookie and, instead, guide themselves towards a different action.[1]

What are the results that suggest that people think of themselves as agent causationists? Two strands of evidence have been put forward in support of that claim. First, certain developmental studies have been interpreted to show that children between the ages of four and six undergo a transition towards thinking of themselves as unconditional free agents (Kushnir et al., 2015; Nichols, 2004). Second, experimental studies indicate that adults think of themselves as agents who can do otherwise under exactly the same circumstances (Nichols, 2006; Nichols and Knobe, 2007; Sarkissian et al., 2010). In this chapter, we present new research that tells against both these strands of evidence. Let us start with the first strand.

The literature on children's understanding of free will is still scarce. To our knowledge, only a few studies have examined conceptions of free will in four- to six-year-old children (Chernyak et al., 2011; Kushnir et al., 2015; Nichols, 2004; Wente et al., 2016). However, these studies seem to agree on the point that young children reason in accord with an unconditional conception of free will. Nichols (2004), for example, concludes that children believe in agent causation:

> [T]he available evidence provides support for the claim that children embrace both claims of the agent-causal account. Apparently children think that an agent is a causal factor in the production of an action.
>
> Nichols, 2004, p. 488

Along similar lines, Kushnir and colleagues (2015) propose that during development an early intuitive theory is replaced by a theory in which free will is conceptualized as some sort of causal force that mediates between desires and action:

> In particular, we propose there might be an earlier intuitive causal theory in place by four, or even in late infancy, in which desires are the immediate and *necessary* cause of choices and actions and so are tightly linked to choice itself. Between four and six that intuitive theory may be replaced by a theory in which a more powerful sense of choice is a further causal factor, choice as a separate mental activity that can itself influence and modify not only actions but desires.
>
> Kushnir et al., 2015, p. 98

In this chapter, however, we will put forward a different view. Based on new empirical data, collected with children aged four to six (Study 1), we argue that children do not necessarily believe in agent causation. Instead, our results show that children think they could have done otherwise only if a conflicting desire is made salient. This suggests that, to children, "could have done otherwise" means "would have done otherwise if I had a different desire." Hence, they may indeed think of their freedom conditionally.

The second strand of evidence comes from questionnaire studies showing that adults think they could have done otherwise even if everything had been exactly the same (Nichols, 2006; Nichols and Knobe, 2007; Sarkissian et al., 2010). We do not dispute that data. In fact, our own data shows that people strongly agree that they can do otherwise in exactly the same situation. However, we will argue that a further ambiguity in the phrases "could have done" and "can do" has gone largely unnoticed.

These phrases can be interpreted to mean either "it is possible to do" or "having the ability to do" (see for example, Kratzer, 1991). To show that people think of themselves as agent causationists, one needs to make sure that the phrase "can do otherwise" is being interpreted (by study participants, for example) as *possibility* and not as an *ability*. The results of Study 2 reveal that the crucial question is, by and large, interpreted as a question about ability. When people are asked to state whether it is possible that an agent does otherwise when everything remains the same, a majority of people say that it is not, which suggests that adults think of their freedom conditionally.

This is how we will proceed. In section 2, we will discuss recent empirical work that seems to demonstrate that children think of themselves as agent causationists. We then present the results of Study 1, in which we tested children's intuitions across different conditions, thereby investigating the influence of conflicting desires on the ascription of freedom of choice. Our empirical work on adults' intuitions on free will (Study 2) is presented and discussed in section 3. In section 4, we will summarize our results, and discuss how our studies bear on the metaphysical account of agent causation.

2 Study 1: Children and agent causationism

Researchers usually opt to examine children's intuitions about free will by first letting them (or another agent) perform a certain action and subsequently asking them, "Could you (the agent) have done otherwise or did you (the agent) have to act that way?" (see for example, Chernyak et al., 2011; Kushnir et al., 2015; Lane et al., 2016; Nichols, 2004; Wente et al., 2016). Attributing the ability to do otherwise (to yourself or another agent) is a necessary condition for attributing agent causationism: without the ability to do otherwise, the question of whether the agent can start and prevent causal chains doesn't even arise.

Nichols (2004) found that young children distinguish between the ability of objects and that of agents to behave otherwise. For example, children were asked whether a ball that fell to the floor due to gravity and an agent who touched the floor with her hand due to a desire could have acted other than they did. All the children attributed the ability to do otherwise to agents but not to the ball, suggesting that children between the ages of four and six develop intuitions fitting the agent causation view. Against this interpretation, Nichols himself raises the following possibility: "the compatibilist might say that when the children claimed that the agent could have done otherwise, they were only claiming that the experimenter would have done otherwise under different conditions" (p. 486). To address this concern, Nichols ran a second study, in which children were told that all the conditions were exactly the same. The results of the second study were somewhat less clear, but there was still a tendency for children to attribute greater ability to do otherwise to agents compared to objects. Nichols therefore concludes that "children regard agents as having the capacity to have done otherwise in a way that can't merely be reduced to a conditionalized analysis" (p. 488). Some scholars have raised doubts that these experiments show that people's conception of choosing indeed fundamentally differs from their conception of physical causation (Turner and Nahmias, 2006). The found differences could rather be explained by a difference in the complexity-level of the two processes (human decision making vs. ball dropping). Indeed, Turner and Nahmias showed that when adults were confronted with two processes which are better matched for their complexity (human decision making vs. a lightning strike) and had to rate how these processes played out each time a hypothetical universe was recreated, they no longer assumed that the physical processes are different from the process of choosing in terms of their inevitability. Turner and Nahmias summarize their findings stating that "our results suggest that most people do not believe that all physical processes are deterministic while human choices are indeterministic, even if they might believe that certain simple physical events are deterministic" (2006, p. 605).

Kushnir and colleagues (2015) ultimately arrive at the same conclusion as Nichols, although the primary aim of their research was not to establish an unconditional reading of the ability to do otherwise, but rather to detail the transitional phase in children's reasoning that happens between the ages of four and six. In this research, experimenters asked four- and six-year-olds whether a certain agent (either a toy character or the child him- or herself) could choose to act against their desire. Across several presented stories, the agent was either about to perform an undesired action (action stories) or to inhibit a desired action (inhibition stories). Children were then asked whether the agent has to do x or whether s/he could choose not to do x. A "have to" response would indicate that the children conceived of the agent's choice as constrained by her desire and that this desire led necessarily to the corresponding action. In contrast, a "choose to" response would indicate an intuition according to which a person can choose to act against her desire.

The results showed that six-year-olds give significantly more "choose to" responses than four-year-olds. While six-year-olds performed above chance level in most cases, this was not true for four-year-olds.[2] Crucially, Kushnir and colleagues (2015) also invited children to provide qualitative explanations for their responses. Looking at explanations of "choose to" responses, they found that most children either said they didn't know or referred to alternative desires or alternative external conditions. Other explanations mentioned the agent's autonomy to act against her desire (17 percent when explaining another agent's freedom of choice, and 10 percent when explaining their own freedom of choice).

These latter explanations were interpreted as reflecting the beginning of an unconditional understanding of free will. In contrast, "have to" responses were viewed as indicators for a concept of free will in which desires necessarily lead to corresponding actions (necessary-link concept). The conditional explanations of "choose to" responses were understood as reflecting some sort of developmental transitional stage in which precursor intuitions are giving way to intuitions about an autonomous free will. Although this picture seems perfectly consistent with the data, we propose another possible interpretation: What if the ascription of freedom of choice was in every case based on the availability of another desire? That is, children might start to "pass the test" not because they start to think of themselves as endowed with absolute autonomy over their actions and desires, but rather because other desires—which are not implied by the story—start to become salient to them. Knowing that other desires are present could make children aware of the fact that, had they followed such *alternative desires*, they would have done otherwise.[3] If that were the case, we could no longer conclude that data from developmental studies support an unconditional interpretation of their freedom of choice.

So, even though both Nichols (2004) and Kushnir and colleagues (2015) conclude that children aged five to six have an unconditional reading of the ability to do otherwise, we are skeptical about their conclusion. The children might have managed to answer the question simply because they were aware of the possibility of an alternative desire—a desire that might have guided their actions differently. If children in both studies were accessing an alternative desire, then children's answers are fully consistent with a conditional reading of the ability to do otherwise. To test this alternative hypothesis, we conducted an empirical study where we manipulated the availability of alternative desires systematically.

2.1 Manipulations and hypotheses

To provide such a manipulation we adopted the design of Kushnir and colleagues (2015) and added similar cases in which two desires are implied by the story. If no significant differences are recorded between cases implying an alternative desire and cases not implying an alternative desire (H0), this would suggest that the availability of an alternative desire plays no crucial role in children's ascriptions of freedom of choice. If, however, significant differences are shown (H1), we will have reason to surmise that the saliency of an alternative desire influences children's responses.[4] Additionally, such a result would provide support for the view that children hold a conditional understanding of freedom of choice, even though we cannot decisively reject the conclusion that children believe in agent causation based on such results.

To investigate the influence of the agent's perspective as well as the compatibility of desires, two additional manipulations were implemented: (1) Children had to answer questions not only about themselves but also about another agent. Note that Kushnir and colleagues (2015) found that children endorse freedom of choice more often for another agent than for themselves. Given that the concepts involved in first-person ascriptions and third-person ascriptions are the same, however, we expect no differences between the two conditions (i.e., self/other agent). (2) The desires of the other agent were either compatible or incompatible with the child's own. Considering that an additional aspect (subjectivity of desires) has to be integrated, we expect there to be differences in response patterns, showing that incompatible cases are more difficult to understand. To investigate the developmental trajectory, we tested four-, five-, and six-year-olds, generally expecting to replicate the increase in "chose to" responses between four and six that were found by Kushnir and colleagues (2015).

2.2 Methods

2.2.1 Participants

Three age groups participated: 16 four-year-olds ($M = 4.66$ years; $SD = .21$), 16 five-year-olds ($M = 5.47$; $SD = .29$) and 16 six-year-olds ($M = 6.24$; $SD = .26$). All age groups were counterbalanced for sex. The children were recruited from five nursery schools in and around Bern (Switzerland).

2.2.2 Material

The material consisted of two drawings for the control questions and fourteen photographs (10cm × 10cm) of different foods (seven generally liked and seven generally disliked). There were also four Playmobil toy characters (two female and two male) used for the control questions and the focal cases involving another agent (the exact phrasing of the focal questions, as well as some examples of the stimuli, can be accessed through this online repository: https://osf.io/gfut8).

2.2.3 Procedure

Children were interviewed individually in a separate room or quiet place in their nursery schools. After a short icebreaker talk, the interview started with two warm-up questions, which also served as control questions. These were designed to test whether the child was able to reason adequately about questions concerning freedom of choice where no motivational constraints were involved. Two drawings were shown in succession (order counterbalanced): One drawing displayed a house located on an island, surrounded by ice-cold water, which could only be reached by a bridge. The other drawing showed a house located on land, with two routes leading to it. The child was then introduced to two toy characters (matched for gender), each living in one of the houses. The child was told that the toy characters were both on their way home after long exhausting days at work. The investigator took each toy character to the door of his or her house, taking the bridge to the island house and randomly choosing one of the routes to the other house on land. The child was then asked whether, in order to get home, the toy character *had to* take the specific route or the bridge (to the dry land or island house, respectively), or whether the character *could have chosen not to* take it (this was the same dichotomous answer format later used in the focal questions).

After answering these two control questions, the main body of the experiment started. It was structured as follows: First, the child was shown fourteen food items (seven generally liked and seven generally disliked). Second, to adjust the focal questions, the child was invited to pick those two food items s/he liked most and those two s/he disliked the most (the order of choosing was counterbalanced). Third, the child was presented with six different cases featuring slightly different stories (order randomized). For each case the child answered a focal question (see Table 9.1 for two examples).

In half of the cases, two different food items were mentioned (c1, c3, and c5). The child, or the other agent respectively, was only allowed to take one of them. In the other cases, only one food item was mentioned (c2, c4, and c6). Thus, cases c1, c3, and c5 imply that the agent holds two desires which are conflicting because, for the given situation, only one can be fulfilled. From a post-choice perspective, there is an alternative desire involved in cases c1, c3, and c5, but not in cases c2, c4, and c6. While

Table 9.1 Examples of two cases: c3 implies two desires, while c4 only implies a single desire. Since the agent is only allowed to take one food item, the two desires in case c3 are conflicting. Note that the food items were always matched to the taste (or distaste, in c5 and c6) of the children and shown by a picture. While in the two cases shown here (and in c5 and c6) the second part consists of a simple statement about the other agent, this was not the same in c1 and c2. In c1, children were asked which of the food items they wanted to take and in c2 *if* they wanted to take the only food item that was presented (all children answered this question affirmatively).

	c3	c4
1. Introduction	Imagine Simon is hungry and sees a cookie *and a candy*, which he both likes. His mum says it's ok to eat something sweet but he is only allowed to take one of the two.	Imagine Simon is hungry and sees a cookie which he likes. His mum says it's ok to eat something sweet.
2. Act	He takes a cookie.	He takes a cookie.
3. Focal Question	Did he *have to* take the cookie or could he have *chosen not* to take it, even though he likes it?	Did he *have to* take the cookie or could he have *chosen not* to take it, even though he likes it?

in c1 and c2, children had to answer the questions about themselves, in the remaining cases (c3–c6) children had to answer the questions about another person. This other agent was in each case one of the toy characters, already known from the control questions (one character for c3 and c4 and the other for c5 and c6). Additionally, the food items in cases c1, c2, c3, and c4 referred to food items the child liked and those in cases c5 and c6 to those s/he disliked. The latter accounted for the agent having incompatible desires and thus required the children to integrate the aspect of the subjectivity of desires (see Table 9.2 for an overview of the different cases).

Table 9.2 Features of different cases. In some cases (c1, c3, and c5) the story implies two desires; in the other cases (c2, c4, and c6) only one. In c1 and c2, the children had to answer the focal question about themselves, in all other cases (c3, c4, c5, c6) about an other agent. In c4 and c5, the other agent held compatible desires, while in c5 and c6, the other agent held incompatible desires.

Case	Second Desire	Agent	Congruence
c1	yes	self	–
c2	no	self	–
c3	yes	other	yes
c4	no	other	yes
c5	yes	other	no
c6	no	other	no

2.3 Results

To check whether children were able to adequately answer questions having the same format as the focal questions but not involving motivational constraints, we looked at the two control questions. Almost all the children, 46 out of 48 succeeded in answering those questions. Only two six-year-olds failed; this was due to insufficient familiarity with the language used in the case descriptions (German). They were excluded from further analysis (remaining $N = 46$).

We first looked at the overall percentages of "choose to" responses (see the last row in Table 9.3). Taking all cases together, 62.3% were answered by "choose to." Looking at the percentages within the different age groups, we observed an increase in "choose to" responses with increasing age (and a decrease in "had to" responses). The distribution of responses was found to be significantly different from a distribution expected under independency ($\chi^2(2, N = 276) = 8.82; p = .012$). A look at the adjusted residuals showed that this was true only for the four- ($prs = \pm 2.04$) and six-year-olds ($prs = \pm 2.88$), but not the five-year-olds ($prs = \pm 0.74$): while four-year-olds gave fewer "choose to" answers, six-year-olds gave more "choose to" answers than we would expect under independency.[5] Moreover, the ratio of "choose to" and "had to" answers was not different from chance for the five-year-olds. Summing up, this first overview suggests an increase in "choose to" responses as a function of age and therefore, a successful replication of previous studies (Kushnir et al., 2015; Nichols, 2004). Next, when considering the responses of all children (the rightmost column in Table 9.3), we noticed that not every case contributed equally to this result. To test our predictions, we looked at each case individually. We found that the distribution of responses differed from the distribution expected under independency only in cases c1 and c3 (Fisher's exact test c1: $p = .045$; c3: $p = .012$).

To see when (between which ages) significant differences emerged, we computed pairwise comparisons for cases c1 and c3 (see Table 9.4). This revealed that the response pattern of four- and six-year-olds was significantly different (Fisher's exact test, c1: $p = .017$; c2: $p = .007$). Moreover, in case c3, this was true for the five- and six-year-olds

Table 9.3 Number and percentages (in brackets) of "choose to" responses, separated by age groups. Note that the complement to 100% of one cell reflects "had to" answers (e.g., c1, five-year-olds: 68.8% "choose to" and 31.2% "had to" responses). Asterisks mark cases in which the distribution of "choose to" and "had to" responses were found to be significantly different than expected under independency (Fisher's exact test).

Case	4-year-olds ($n = 16$)	5-year-olds ($n = 16$)	6-year-olds ($n = 14$)	All Children ($n = 46$)
c1*	8 (50.0%)	11 (68.8%)	13 (92.9%)	32 (69.6%)
c2	9 (56.3%)	8 (50.0%)	7 (50%)	24 (52.2%)
c3*	9 (56.3%)	10 (62.5%)	14 (100.0%)	33 (71.7%)
c4	8 (50.0%)	10 (62.5%)	7 (50.0%)	25 (54.3%)
c5	9 (56.3%)	8 (50.0%)	11 (78.6%)	28 (60.9%)
c6	9 (56.3%)	10 (62.5%)	11 (78.6%)	30 (65.2%)
All Cases	52 of 96 (54.2%)	57 of 96 (59.4%)	63 of 84 (75.0%)	172 of 276 (62.3%)

Table 9.4 Pairwise comparisons between age groups using Fisher's exact test.

Case	4- vs. 5-year-olds	5- vs. 6-year-olds	4- vs. 6-year-olds
c1	$p = .473$	$p = .175$	$p = .017$
c3	$p = 1$	$p = .019$	$p = .007$

(Fisher's exact test, $p = .019$). That is, a significant change in response patterns was found only in cases in which a second conflicting desire was mentioned explicitly. Considering the percentages, this tells us that for the significant pairwise comparisons, the older children responded significantly more with "choose to" answers than the younger ones. In all other cases (including c5, where a second conflicting desire was mentioned, but questions had to be answered regarding another agent holding incompatible desires), there was no significant change in response patterns as a function of age.

Finally, to get a more concrete description of the relationship between age and "choose to" answers, odds ratios were calculated using binomial logistic regression. Whereas in case c1 an increase of one year resulted in a 3.1 times higher probability of a "choose to" response ($B = 1.15, p = .017, OR = 3.14, 95\%$ CI $[1.23, 8.02]$), it resulted in a 3.4 times higher probability in c3 ($B = 1.23, p = .015, OR = 3.42, 95\%$ CI $[1.27, 9.17]$).

2.4 Discussion

This study was designed to check whether the availability of an alternative desire has an impact on children's ascriptions of free choice. Indeed, our results suggest that this is the case. While we observed a significant increase of "choose to" responses in cases where a second conflicting desire was mentioned explicitly, this was not true for cases without an explicit mentioning of a second conflicting desire.[6]

Our results provide evidence for hypothesis (H1) and against hypothesis (H0), according to which there are no significant differences between cases implying an alternative desire and cases implying no such desire. On the assumption that children entertain an unconditional interpretation of "could have done otherwise," we would expect to find that the availability of alternative desires does not influence children's responses: we would expect them to indicate that an agent can simply choose to act against his or her desire, whether or not an alternative desire is implied. However, it turns out that awareness of alternative desires matters. It is therefore no longer plausible to conclude that children entertain an unconditional understanding of the phrase 'could have done otherwise'.

Of course, it might still be the case that children think of themselves as agents with self-originating causal powers. This conjecture is most plausible if adults are indeed agent causationists; at some stage, agent causationist intuitions will become dominant and measurable. When it comes to adults, the debate is still not settled. However, most studies suggest adults to be agent causationists (Nichols, 2006; Nichols and Knobe, 2007; Sarkissian et al., 2010). Therefore, in a second study we investigated adults' intuitions about agent causation.

3 Study 2: Adults and agent causationism

As adults, we do not hold the intuition that each and every desire of ours impairs our freedom of choice. Of course, in some sense, our (at least partial) autonomy from desires is a trivial matter: If we hold two conflicting desires, both desires cannot be implemented simultaneously. For instance, when an adult actively chooses not to eat a cookie, even though she would really like to eat it, then her choice is usually motivated by a further desire—perhaps a desire to eat healthy. In other words, if the agent's desire to eat healthy is stronger than her desire to eat the cookie, it follows that her desire to eat the cookie did not constrain her choice. However, a stronger claim can be made according to which agents are not only free to resist acting upon weaker desires, but also capable of acting against their strongest desires and interests. The existence of such an ability would provide support for an unconditional reading of the ability to do otherwise, and, *a fortiori*, for the claim that we conceive of ourselves as agent causationists, who can prevent even our strongest desires from ruling our actions.

As mentioned above, the standard way to investigate adults' intuitions about agent causation features a "can do otherwise" or "could do otherwise" question. The exact meaning and ambiguity of the phrase has been debated for centuries. For Hobbes, the idea that an agent could do otherwise was a contradiction: it would be equivalent to saying that a cause is necessary and sufficient for a certain effect but this effect does not necessarily follow its cause (Hobbes, 1839/1646). Others argued that it is true but trivial that any given agent could have done otherwise if that agent had chosen to do otherwise—but that it's not possible for an agent to have chosen otherwise given the exact same circumstances (see for example, Schlick, 1939). It has also been claimed that even if we accept that an agent could have done otherwise given the exact same circumstances, this would lead to the conclusion that such a choice is arbitrary and irrational (Double, 1990; Kane, 1985), given that we want our psychological circumstances (such as character traits, reasoning processes, and motives) to account for our choices.

The experimental-philosophical literature has made giant leaps in furthering our understanding of our intuitions concerning free will, moral responsibility, and determinism. A large chunk of this research has focused on whether laypeople are natural compatibilists or natural incompatibilists (Feltz, Cokely, and Nadelhoffer, 2009; Murray and Nahmias, 2014; Nahmias, Coates, and Kvaran 2007; Nichols and Knobe, 2007; and many others). The approach these papers take is different from ours in presupposing a deterministic universe to find out whether people believe free will and moral responsibility to be compatible with such a universe. In contrast, we investigate if laypeople believe they could have done otherwise in exactly the same circumstances. A negative answer would suggest that the folk believe that their choices are determined. In other words, determinism would follow from our studies and is not already presupposed.

Other experimental studies have indeed grappled with a similar problem that we try to tackle in this paper. Nichols (2006) asked participants to rate whether a conditional or an unconditional analysis of "could have done otherwise" sounded more reasonable.[7] The results clearly favored an unconditional analysis. Nichols and Knobe (2007) asked participants whether they thought they lived in a universe in which our decisions were either completely caused by the past or not. Again, a majority of people seem to have indeterminist intuitions. Sarkissian and colleagues (2010) demonstrated the cultural universality of responses to the scenarios from Nichols and Knobe (2007). Knobe (2014) suggests that the current state of experimental-philosophical research favors a view according to which we view ourselves as beings who "transcend the whole causal order" (2014, p. 70).

While these results are impressive, we believe an important aspect has so far been neglected. Even if the circumstances are held constant, and participants understand that aspect of the scenarios given, it is unclear whether the question at stake aims at a person's *ability* or at the *possibility* to do otherwise. That is, even if participants claim that an agent could have done otherwise if everything had been exactly the same, it is not clear whether they mean that given these circumstances, the agent has the ability to follow a different desire, or that given the actual circumstances, it is possible to do otherwise.

To illustrate our point, consider the following case, which does not involve desires. A pro surfer called Jimmy faces an ocean devoid of waves. Can he catch a wave? Well, he is a pro surfer and has—as a matter of fact—the ability to catch waves, so it seems perfectly fine to state that he can catch a wave. On the other hand, there is no possibility of him catching a wave on this particular day because the enabling condition—there being waves—is not met by the actual circumstances. To show the empirical adequacy of this distinction, we conducted a small-scale study, involving 102 participants, to confirm that response patterns indeed differed when the question type was manipulated. Given the scenario described above, participants disagreed with the claim "It is possible that Jimmy catches a wave" ($M= -1.39, SD = 1.78$), but they tended to agree that "Jimmy has the ability to catch a wave" ($M= 0.2, SD= 2.55$) (Ratings were obtained using a seven-point Likert Scale anchored at '-3' (Totally Disagree), '0' (Neutral), and '+3' (Totally Agree.))[8]

These results suggest that people indeed interpret questions about possibility and ability differently. Questions about ability ask whether there exists at least one set of circumstances under which an agent can perform a certain action. That set of circumstances is largely independent of the actual circumstances. Questions about possibility, on the other hand, ask whether, given the actual circumstances, an agent is in the position to perform a certain action.

When investigating intuitions about agent causation, we are interested in whether people think an agent could have done otherwise given a fixed set of circumstances. Therefore, we should ask participants whether it is possible for an agent to do x, but not whether he or she has the ability to do *x*. "Can" questions are often interpreted to align themselves with an ability reading, also known in the literature as circumstantial possibility (Kratzer, 1991). However, "can" questions are ambiguous between these meanings. It remains unclear what exactly adults mean when they state that an agent could have done otherwise. To resolve this ambiguity, we conducted a second empirical study, in which we investigated the effect of different modal formats on adults' intuitions about freedom of choice.[9]

3.1 Manipulations and hypotheses

We designed a questionnaire study, in which we systematically manipulated the wording of certain statements. Three groups of participants read a short story in which an individual decides to take an action. They were then asked to rate a statement (a "can," an "ability," or a "possibility" statement) about the agent's decision to take that action. We hoped thereby to assess whether people think of "can" as indicating the ability to do otherwise in general or the capacity to perform a different action under the very same circumstances. That is, we intended to clarify whether adults interpret 'could have done otherwise' conditionally or unconditionally, and thus whether adults tend to hold agent causationist intuitions or not.

If "can" is interpreted as indicating ability, we would expect agreement ratings not to differ significantly between "ability" and "can" statements. However, if "can" is interpreted as indicating possibility, we would expect agreement ratings not to differ significantly between "possibility" and "can" statements. Furthermore, if people are agent causationists, we would expect high agreement ratings for both the "ability" and the "possibility" statements. That is, ratings should indicate both that the agent has the general ability to do otherwise and that, given the current circumstances, it is actually possible for her to do otherwise. Therefore, independent of whether the "can" statement is interpreted as a statement about ability or a statement about possibility, ratings should also be significantly above the midpoint for this statement. If people do not have agent causationist intuitions, we would expect average ratings for the "possibility" statement to be significantly below the midpoint.

3.2 Methods

3.2.1 Participants

Two hundred and eighteen participants were recruited online via Prolific and randomly assigned to one of three conditions (ability, possibility, can). An *a priori* power analysis with an effect size of 0.6 and a p-value of 0.05 yielded a total sample size of 183 to reach a power level of 0.8. Because we expected some dropouts and did not know how many participants would fail the attention check (described below), we set the number of participants to 200 (usually, slightly more participants are then recruited given the way Prolific operates). There was a dropout rate of 5.5% ($n = 11$). Additional participants were excluded either because they did not indicate English as their first language ($n = 10$) or because they failed to pass the attention check ($n = 42$). The remaining sample ($n = 155$, $M_{Age} = 32.98$, SD = 12.43) consisted of 65% females and 35% males. The experimental design, predictions, and statistical tests were preregistered with the Open Science Framework: https://osf.io/mcpbr.

3.2.2. Questionnaire

After participants were asked for consent, they were instructed to read a short story and then rate a provided statement. The short story featured an agent who desires to move her belongings from one desk to another:

Sarah works in an open office space and moves her belongings from one desk to another. She is almost finished. On her old desk are only her printer and a pile of books. Sarah desires to move the pile of books and she desires to take the printer to her new desk. Her desire to take the pile of books is greater than her desire to take the printer. So she chooses to take the pile of books and moves them to her new desk.

Now, imagine we can turn back time to the point where Sarah makes her decision. Everything is exactly the same as before: Sarah has the same two desires and no other desire: She wants to take the pile of books and she wants to take the printer. Sarah's desire to take the pile of books is stronger than her desire to take the printer.[10]

After reading this short vignette, participants were presented with one of the following three claims and asked to rate how much they agreed with it:

- *Ability condition*: Sarah has the ability to choose to move the printer first.
- *Possibility condition*: It is possible that Sarah chooses to move the printer first.
- *Can condition*: Sarah can choose to move the printer first.

Ratings were obtained using a seven-point Likert Scale anchored at -3 (Totally Disagree), 0 (Neutral), and +3 (Totally Agree). After answering the focal question, participants were asked to qualitatively explain their answers in a short sentence. To check whether the short story was read carefully, participants were also asked to indicate how many desires were involved in Sarah's decision. If participants indicated that either more or fewer than two desires were involved, they were excluded from the analysis.

3.3 Results

Participants in the *Ability* condition agreed most strongly with the rated statement ($M = 2.69$, $SD = .79$). In the *Can* condition, participants generally agreed with the statement ($M = 1.81$) but showed greater variability in their ratings ($SD = 1.71$). Crucially, participants in the *Possibility* condition tended to disagree with the statement ($M = -0.56$, $SD = 2.04$). Figure 9.1 shows the mean results of the three conditions; Figure 9.2 depicts the distribution of responses grouped by different conditions.

Because a Levene's test indicated unequal variances ($F(2, 151) = 13.804$, $p < .001$) and a Shapiro-Wilk test showed a significant departure from normality ($W = .946$, $p < .01$) we used Kruskal–Wallis one-way analysis of variance to check whether the means of the conditions differed significantly. Employing this non-parametric test we found a significant effect of treatment ($\chi^2 (2) = 65.37$; $p < .0001$). To examine how different mean differences contributed to this result we used Dunn's test for pairwise post-hoc comparisons. While the *Ability* and *Can* conditions differed significantly from the *Possible* condition (both $p < .01$), this was not the case for the comparison between the *Ability* and the *Can* condition ($p = .20$).

As a next step we investigated whether agreement ratings for the three conditions were significantly different from the midpoint of 0. Because data was not normally

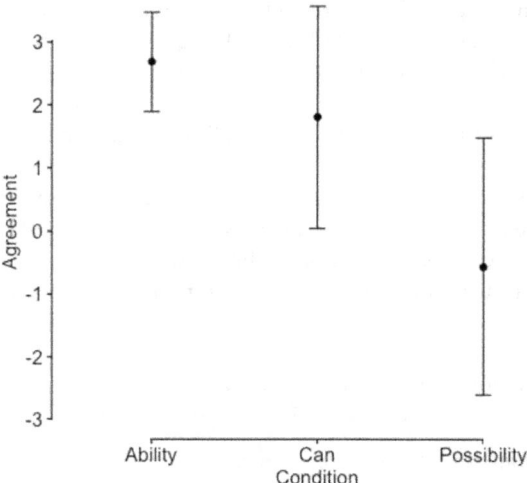

Figure 9.1 Means of agreement ratings across conditions. Error bars represent standard deviations.

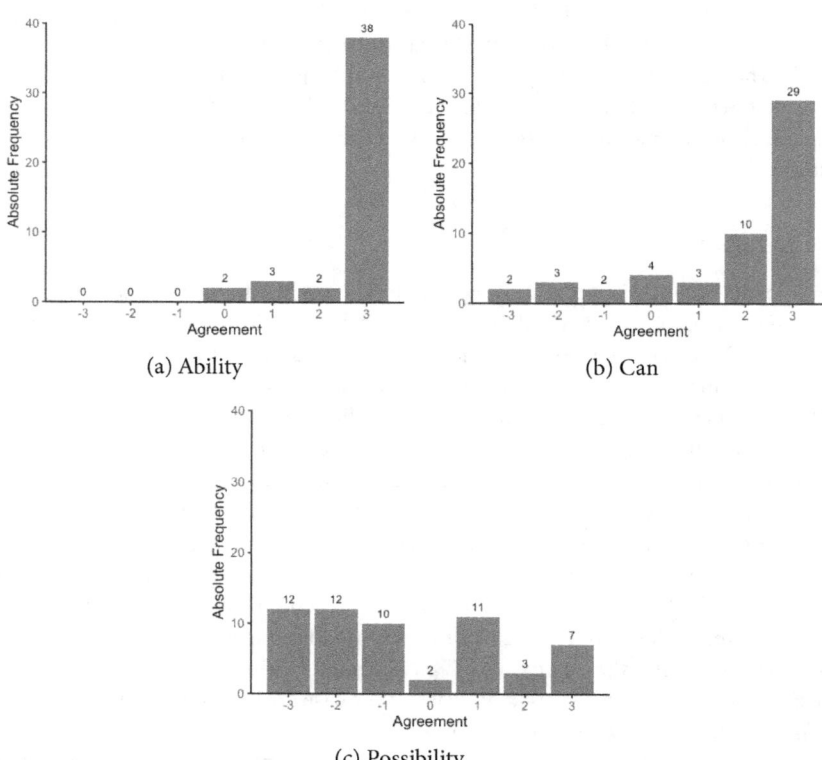

Figure 9.2 Distribution of agreement ratings across conditions (**a–c**).

distributed within conditions (Shapiro-Wilk's test yielded *Ability*: $W = .447, p < .001$; *Can*: $W = .712, p < .001$; *Possibility*: $W = .885, p = .039$), we used the Wilcoxon signed rank test to evaluate whether the observed differences from the neutral midpoint of 0 were significant. This analysis showed that the medians in the *Ability* and *Can* (*Mdn* = 3 for both) conditions were significantly above 0 (both $p < .01$), whereas the median of the *Possibility* condition (*Mdn* = -1) was significantly below 0 ($p = .042$). In other words, participants in the *Ability* and *Can* conditions agreed with the rated statement, while participants in the *Possibility* condition disagreed.

3.4 Discussion and possible objections

Having agent-causationist intuitions would inevitably include the belief that an agent has the ability to do otherwise as well as the belief that, given the current circumstances, it is possible that the agent does otherwise. However, our results show that there is a significant difference between ratings for "ability" vs. "possibility" statements. While people agreed that the agent has the ability to do otherwise, they tended to disagree that it is possible that the agent does otherwise given the actual circumstances. Thus, our results suggest that most adults do not hold agent-causationist intuitions. Admittedly, the large variance of responses indicate that people may disagree on the question of whether it is possible to do otherwise in such situations. Unfortunately, our study was not designed to investigate the source of the large distribution of responses.

Furthermore, the absence of a significant difference between ratings for the "can" vs. the "ability" statement combined with the significant difference found between ratings for the "can" vs. the "possibility" statement suggest that "can" questions are interpreted as questions about ability and not about possibility. This means that positive ratings for "can" statements do not provide information about whether people think an agent could have done otherwise given the actual circumstances. They instead target the general capacity of an agent to choose another desire independent of the actual circumstances. Therefore, "can" questions seem unsuitable for determining whether people hold agent causationist intuitions or not.

To avoid this conclusion, one might object that the "possibility" statement was not interpreted by participants as we intended. Instead, the "possibility" statement might have been interpreted as a statement about the likelihood of the action in question, i.e., when participants stated that it is not possible that Sarah chooses to move the printer first, they actually meant that it is not very likely that Sarah chooses to move the printer first. Looking at the qualitative responses we collected, this alternative explanation seems rather implausible. Out of thirty-four responses disagreeing with the "possibility" statement (responses of "-3," "-2," and "-1"), only a single person explained her response in reference to likelihood. All other responses do not allow for such an alternative interpretation.

One might also argue that whereas the "ability" and "can" statements have a natural agential reading, this is not the case for the "possibility" statement, which participants might have interpreted in terms of physical possibility at the level of events and state of affairs.[11] Such a physical reading might be triggered because the agent's name "Sarah" was not in the subject NP position as in the other statements. Furthermore, statements phrased in the form "it is possible that" might be most frequently used when talking about events and less so when talking about agents. Accordingly, disagreeing with the "possibility" statement would no longer speak against agent causationism. Again, even though some of the qualitative explanations are neutral in regards to how participants interpreted the main statement, the majority of responses do not support such an alternative reading (we have uploaded the complete data file in the online repository: https://osf.io/gfut8, including participants' responses). Additionally, we take the design of our Study 2 to be analogous to the preliminary study about Jimmy the surfer, for which we have shown that participants have the tendency to affirm the 'possibility' statement only if favorable circumstances hold.

4 General discussion

While the metaphysical account of agent causation has only few followers, most scholars agree that we *think* of ourselves as agent causationists. The popularity of that latter view is not surprising. While free will might well be an illusion (Wegner, 2002), the illusion itself provides initial support for the idea that we think of ourselves as agent causationists: If we *feel* or *perceive* that we are able to start new causal chains, then perhaps we also *conceive* of ourselves as beings with such (mystical) powers. As such, previous experimental studies—like those we discussed above—that suggest that children and adults think of themselves as agent causationists, struck a chord with many scholars.

However, perceiving and conceiving are two different pairs of mental shoes. We perceive the Müller-Lyer lines as being different in length, but conceive of them as having the same length. Thus, we need additional, independent evidence that shows that people *conceive* of themselves as agent causationists. We started this chapter by highlighting two such strands of evidence. We then conducted two studies to investigate possible flaws in those strands. In this General Discussion, we first assess our results in light of the current debate. We will then discuss the impact of our results for the metaphysical account of agent causation.

4.1 The "new" empirical situation

Developmental research on children aged four to six suggests that around the age of five, children gain the conceptual sophistication required to state that they did not have to act a certain way but could have chosen otherwise. This achievement leaves open a crucial question: How are we to interpret children's cognitive development? As we claimed in the introduction, (at least) two interpretations are possible. According to the unconditional interpretation, children believe that they could have done otherwise even if the situation were exactly the same. This unconditional reading is very much in line with the agent causation model, which states that agents can interfere in the causal process that leads from desire to action. Both Nichols (2004) and Kushnir and colleagues (2015) are sympathetic to the agent causation model. They argue that the empirical evidence they have collected from their research is best explained by this model. The agent causation model is, however, not the only game in town. According to the conditional interpretation, children believe that they would have done otherwise if they'd had a different desire. Thus, when children contemplate whether they could have done otherwise, they answer affirmatively, because they believe that had they entertained an alternative desire, they would have acted differently.

Our own results indicate that by the age of six, almost every child succeeds at the given task as long as two conditions are met: (i) at least two conflicting desires have to be mentioned explicitly, and (ii) the two conflicting desires have to be compatible with the child's own desires. These results do not square easily with the idea that children's ability to understand freedom of choice is best explained via the agent causation model. This model does not predict that explicit reference to alternative desires facilitates children's conceptual transformation, nor that children's responses depend on the compatibility of the stated desire with the child's own preferences. After all, if children believe that they can do otherwise by intervening in the causal flow from desire to action, alternative desires should not play a crucial role in that process. As we have shown, however, the availability of alternative desires seems vital in prompting an affirmative response to the question "Could you have done otherwise?" This suggests that children believe they could have done otherwise only if an alternative desire had been stronger than the actual desire. If true, this would provide support for the conditional interpretation.

Admittedly, the data we obtained do not rule out the possibility that children harbor agent-causationist intuitions on free will. Perhaps the two conditions that seem to be required for six-year-olds to consistently answer such questions affirmatively (to wit: the availability of explicitly stated alternatives and the compatibility of the desires under consideration with the child's own desires) foster agent-causationist thinking. For instance, it is indeed possible that, in the absence of an explicitly stated second conflicting desire, a young child is not sufficiently motivated to think of herself as an agent who can resist her desires. Nonetheless, our results put considerable pressure on those arguing that developmental data tells in favor of the agent causation model. At a minimum, our results open up the possibility that children reason conditionally about free will under motivational constraints.

Several empirical studies on adults' intuitions on free will suggest that adults conceive of themselves as agent causationists (Nichols, 2006; Nichols and Knobe, 2007; Sarkissian et al., 2010). In fact, if we were to focus only on those parts of our second study in which we asked participants to tell us whether Sarah is able to (or can) choose to follow an alternative desire in a situation in which 'everything is exactly the same as before', an overwhelming majority of participants agree that Sarah can do so. Taken in isolation, this outcome favors the agent causation model. However, people's responses change dramatically if the question is asked differently. Most people disagree with the suggestion that *it is possible* that Sarah chooses an alternative desire. How can these contrasting results be explained? As our study on ability and possibility shows, people interpret ability claims to mean something akin to "possible if the circumstances are favorable": a professional surfer is able to catch waves even if there are no waves, because if the situation were favorable (i.e., if some waves emerged), it would be possible for him to catch them.

A similar understanding of ability and possibility seems to hold for free will intuitions. If the situation favors an alternative desire, then we can follow that alternative desire. Consequently, people conceive of themselves as able to follow alternative desires. However, and crucially, people do not think it is possible for an agent to have followed an alternative desire if that desire has (in fact) proven weaker than another. If, in a hypothetical situation, everything is held exactly the same as in a (hypothetical or real) past situation in which an agent ate a cookie, then people do not think that it is possible for the agent to have chosen not to eat the cookie.

Our studies show that the ability question is clearly tied up with a conditional understanding of free will. Most (if not all) people believe they could have acted differently if the situation had been different. Unsurprisingly then, these results show support for a conditional understanding of free will. However, philosophers who argue for the agent causation model need more than just the ability to do otherwise—they are after an unconditional understanding of free will, which our studies suggest can be tracked by asking whether *it is possible* to do otherwise in the exact same circumstances. By and large, people do not think so. In other words, our studies suggest that people do not think we are the kind of agents who have causal powers to prevent our strongest desires from happening. Interestingly, questions about whether people *can* behave differently are largely interpreted as questions about ability, not possibility. The agreement ratings for the *Can* condition were slightly lower but not significantly different from those for the *Ability* condition. Note that we do not claim that this result can be generalized across a wide range of scenarios. Whether "can" is read as "ability" or "possibility" likely depends on a number of factors, for instance, whether a certain "can" question is more frequently raised in situations in which actual possibility is at stake or, alternatively, in situations relating to a person's ability and skills. In the scenarios we investigated, the "can" formulation is more often interpreted as a question about ability, not possibility. This has important consequences. When researchers design experiments (whether real experiments or thought experiments) featuring such scenarios, they should be careful to ask the right questions. Thus, we recommend that researchers use the "possibility" question instead of the "can" question or the "ability" question.[12]

4.2 Folk agent causationism and agent causation

At the beginning of this chapter, we highlighted the importance of distinguishing between folk agent causationism—the view that people think of themselves as agents who can start and prevent causal chains independently from the causal chains of events—and agent causation—the view that agents, regardless of how they think about their agency, can start and prevent such causal chains. It is fully consistent to endorse the former and reject the latter view. In fact, probably the majority of scholars hold that folk agent causationism is true, while agent causation is false. This position is often made plausible by the different perspectives that we can take in regards to agents. From a third-person perspective there is little evidence that agents are causally relevant beyond the physical processes that determine the workings of agents. Hence, agent causation is wrong. In contrast, from a first-person perspective it seems to us that we are not at the mercy of those physical processes but actually determine our own faith. Hence, agent causationism is true.

While there is no deductive link between agent causationism and agent causation, proponents (and some opponents) of agent causation state that folk agent causationism provides a strong motivation and a reason for agent causation. O'Connor, for instance, states that "the agency theory is appealing because it captures the way we experience our own activity. It does not seem to me (at least ordinarily) that I am caused to act by the reasons which favor doing so;" (O'Connor, 1995; 1996).

We think it is not just the "experience of of our own activity," but the putative *actual belief* in free agent activity, that provides the strongest motivation for agent causation. Campbell nicely connects the experience-claim with the belief-claim:

> Let us ask, why do human beings so obstinately persist in *believing* that there is an indissoluble core of purely self-originated activity which even heredity and environment are powerless to affect? There can be little doubt, I think, of the answer in general terms. They do so, at bottom, because they *feel* certain of the existence of such activity from their immediate practical experience of themselves.
>
> 1967, p. 41, our italics

If Campbell were right, then most scholars actually believe—in the unguarded moments of life that comprise almost all our cognitive activity—that they can start new causal chains, but reject this ability only from a third-person perspective: "So far as we confine ourselves to external observation, I agree that this notion must seem to us pure nonsense" (Campbell, 1967, p. 48).

Our results suggest that this view is mistaken. While perhaps most people may feel the existence of self-originated activity, it would be wrong to infer that those people also believe in such activity. In Figure 9.3, we depict the relation between the claims at stake. Many scholars object to the claim that belief in self-originating causal agency provides a good reason for agent causation. Independently of whether they are successful, our results dispute that people even entertain the belief in self-originating causal agency. Consequently, our results also provide evidence against the metaphysical account of agent causation, in the sense that if we can show that one of the main motivations for agent causation falls apart, advocating agent causation becomes that much harder.[13]

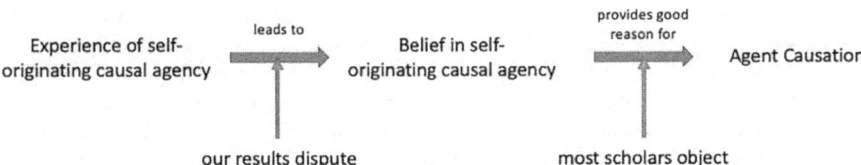

Figure 9.3 The results of Study 2 threaten a successful inference from the experience to the belief in causal agency.

5 Conclusion

The present studies offer a detailed look at how different features influence our intuitions about choice under motivational constraints. The data of Study 1 suggest that children might reason conditionally about free will: six-year-olds succeed in consistently answering affirmatively that they could have done otherwise only if at least two conflicting desires are implied, which are compatible with their own desires. We also demonstrated (Study 2) that adults are likely not to conceive of themselves as agent causationists. When participants were questioned about the possibility of having done otherwise (rather than their ability to have done otherwise), they denied, in the main, that any such possibility exists.

Acknowledgement

The authors would like to thank Luca Barlassina, Beat Huber-Eicher, Joshua Jäger, Miklos Kürthy, Romano De Maddalena, Shaun Nichols, Louis Oberli, Fabio Del Prete, Alex Wiegmann, Pascale Willemsen, and an anonymous reviewer for very helpful discussions and comments on earlier versions of this manuscript. An earlier version of this paper was presented at the Experimental Philosophy Conference in Bern 2019. We thank the participants for the valuable feedback.

This research was supported by the Swiss National Science Foundation (grant number: 100012 169484).

Notes

1. While our focus is on whether people believe they can start and stop causal chains, these beliefs are often put forward as a motivating reason for arguing for agent causation (Campbell, 1967; O'Connor, 1995). Thus, the debate on agent causationism has a direct bearing on the metaphysical account of agent causation (see our General Discussion for further details.)
2. However, there were exceptions to this general pattern: In action stories, where children had to reason about another agent, the results did not significantly differ between the age groups. Additionally, in inhibition stories where children had to reason about themselves, neither the six-year-olds nor the four-year-olds performed significantly above chance level.
3. Note that the term "alternative desire" makes only sense from a post-choice point of view. Throughout this chapter, we use the term "alternative desire" to refer to an agent's desire *which might have but did not* result in an action. The term can thus only be ascribed after a choice has been made.
4. Note that we cannot exclude the possibility that even without implying a second desire, children make an implicit inference to such a desire. Consequently, we would not find any differences even though the availability of an alternative desire plays a crucial role. However, some studies have shown that it seems to be difficult for young children to reason about conflicting desires when one of those desires has to be inferred first (see for example, Cassidy et al., 2005).

5 "*prs*" denotes the standardized Pearson residual which is the residual divided by the standard error. Standardized Pearson residuals are asymptotically and normally distributed, which means that values > 1.96 indicate significant differences.
6 This did not hold for cases in which questions were asked about another agent holding incompatible desires. This suggests that the integration of incompatible desires sets an additional degree of difficulty and is not—at least not fully—achieved at the age of six.
7 More specifically, Nichols asked participants to consider that Bill lied about his income when filling out his tax form. Subsequently, he inquired how right or wrong it sounded that "Bill could have decided to be honest at 10:30, 4/13/2005, but only if some things [even if nothing] had been different before the moment of his decision."
8 For details about the methods of this study please go to the online repository: https://osf.io/gfut8/
9 While we are not aware of any studies in the free will literature that have questioned the effects of different modal formats, some authors have recently started to investigate different modal interpretations when it comes to the ought-implies-can principle (see for example, Kürthy, Del Prete, and Barlassina, ms; Turri, 2017; Willemsen and Wiegmann, ms).
10 It would have been interesting to use similar vignettes in Study 1 and Study 2 that would allow for comparisons between responses in both studies. However, the questionnaire in Study 1 was designed to match the structure and wording of Kushnir and colleagues (2015) as close as possible. In contrast, in Study 2, our aim was to use a scenario that would allow for the different modal questions, and also to describe a situation that would be very unlikely to involve any emotional agitation.
11 We would like to thank Miklos Kürthy for suggesting this alternative reading to us.
12 Such a recommendation might not hold for developmental studies. In our Study 1, we used a "can" question to get at children's intuitions about free will. Arguably—though we lack the data to support this—it is easier for young children to understand a sentence like "Can you do this," as opposed to "Is it possible for you to do this?"
13 While the results of both studies suggest that people by and large do not conceive of themselves as agent causationists, our results do not allow us to draw a decisive conclusion against folk agent causationism in all its varieties (for different ways to cash out agent causation, see, e.g., Clarke (1993); O'Connor (1996)). In fact, folk agent causationism can provide a compelling response. Two different versions of agent causationism need to be kept apart. First-order agent causationism is the view that agents can directly intervene between a desire—like a desire to eat a cookie—and a subsequent action. Second-order agent causationism allows agents to select which of their first-order desires (e.g., a desire to eat a cookie vs. a desire to eat healthy food) is effective in causing an action. The results of our empirical studies are consistent also with second-order agent causationism. In future studies, we aim to investigate the role of second-order desires in free will intuitions to find out whether a more sophisticated version of folk agent causationism stands a better chance of accounting for people's intuitions.

References

Campbell, C.A. (1967). *In Defence of Free Will, with other Philosophical Essays*. London: Allen Unwin.

Cassidy, K.W., M. Cosetti, R. Jones, E. Kelton, V. Meier Rafal, L. Richman, and H. Stanhaus (2005). "Preschool children's understanding of conflicting desires." *Journal of Cognition and Development* 6(3): 427–54.

Chernyak, N., T. Kushnir, K. Sullivan, and Q. Wang (2011). "A comparison of Nepalese and American children's concepts of free will." In *Proceedings of the Annual Meeting of the Cognitive Science Society*, Vol. 33: 33.

Clarke, R. (1993). "Toward a credible agent-causal account of free will." *Noûs 27*(2): 191–203.

Double, R. (1990). *The Non-reality of Free Will*. Oxford: Oxford University Press.

Feltz, A., E.T. Cokely, and T. Nadelhoffer (2009). "Natural compatibilism versus natural incompatibilism: Back to the drawing board." *Mind & Language 24*(1): 1–23.

Hobbes, T. (1839/1646). "The questions concerning liberty, necessity, and chance." In S.W. Molesworth (ed.), *English Works of Thomas Hobbes*, Vol. V. London: Routledge.

Kane, R. (1985). *Free Will and Values: Adaptive Mechanisms and Strategies of Prey and Predators*. Albany: SUNY Press.

Knobe, J. (2014). "Free will and the scientific vision." In. E. Machery and E. O'Neill (eds.), *Current Controversies in Experimental Philosophy*. London: Routledge.

Kratzer, A. (1991). "Modality". In A. von Stechow and D. Wunderlich (eds.), *Semantics: An International Handbook of Contemporary Research*. Berlin: Walter de Gruyter.

Kürthy, M., F. Del Prete, and L. Barlassina (ms). "'Must'' implies ''can.'"

Kushnir, T., A. Gopnik, N. Chernyak, E. Seiver, and H.M. Wellma (2015). Developing intuitions about free will between ages four and six. *Cognition 138*: 79–101.

Lane, J.D., S. Ronfard, S.P. Francioli, and P.L. Harris (2016). "Children's imagination and belief: Prone to flights of fancy or grounded in reality?" *Cognition 152*: 127–40.

Murray, D., and E. Nahmias (2014). "Explaining away incompatibilist intuitions." *Philosophy and Phenomenological Research 88*(2): 434–67.

Nahmias, E., D.J. Coates, and T. Kvaran (2007). "Free will, moral responsibility, and mechanism: Experiments on folk intuitions." *Midwest studies in Philosophy 31*: 214–42.

Nichols, S. (2004). "The folk psychology of free will: Fits and starts." *Mind & Language 19*(5): 473–502.

Nichols, S. (2006). "Free will and the folk: Responses to commentators." *Journal of Cognition and Culture 6*(1–2), 305–20.

Nichols, S. and J. Knobe (2007). "Moral responsibility and determinism: The cognitive science of folk intuitions." *Noûs 41*(4): 663–85.

O'Connor, T. (1995). "Agent causation." In T. O'Connor (ed.), *Agents, Causes, and Events: Essays on Indeterminism and Free Will*. Oxford: Oxford University Press.

O'Connor, T. (1996). Why agent causation? *Philosophical Topics 24*(2): 143–58.

Sarkissian, H., A. Chatterjee, F. De Brigard, J. Knobe, S. Nichols, and S. Sirker (2010). "Is belief in free will a cultural universal?" *Mind & Language 25*(3): 346–58.

Schlick, M. (1939). *Problems of Ethics*. New York: Dover Publications.

Turner, J. and E. Nahmias (2006). "Are the folk agent-causationists?" *Mind & Language 21*(5), 597–609.

Turri, J. (2017). "How 'ought' exceeds but implies 'can': Description and encouragement in moral judgment." *Cognition 168*: 267–75.

Wegner, D.M. (2002). *The Illusion of Conscious Will*. Cambridge, MA: MIT Press.

Wente, A.O., S. Bridgers, X. Zhao, E. Seiver, L. Zhu, and A. Gopnik (2016). "How universal are free will beliefs? Cultural differences in Chinese and US 4-and 6-year-olds." *Child Development 87*(3), 666–76.

Willemsen, P. and A. Wiegmann (ms). "I must although I can't?! Suggestions for a two-level theory of 'ought implies can.'" doi:10.31234/osf.io/hyq9u

Index

abductive reasoning 105
ability to do otherwise 191 ff., 197 ff.
actual causal contribution 36, 45, 52 ff.
agent 189 ff.
    causation 189 ff., 197 ff.
alternative causes 103 ff.
Anscombe, G.E.M. 123 ff.
association 7 ff.

bias account/bias model 145, 150f., 160, 172, 176
blame 58, 70 ff., 127, 132 f., 140, 150, 154 ff., 173 f., 176 f.

causal
    attribution 125, 147 ff., 172, 174, 177
    Bayes net 103, 112, 117
    induction 7 ff.
    inference 7 ff., 81 ff.
    information
    latency 108 ff.
    mechanism
    mechanism information 102, 111 ff.
    model 101 ff.
    monism 84, 88 ff.
    overdetermination 41, 56
    perception 10 ff., 81 ff., 138, 148
    pluralism 82 ff.
    pre-emption 48, 55 ff., 65 ff., 102, 105 ff.
    reasoning 24 ff.
    selection p, 36, 38, 43 ff.
    strength 18 ff., 102 ff.
    structure 108 ff.
    sufficiency 105
    verbs 123 ff., 139
causation
    actual 10, 35 ff.
    observability of 10 ff.
    singular 18
    type 18
children 189 ff.

choice 189 ff.
cognitive representations 81 ff.
compatibilism 189 ff.
competence model (account) 173 ff.
construct 8 ff.
context
    application 8
    learning 8
counterfactual 22, 31, 40, 65, 68, 81. 84, 87, 92, 116, 129, 133, 150 ff., 172 f., 175 f.
    account 116, 145, 150 ff.
covariation 101 ff.
criminal law 174 ff.

decomposition function 20 ff.
desires 189 ff.
developmental study 189 ff.
directed graphs 35 f., 45 ff.

email case 148, 157
experimental jurisprudence 165 ff.
explanation 63 ff.

free will
    conditional 189 ff.
    unconditional 189 ff.

generalizability 20 ff.
grounding 63 ff.

Hart and Honoré 140 f., 166 ff.
Holmesian inference 105

independent influences 22, 28
integration function 23 ff.
intuition 165 ff.
    causal 63 ff.
    explanatory 63 ff.
    grounding 63 ff.
    responsibility 63 ff.
invariance 22, 49, 54, 58

Knobe, Joshua 38, 44 ff., 124 ff., 138 ff., 145 ff., 172 ff.

launching effect 82 ff.
law 140 f., 165 ff.
legal theory 166 ff.
Levin, Beth 127

moral responsibility (responsibility) 63 ff.
motivational constraints 194, 196, 205, 208

norm 51, 126 ff., 138 ff., 145 ff., 167ff.
    effect 129, 132, 146 ff.
    injunctive 152 ff.
    legal 165 ff.
normality in actual cause judgments 36, 44 ff.
normative 7, 28, 32, 35 ff., 63, 67f., 125 f., 128 ff., 139ff., 147ff., 167 ff.,174 ff.

omission 65 ff.
onset time 108
overdetermination
    asymmetric 65 ff.
    causal 65 ff.
    symmetric 65 ff.

pen case/vignette 57, 124. 127 ff., 135, 145 ff., 152 f.
possibility 191f., 199 ff.

power PC model 102 ff.
pragmatic account/model 145 ff., 150 f., 156 ff., 172
preemption *see* causal preemption
principle of univariance 14

rational constraint 17 ff.
reasoning
    abductive 105
    causal *see* causal reasoning
    by elimination 105
reflective equilibrium 64, 74
representation 8 ff.
responsibility 63 ff., 124 ff., 132, ff, 145 ff., 172 ff., 198
responsibility model/ account 145 ff., 172, 174, 176, 178

statistical cues 92 f.
statistical inference 32
structural equations 35 f., 45 ff.
symmetry 20, 25 ff.

time 101 ff.

unobserved background cause 117 f.

voting scenarios 51 f.

Wolff, Phillip 124

www.ingramcontent.com/pod-product-compliance
Lightning Source LLC
Chambersburg PA
CBHW062223300426
44115CB00012BA/2195